Stability and Change in American Education
Structure, Process, and Outcomes

Stability and Change in American Education
Structure, Process, and Outcomes

Edited by

Maureen T. Hallinan
University of Notre Dame
Notre Dame, Indiana

Adam Gamoran
University of Wisconsin-Madison
Madison, Wisconsin

Warren Kubitschek
University of Notre Dame
Notre Dame, Indiana

Tom Loveless
Brookings Institution
Washington, D.C.

ELIOT WERNER PUBLICATIONS, INC.
Clinton Corners, New York

Library of Congress Cataloging-in-Publication Data

Stability and change in American education: structure, process, and outcomes /
    edited by Maureen T. Hallinan ... [et al.].
        p. cm.
    The chapters in this volume were originally presented at a conference
held at the University of Notre Dame in November 2001.
    Includes bibliographical references and index.
    ISBN 0-9719587-8-5 (pbk.)
    1. Educational sociology—United States—Congresses. 2. School management and
organization—United States—Congresses. 3. Educational change—United States—
Congresses. 4. Dreeben, Robert. I. Dreeben, Robert. II. Hallinan, Maureen T.
LC189.85.S72 2003
306.43—dc21
                                                                    2003053815

ISBN 0-9719587-8-5

Copyright © 2003 Eliot Werner Publications, Inc.
PO Box 268, Clinton Corners, New York 12514
http://www.eliotwerner.com

Printed in the United States of America
Boyd Printing Company, Inc., Albany, New York

To Robert Dreeben

Scholar, Teacher, and Mentor

and to the memory of Rebecca Barr

Foreword

Robert Dreeben's research cuts across many aspects of sociology of education, but throughout his work there is a consistent focus on teaching and/or the classroom as a social structure: the organization of the school and classroom, the work of teaching, and the curriculum and its structure. The chapters in this book reflect these concerns, all of which are at the center of contemporary research and all of which are seen as foci of important policies.

Most influential, from Dreeben's early work, is a concern with the impact of the school and classroom as social institutions that reflect and maintain core cultural values and conceptions. *On What Is Learned in School* remains a most important document: it has been on my own course reading list for decades, remains there now, and has many followers. Some of these are almost unrecognizable, such as some critical theorists on the Left who see the core values carried along by the social forms and pageantry of the school as masking the inequalities and oppressions of modern society at best and reinforcing these inequalities at worst. But most analyses, including those of the chapters in this book, simply take the basic vision for granted.

The work is at the background of a whole range of discussions in the field. It is in the background, but not the foreground, for interesting reasons. The extraordinary success of education in the modern system—with its expansion across countries, age groups, social strata, and topics—leads us to take for granted the ultimate validity of the social structure that Dreeben analyzed. His research focused on the impact of schooling as a distinctive moral order. The implied contrast was with all those other social arrangements besides schooling by which people are channeled into roles and role performances in society. This implied contrast makes little sense to researchers and scholars who take for granted the distinctive virtues of schooling as a social form, and who assume its necessity in any vision of any sort of modern society.

There is, thus, an enormous amount of research comparing schooling of type "A" with schooling of type "B." Lectures are compared with participatory modes of instruction. The Bluebird reading groups are compared with the Turkeys, and two-year with four-year colleges. The essential focus of modern sociology of education is on comparisons of the educational achievement and attainment of individuals varying in class, ethnicity, race, and gender. In a recent overview of the field in its leading journal, *Sociology of Education*, more than three-quarters of the papers focused entirely on these kinds of issues.

Modern research in sociology of education drops off sharply when it comes to comparing schooling with nonschooling. Those studies that do exist often suggest that huge differences can be found, for instance, between communities that are a bit schooled and literate and those that are not. Differences attenuate sharply at more advanced levels, and it is difficult to find effects of many occupational training programs added to fourteen or sixteen years of regular schooling.

One learns a broader perspective, and one closer to the original conceptions put forward by Dreeben, when one looks at schooling outside the developed world context. Something close to chance has sent me out, on a good many occasions, to look at schools in the sub-Saharan African peripheries. However jaded one is, such trips across so much time and space are accompanied by a bit of romantic sensibility, and one expects to find syncretic (and perhaps exotic) mixtures of tribal village society and the modern school.

One finds instead an entirely recognizable world according to Dreeben. The schooling forms, carrying their rituals of universalism and achievement orientation, appear before one's eyes out of the bush. In actual content, effectiveness, and so on, this may all be something of a charade. But the form is there and everybody involved seems to understand it pretty well. Even to a complete outsider, it is obvious: what is going on is school. It is all very clear, very recognizable, very routine. Even under unfortunate conditions, such as the absence of an actual school building with walls and classrooms, passable and unmistakable enactments of the form occur.

I recall a school in Lesotho (in southern Africa) that lacked a building and functioned with classes meeting on the bare ground. The children were sitting on soil carefully raised in low straight-line benches by the parents. Everything was in order, except for me: I was a bit overwhelmed by my own expectations that when one visits a school there ought to be a school building there. But the head teacher and inspector who accompanied me treated the situation as normal. Their interaction was precise. The head teacher apologized to us for several violations of modern progressive doctrine: "I know I should have the children's work displayed on the walls, but I have no walls." The inspector accepted this explanation, but found other and correctable violations of the principles of modern child-centered instruction: "It's good that you have those [low mud] benches for the children, but they are in straight rows. If you had them in semicircles, the teachers could better hear and respond to each individual child." The head teacher understood the point immediately and promised improvement.

In order to sustain this order of proper schooling in a context of village rules and roles that are far removed from it, sharp boundaries are needed—sharper than in modern communities in developed countries. In a schooled community in the United States, casual interpenetration of school and community and a relaxation of boundaries make sense. But maintaining the moral order of the school in the developing countries requires effort: the physical boundary of the school, the patterns of teacher and pupil dress, and often the language of instruction and interaction are kept distinctive. Schooled knowledge is enacted in special tones of voice and carefully written down in forms not available for ordinary knowledge. Schoolbooks and other materials, precious by village standards, may be kept under lock and key (and are actually unavailable for the daily use of the students and teachers). The values and schooling form are maintained but at some distance from anything that we might call local social practice. It all has a religious quality reminiscent of the storing of similar truths in Western history, locked up in special buildings and organized in a Latin language that no one understood or used.

In northern Namibia I saw a social studies lesson built on modern democratic and child-centered principles. The idea was for the children to draw a schematic picture of their own village, with their own homes in it. The textbook provided a helpful example, a schematic picture of an obviously English village with green grass, well-defined streets, a church, a school, a store, and so on. Both teacher and pupils clearly understood that their task was to carefully copy the picture of the English village, not to draw their own. Green crayons were distributed to depict the grassy lawns of a completely alien world. It all made sense in this context: the privileged world of schooling is far from the normal one, and when entering it one sacrifices many links to ordinary local reality.

I think we as researchers in the field, especially those operating entirely in the developed world, may take too much for granted the basic social form of schooling, its dominance, and the degree to which it is simply functional or natural. It carries a coded value system, obviously, and one of worldwide force and power. Dreeben's analysis of that, probably moreso than the subsequent tendentious discussions of hidden curricula, retains a great deal of force.

Dreeben's comprehension of this core point, the sweeping cultural or religious vision built into modern universalized schooling, helped him in his later work to understand and creatively study the problematics of schooling organization. The school as organization must link universal visions to very practical and prosaic daily activities in classroom and community. In a sense this is an impossible task. Given the grand visions infusing expectations for modern education, it is almost certain to fail most of the time. Whereas other researchers expected successes from each new organizational innovation in education, Dreeben had good theoretical grounds for more skepticism.

Understanding Dreeben's perspective helps us understand why so many educational innovations that violate aspects of the basic schooling form tend to fail to gain acceptance, implementation, and use. It also helps us understand why some forms that are obviously inefficient in instructional terms (the lecture method, for instance) survive so well on ritual clarity, and why — despite the prescriptions of most pedagogical theorists—the sharp formal separation of classroom and school, and school and society, retain such power in so much of the world.

The authors of the chapters in this book focus principally on the organizational puzzles that infuse Robert Dreeben's later work. In the main they retain some optimism about the ways in which organizational changes can make modern schooling more effective. They do this by at least partially incorporating the core original story of *On What Is Learned in School*—that education carries a great and universalized cultural vision of a kind that transcends purely organizational capture and management. Thus the chapters here tend to celebrate ultimately nonorganizational aspects of education as keys to reform and improvement: the interactions among teachers as persons, professionals, and coworkers; the networks linking students; and the educational costs of hyperrationalization of the schooling system. In these ways they carry on Robert Dreeben's own themes, starting with his landmark early achievement.

John W. Meyer
Stanford University
Stanford, California

Contributors

CHARLES E. BIDWELL, Department of Sociology (Emeritus), University of Chicago, Chicago, Illinois 60637

MATTHEW BOULAY, Teachers College, Columbia University, New York, New York 10027

ROBERT DREEBEN, Department of Education (Emeritus), University of Chicago, Chicago, Illinois 60637

WILLIAM A. FIRESTONE, Graduate School of Education, Rutgers University, New Brunswick, New Jersey 08901

ADAM GAMORAN, Department of Sociology, University of Wisconsin-Madison, Madison, Wisconsin 53706

MAUREEN T. HALLINAN, Department of Sociology, University of Notre Dame, Notre Dame, Indiana 46556

ALEX INKELES, Department of Sociology (Emeritus), Stanford University, Stanford, California 94305

MELINDA MECHUR KARP, Teachers College, Columbia University, New York, New York 10027

SEAN KELLY, Department of Sociology, University of Wisconsin-Madison, Madison, Wisconsin 53706

P. HERBERT LEIDERMAN, Department of Psychiatry and Behavioral Sciences (Emeritus), Stanford University, Stanford, California 94305

TOM LOVELESS, Brown Center on Education Policy, Brookings Institution, Washington, D.C. 20036

DANIEL A. McFARLAND, School of Education, Stanford University, Stanford, California 94305

JOHN W. MEYER, Department of Sociology (Emeritus), Stanford University, Stanford, California 94305

AARON M. PALLAS, Teachers College, Columbia University, New York, New York 10027

BARBARA SCHNEIDER, Department of Sociology, University of Chicago, Chicago, Illinois 60637

KENNETH K. WONG, Department of Leadership, Policy, and Organizations and Department of Political Science, Vanderbilt University, Nashville, Tennessee 37203

Preface

In January 2002 President Bush signed into law the No Child Left Behind Act of 2001. The first requirement of this law is that states create curriculum standards for students at every grade level. Most states have developed these standards for reading and mathematics. The second requirement is that beginning in 2002–03, states conduct annual assessments of students' academic progress. Schools whose students fail to make progress will suffer significant consequences. These two pillars of the law, standards and assessment, are absorbing the energy and limited financial resources of states and local school districts.

The effectiveness of the far-reaching No Child Left Behind Act in reforming public education will not be known for some time; however, sociological research on schools suggests caution in anticipating positive results. Two major studies of schooling by Robert Dreeben, whose scholarship and career we honor in this book, provide the reasons for concern. In his early classic *On What is Learned in School,* Dreeben described how the formal and informal organization of a school influences student socialization. In a complementary treatise, *How Schools Work,* Dreeben and his coauthor Rebecca Barr analyzed school influences on student learning. These two theoretically insightful and empirically rigorous studies identify the mechanisms that link school inputs to student outputs. The school and classroom processes described in these books explain how curriculum standards can affect student performance, as measured by some assessment strategy.

While curriculum standards indicate what should be taught, they do not directly improve teacher pedagogy; and although assessments measure what students have learned, by themselves they do not raise student achievement. In contrast, the social organization of students and the interpersonal processes that characterize a school and classroom are powerful influences on student learning, as Dreeben's analysis makes clear. Educators and policymakers would benefit from studying Dreeben's work to help them implement obligatory curriculum standards in a manner that improves teacher pedagogy and classroom practice and increases student achievement.

The chapters in this volume were originally presented at a conference entitled "Stability and Change in Education: Structure, Processes, and Outcomes" held at the University of Notre Dame in November 2001. The editors are grateful to the University of Notre Dame's Institute for Scholarship in the Liberal Arts for funding this conference as part of the Henkels Visiting Lecture Series. Sylvia Phillips handled the organizational details associated with the conference; her graciousness and skills were evident in the smooth running of the event. Cheryl Pauley prepared the manuscripts for publication; her editorial experience and hard work enabled us to remain on a tight production schedule.

The purpose of the conference was to celebrate Robert Dreeben's lifelong contributions to sociology of education. Participants and subsequent chapter authors include Dreeben's colleagues, former students, and friends. The high quality of their contributions to this volume underscores their desire to express appreciation to Dreeben for his important influence on their scholarship. We are grateful to the authors for their cooperation with our rigid deadlines and their patience with the strict editorial regulations that we imposed on them.

Finally, we express appreciation to Eliot Werner, president of Eliot Werner Publications, for publishing this volume. The time, energy, and attention to detail—both substantive and technical—that Eliot devoted to this book single him out as a knowledgeable and conscientious professional. Watching him make up the rules as he went along provides material for many future exchanges. We also are grateful to Jane Carey, president of Boyd Printing Company, for printing the volume. Jane's reputation for outstanding service to all of her clients is well known. Collaborating with Jane on this book reminded me of the pleasure that I used to experience in working with her late father, Henry Quellmalz, when I edited *Sociology of Education*. Both Eliot and Jane have made the publication of this book a smooth process. It is my privilege to know and work with these two special people.

Maureen T. Hallinan

Contents

Contents

III. HOW SCHOOLS WORK: ORGANIZATION AND EFFECTS

IV. TEACHING AS AN OCCUPATION

V. SOCIOLOGY OF EDUCATION AS A FIELD OF INQUIRY

VI. CONCLUSION

I

Introduction

Robert Dreeben's Contributions to Sociology of Education

Adam Gamoran
Tom Loveless

The chapters in this book were inspired by the work of Robert Dreeben, one of the most widely read and influential sociologists of education of the second half of the twentieth century. The papers were first presented in a conference held at the Institute for Educational Initiatives at the University of Notre Dame in November 2001; they reflect original work written specifically for the conference and this book. The influence of Dreeben's scholarship has been pervasive, but are the ideas from decades ago still applicable today? In light of many changes in American education—shifts in youth culture and socialization, changes in the American family, a new regime of accountability for schools—one may ask whether concepts that were important in the last century are still relevant. We pursue that question in this introductory chapter.

Robert Dreeben is best known for two books, *On What Is Learned in School* ([1968] 2002) and *How Schools Work* (1983, cowritten with Rebecca Barr). The latter has remained in print for two decades, and the former was just brought back into print as a Foundations of Sociology classic by Eliot Werner Publications. Curiously, *On What Is Learned in School* said little about what comes easily to mind when one thinks of school learning: "reading, writing, and 'rithmetic." Instead, the book argued that schools serve a critical function in the socialization of youth, serving as a bridge between the family and the world of adulthood. Structural features of contemporary schools—such as instruction organized into classrooms consisting of one teacher and many students, and teachers who change from year to year in contrast to the permanence of family relations—helped inculcate norms of achievement, independence, universalism, and specificity that young people need to navigate the

Adam Gamoran • Department of Sociology, University of Wisconsin-Madison, Madison, Wisconsin 53706.
Tom Loveless • Brown Center on Education Policy, Brookings Institution, Washington, D.C. 20036.

Stability and Change in American Education: Structure, Process, and Outcomes edited by Maureen T. Hallinan, Adam Gamoran, Warren Kubitschek, and Tom Loveless. Eliot Werner Publications, Clinton Corners, New York, 2003.

transition to adulthood. The important learning that occurred in school, this book asserted, was how to live in adult society.

Then, fifteen years after achieving prominence for *On What Is Learned in School* (which all but ignores cognitive learning), Dreeben published *How Schools Work*, which is about the production of cognitive learning in schools. The latter work reflected Dreeben's partnership with his wife Rebecca Barr, a noted reading scholar who had collected for another purpose fine-grained data on classroom instruction and children's learning in first grade reading (Barr, 1973–74). Barr's expertise on reading instruction and the rich empirical evidence she brought combined with Dreeben's sociological insights to produce a work that contributed to a dramatic and long-lasting shift in thinking about the organization of schooling and achievement. Prior to *How Schools Work*, few sociologists gave thought to what occurred inside schools and classrooms—what Barr and Dreeben referred to as the "technology of schooling"—limiting their attention instead to the inputs and outputs of schooling while ignoring the process through which achievement is produced. *How Schools Work* showed that schooling is organized in "nested layers" of districts, schools, classrooms, and (in the case of first grade reading) instructional groups, and that learning is produced when resources such as personnel, time, and curricular materials are passed from one organizational level to the next until they are applied by teachers in classrooms and experienced by students as classroom instruction.

Although the subject matter of *How Schools Work* seems to represent an about-face from *On What Is Learned in School*, important parallels become evident on close reading. First, both draw on a Parsonsian theoretical framework although they stem from different elements of Parsons's oeuvre. The norms to which Dreeben attends in *On What Is Learned in School* reflect Parsons's (1959) concern with schooling and socialization and the transmission of norms more generally, and the attention to organizational levels in *How Schools Work* parallels Parsons's (1960) distinctions between the institutional, managerial, and technical levels of organization—for which educational organizations served as a key example. Second, Dreeben's two most famous works are similar in their attention to school structure as the mediator of social norms in the one case and resource allocation in the other. Third, both major works reflect originality, flexibility, and an ability to reinvent oneself that are characteristic of seminal scholarship in any discipline. Fourth, the works are complementary rather than contradictory. Indeed one may see *How Schools Work* filling an important void that was left by *On What Is Learned in School*: cognitive learning is an important part of the socialization process to which the earlier book did not give sufficient attention. Despite these contributions, times have changed; how do these works hold up today? Part II of this book, "Schooling and Socialization," contains three chapters stimulated by *On What Is Learned in School*. Part III, "How Schools Work: Organization and Effects," consists of contemporary reflections on *How Schools Work*.

Shortly after *On What Is Learned in School* appeared, Dreeben published another book called *The Nature of Teaching* (1970). Although less well known than the other two, *The Nature of Teaching* stands as an important link between the two classics, depicting the structural elements of teaching as an occupation that set conditions for everyday activities that underlie both cognitive and noncognitive learning in schools. Now in a time of increasing state regulation over curriculum, instruction, and assessment, the occupation of teaching has undergone fundamental changes. Thus, reflecting on the chapters in this book, it is also appropriate to ask whether *The Nature of Teaching* still offers lessons to sociologists. Finally, in 1994 Dreeben published a retrospective analysis of the development of the field of sociology of education. This paper, which won the Willard Waller Award as the best paper in sociology of education, traced the development of the field over the course of the twentieth century. Is the account still relevant for the twenty-first? Part IV of this book, "Teaching as an Occupation," reflects on Dreeben's notions of teaching in light of changes in the profession, and Part V, "Sociology of Education as a Field of Inquiry," provides an update to Dreeben's award-winning survey. In the remainder of this introductory chapter, we briefly summarize the chapters that appear in each part and reach an overall assessment of the applicability of Dreeben's ideas in light of changes in American education.

SCHOOLING AND SOCIALIZATION

What is learned in school? Since the formal curriculum is organized by subject matter—reading, math, history, science, and so on—the skills and knowledge from these disciplines provide a logical starting point for answering that question. It is significant that Dreeben's *On What Is Learned in School*, published in 1968, does not start there. In fact, the book spends very little time discussing academic subjects and no time at all scrutinizing the knowledge found in textbooks or the typical course syllabus. Instead, the book focuses on the informal teachings of schools. It is especially interested in analyzing the school's role in preparing children for life as an adult in a modern, democratic society. The book lays out a theory for *why* the school's socializing functions have evolved as they have, primarily by exploring the school's connections with other institutions: the family, workplace, and institutions of civil society.

Dreeben's argument rests on the premise that modern societies rely on schools to act as bridges between childhood and adulthood, easing the child's transition from being the protected, dependent member of a family to an independent, contributing member of society. The social organization of school affects the teaching of norms. Letter grades and report cards, for example, do more than inform parents of student progress; they also convey to students what "achievement" means in concrete terms. In addition to achievement, Dreeben examines the learning of independence, universalism, and specificity, broad categories describing what Dreeben calls "psychological" outcomes of schooling. Are these categories as relevant in 2003 as they were in 1968? Considering the remarkable changes in society since 1968, do schools at the turn of the twenty-first century socialize students differently than in 1968?

Chapter 2, by Aaron Pallas, Matthew Boulay, and Melinda Mechur Karp, takes a novel approach to shedding light on these question by plumbing the memories of a random sample of Lansing, Michigan, adults, between the ages of 25 and 65. The researchers asked subjects to talk about what they remembered learning in school. Academic knowledge was mentioned by most; however, as if to verify Dreeben's thesis, respondents rarely talked about the specific content they had studied. Instead, they more often spoke of learning "how to learn" or of learning the value of learning for its own sake, noncognitive aspects of schooling that transcend formal curriculum. Similarly, the interviewees discussed learning social norms, learning about oneself, and learning about differences among people. In general, the respondents described how schools contributed to the formulation of general dispositions rather than to the mastery of particular skills or particular intellectual fields.

Pallas, Boulay, and Karp's chapter embellishes and updates Dreeben's thesis. First, it suggests that what is learned in school reflects a historical time. The war in Vietnam and the civil rights movement influenced the college education of Rich Dalton, a case study in the chapter, just as the Great Depression and two world wars shaped the education of earlier generations. Second, if the psychological outcomes that Dreeben analyzed in the 1960s evolved from industrial societies' demand for particular dispositions in young people, then a new set of dispositions may have risen to prominence in the past few decades. Undoubtedly, globalization of markets and increased racial and ethnic diversity in the United States have elevated the value of knowing about other cultures and understanding and appreciating human differences.

Colleges may be better equipped to teach these skills than grade schools. Whereas Dreeben focused on elementary and secondary education, less is known about how the social organization of postsecondary institutions prepares young adults for social roles. Typically, attending college physically separates young people from their families and home communities and—because classroom time is limited—exposes them to students of varying ages, races, and social backgrounds. Interactions often take place in informal, out-of-school settings. The social organization of colleges and universities may fulfill functions that were not as important a few decades ago as they are in contemporary societies.

Dreeben's ideas concerning the school's capacity to inculcate characteristics such as psychosocial maturity rests on his analysis of teacher-student relations in the classroom. Crucial to the relationship is the creation of what Dreeben calls "classroom goodwill," the subject of Chapter 3 by Charles Bidwell. Teachers motivate students by convincing them of the legitimacy of the classroom's instructional regime. This task requires that a bargain be struck in which the rewards and sanctions offered by teachers (grades, criticism, and praise) are regarded by students as a fair exchange for their effort.

Bidwell describes how random shocks to the school environment, such as sudden changes in student composition, may disrupt the arrangement. Bidwell notes that in many of the highly successful schools that he has studied, students seem to replicate their parents' relationship with work. Staying late after school to complete projects and taking home backpacks stuffed with work on weekends are two ways in which ambitious, conscientious students model their parents' work habits. Schools that serve many students behaving like this find generating goodwill an easier task than schools with students who are apathetic toward academic accomplishments or hostile to schoolwork and teachers' expectations. If a school's population shifts from a preponderance of cooperative students to a preponderance of noncooperative students, teachers find their skill at generating goodwill severely tested.

That is not to say that Bidwell thinks schools are helpless. Bidwell believes schools can learn as organizations how to create goodwill with different kinds of students. Schools that engage in collective problem solving often evidence bounded solidarity among faculty, school cultures in which teachers are encouraged to seek solutions to common problems. School principals and other administrative leaders are important to fostering cooperative rather than adversarial relationships within the faculty, allowing teachers to forge ties with professional communities and organizations outside the school. Under such conditions teachers can increase their capacity to create goodwill and sustain it over time.

Alex Inkeles and Herbert Leiderman are also interested in the interplay of sociological and psychological factors in student learning. In Chapter 4 these authors gauge the influence of *psychosocial maturity* on two student outcomes: high school grades and expectations of going to college. By psychosocial maturity Inkeles and Leiderman are referring to characteristics such as cooperativeness, efficacy, individualism, perseverance, planfulness, and responsibility. In a sense Inkeles and Leiderman flip Dreeben's argument on its head. Dreeben's primary project was to explain the effects of schooling on the cultivation of habits and dispositions required in adulthood; Inkeles and Leiderman are interested in measuring the impact of habits and dispositions on schooling's outputs. Society may depend on schools to socialize youth for the economic and civic roles that students will assume as adults, but this chapter reminds us that to function properly, schools must also depend on the adequate fulfillment of a social role—that of student. One benefit of this perspective is that young people are viewed as participants in determining their own success as students. Another is that it reinforces the notion that the role of student mediates an individual's growth from the social roles typical of childhood to those demanded by the adult world.

How does psychosocial maturity affect success at school? In a cross-cultural study of U.S. and Japanese students, Inkeles and Leiderman found that psychosocial maturity matters a great deal in predicting high school grades. Maturity is not as influential in predicting college expectations, which are correlated highly with socioeconomic status. However, among low-SES students maturity strongly influences college expectations. This suggests that college expectations are not merely a product of family history and that greater social mobility can be encouraged by developing psychosocial maturity in adolescents. The policy consequences are important. Programs that seek to boost the attendance of groups traditionally underrepresented on college campuses usually concentrate on preparing students for advanced academic courses and the SAT and ACT tests. Teaching and encouraging students to cooperate, persevere, and plan ahead may also increase students' opportunities for success, both in high school and in college.

THE ORGANIZATION OF SCHOOLING

The chapters in Part III of this book reflect the levels of schooling that Barr and Dreeben (1983) considered in their classic work: Kenneth Wong examines the district level, Maureen Hallinan focuses on the school, Adam Gamoran and Sean Kelly are centrally concerned with classrooms, and Daniel McFarland explores students within classrooms. While drawing on ideas from *How Schools Work*, each of these chapters offers important developments that reflect the changing times.

Wong (Chapter 5) examines institutional, managerial, and technical aspects of school reform, focusing on the case of school reform in Chicago in the 1990s. Wong characterizes Chicago's approach to reform as "mayor-led integrated governance" in that control over the school system was ceded to the mayor, but new governance structures involved a wide range of actors including educators and community members. At the institutional level, reformers acted to reduce fragmentation and raise accountability for student performance on achievement tests. These reforms helped restore public confidence in the school system. Meanwhile at the managerial level, reorganization of property services, union contracts, and other administrative tasks gave new authority to school-level actors. At the technical level of classroom instruction, however, results of reform were more problematic. Although test scores rose, it is not clear that this change will be long lasting in light of ambiguity about the mechanisms that produced test score changes. Wong's research reveals little impact of reform on classroom instruction, and he concludes that "the technical challenge remains enormous."

This study of Chicago school reform confirms that the insights of *How Schools Work* are useful today, perhaps even moreso now than twenty years ago. Given new accountability for test scores, the technical task of improving instruction as a means of raising achievement comes to the forefront. Insights from Barr and Dreeben's "nested layers" outlook help us understand the importance of moving beyond institutional and managerial activities to affect the resources teachers have at their disposal in classrooms, including their human resources—that is, their capacity to provide high-quality instruction.

In her analysis of the school scheduling process, Hallinan (Chapter 6) builds on Barr and Dreeben's formulation by challenging it. While the hierarchically organized, loosely structured system that Barr and Dreeben describe may accurately reflect normal operations, how does this depiction hold up when a crisis occurs? Hallinan draws on Perrow's (1984) analysis of Three Mile Island and other "normal accidents" to examine a catastrophic break-down in one high school's scheduling process that resulted from a combination of human error and insufficient resources. At the beginning of the school year, 50 percent of the students had scheduling conflicts and there were too few counselors and too little technology to resolve the conflicts quickly. It took six weeks until the scheduling chaos was fully resolved and all students had workable class schedules. Although Hallinan does not find achievement differences between students who missed different numbers of class sessions due to the scheduling conflicts, she reports a variety of negative consequences including strained relations among staff, increased absenteeism among students, and loss of confidence among parents. At the same time, the loosely coupled structure of the school allowed normal operations to continue throughout the period of disruption: classes met, extracurricular activities occurred, the principal's routine did not vary, and so on.

This study of one school's "accident" shows that loose coupling has advantages as well as disadvantages. On the one hand, everyday routines continued in most parts of the school even though one major component, the assignment of students to classes, broke down. On the other hand, tighter organizational connections might have prevented the incident from occurring in the first place. Clearly the system of coordination through resource allocation portrayed in *How Schools Work* cannot stave off major problems, but it can minimize the damage that ensues when such problems occur.

In Chapter 7 Gamoran and Kelly use evidence from a new study of teaching and learning in secondary school English to identify connections between the structure of schools and their productive technology—that is, teaching and learning in classrooms. Structure creates conditions in which technology occurs, but it is technology that produces results. In a sample of nineteen middle and high schools drawn from five states, the authors find that only 10 percent of the variance in writing achievement lies between schools, while 29 percent is between classes within schools and 61 percent is between students within classes. Tracking into high, regular, and low classes is the main axis of differentiation at the class level, and variation in the quality and impact of instruction account for part of the effects of tracking on achievement.

Gamoran and Kelly's analysis follows closely on models developed by Barr and Dreeben (1983) and elaborated by Gamoran (1986, 1987; see also Gamoran et al. 1995). The new data show a similar pattern of results with more contemporary evidence and a much broader sample. Despite decades of deliberations about the organization and effects of tracking, it appears that little has changed: on average, high tracks promote high achievement and low tracks hold students back, at least in part because the quality of instruction is better in high tracks. Instructional conditions of persisting importance include authentic questions and discussion in class and the extent to which students carry out their assigned work. The notion of nested layers does not capture all the factors that account for achievement variation; indeed, most of the variance within classes—where students are receiving similar instruction—remains unexplained, but it remains a powerful conceptual framework for describing class-level effects on achievement.

McFarland (Chapter 8) draws on both *On What Is Learned in School* and *How Schools Work* to focus on the academic and social dimensions of classroom life. His contribution is not a response to changing times since solving the problem of classroom order, which lies at the heart of his chapter, has always been a teacher's first challenge. Rather, McFarland's chapter shows the value of new ideas for understanding persisting problems. Issues that Dreeben addressed in separate works receive an integrated focus in McFarland's analysis. Whereas the notion that students' classroom behavior is central to academic performance is implicit in Gamoran and Kelly's conception of instruction as what teachers and students do together (as opposed to what teachers do to students), McFarland makes this point explicit with a clear focus on students as actors. He uses Goffman's ([1974] 1986) concept of "frame," which McFarland characterizes as "principles of organization that govern the subjective meaning actors assign to social events," to examine multiple and often competing processes within classrooms. Conflict between the academic and social frames may lead to tension. McFarland demonstrates this point with a case study of an Algebra 2 classroom in which the teacher's efforts to maintain the hegemony of the academic frame, mainly enacted through academic task structures, were undermined by students acting within a social frame. Whereas Gamoran and Kelly examine classroom behavior in the aggregate, McFarland explores competing frames as battles between individuals, in this case the teacher versus dominant students or student subgroups.

Sociological analyses of teaching and learning from Barr and Dreeben (1983) to Gamoran and Kelly (Chapter 7) place academic task structures at the heart of the school's productive process. McFarland shows that although this may be correct, it is an incomplete picture. Indeed, much of the unexplained within-class variation in studies of that sort may be attributable to students' varied participation in the social frameworks that McFarland describes. A much closer analysis of students' roles within classrooms than commonly occurs in quantitative studies of achievement would be necessary to test the proposition that students' responses to social as well as academic frameworks govern their learning over the course of the school year. This notion is clearly implied by McFarland's analysis and awaits more nuanced data of the sort he has elsewhere (2001) reported.

TEACHING AS AN OCCUPATION

In *The Nature of Teaching*, Dreeben examined teaching as an occupation, with an extended discussion of several aspects of teachers' work that distinguishes it from other occupations. One of the hallmarks of teaching when the book was published in 1970, and a continuing source of commentary today, is that teachers have considerable autonomy in instructional matters. With supervision by principals and other school administrators infrequent at best, teachers can present material to students in practically any fashion they choose. Thus, although policymaking by higher authorities acts as a counterbalance to teacher autonomy, Dreeben also noted its limited success in constraining teachers' behaviors. In 1970 school boards and district administrators were the most important policymakers in education. But as documented by both William Firestone and Tom Loveless, authors of the two chapters in this section of the book, power has shifted upward in the administrative hierarchy since *The Nature of Teaching* was written. Prodded by various reform movements during the past three decades, states have assumed a greater role in governing schools and have created an impressive array of tools to ensure that local educators follow policies. Have these policy changes made teaching more governable than it was when Dreeben wrote *The Nature of Teaching*?

Firestone (Chapter 9) examines the impetus behind the state-initiated reforms of the last two decades, especially the standards and assessment reforms of the 1990s. Standards were supported by professional educators who hoped to enrich the intellectual content of subject matter, which for years had been criticized as neither interesting nor challenging. Assessment programs were supported by accountability advocates, many of whom believed that education should adopt management practices of the business world. By regularly testing students and gearing incentives toward greater student learning, states could encourage students and teachers to be more productive.

Firestone offers several Dreeben-like insights suggesting that standards and assessments will not dramatically change the conduct of teaching. Teachers' notions about professionalism—that instruction should be driven by the best interests of students and that they and teachers, not policymakers, are in the best position to discern these interests—serve as daunting obstacles to steering instruction from beyond the classroom. Firestone also notes that accountability systems threaten well-established zones of authority in which administrators and upper-level officials decide questions concerning budgets, attendance, and student behavior, leaving instruction and classroom-level decisions to teachers. Moreover, Firestone describes an important split in the political forces supporting standards. Professional educational organizations (on the one hand) support standards for the purpose of changing traditional content and pedagogy, while accountability advocates (on the other) push for rewards and sanctions tied to more traditional conceptions of good teaching and academic achievement. This political conflict led to drastically revamped tests in Kentucky and California, as innovative assessments were overthrown for more traditional tests. In addition, technical problems have plagued tests in several states, undermining political support.

Notwithstanding these difficulties, content may be an area susceptible to influence by centralized authority. Firestone reviews studies of how teachers in three states have responded to standards-based reforms. He concludes that there is some evidence of math teachers, for example, shifting the emphasis from traditional content areas to areas promoted by curriculum reformers. But instructional practices have been less amenable to change. Teachers appear to have added practices that accommodate state tests, such as using manipulatives in instruction, but they have not yet altered their fundamental instructional approaches. Firestone's conclusion that states are able to influence curriculum more than instruction is consistent with Dreeben's observations in *The Nature of Teaching.*

In Chapter 10 Loveless is also skeptical that policies promoting reform, although plentiful, are powerful enough to substantially affect teaching. Loveless believes that instructional policies are generally ineffectual because of the weak science supporting most instructional reform. Put simply, the instructional changes sought by groups such as the National Council of Teachers of Mathematics are not well grounded in research. Loveless argues that teaching's weak technology is to blame. In *The Nature of Teaching,* Dreeben observed that "the central problem of teaching as an occupation is *the state of its technology*" (Dreeben 1970:206; emphasis in original). By technology he was referring to a body of knowledge spelling out the essential tasks of teaching, how to do them, and why they are done. A robust technology of teaching would tie together the ends and means of teachers' work, identifying what teachers are to accomplish and the activities leading to the accomplishment.

Like Firestone, Loveless sees a split in the standards movement but he believes that a critical distinction should be made between two objectives of contemporary policies, between the regulation of teaching and the regulation of learning. Teaching's weak technological base affects both types of policies. Thinking about them (as Dreeben does) as targeting the means and ends of teaching is illuminating. Instructional reformers urge teachers to modify or abandon traditional teaching strategies for progressive techniques. The means of teaching are targeted for change, but the reformers usually can provide little evidence that altering traditional instruction will produce valued ends. The fact that in many communities parents organize to oppose instructional innovations further undermines the reforms' credentials in the eyes of many teachers. Content reformers, on the other hand, attempt to regulate students' learning. The effect of a weak technology is more subtle here, but no less enervating on the power of policy to induce change. Stipulating the content that students must learn—and holding teachers accountable for producing these ends—is a dubious proposition without an ample stock of instructional approaches that will reliably produce the desired outcomes. Otherwise teachers will be held accountable for producing something that no one in a predictable, systematic way knows how to produce.

SOCIOLOGY OF EDUCATION AS A FIELD OF INQUIRY

Part V of this book consists of a single chapter by Barbara Schneider (Chapter 11), which examines developments in the field of sociology of education. Dreeben's (1994) contribution to this literature focused on twentieth century developments in three areas: social mobility and stratification, community studies, and the social organization of schooling. Schneider updates these areas and adds three new topics, which she views as increasingly important to the field: inequality and social justice, globalization and the expansion of schooling, and social networks in education. Of course inequality and social justice have long been of interest to sociologists of education, and Schneider's point is that the current constellation of policies (e.g., choice, resegregation, testing and accountability, ending affirmative action) makes this a compelling issue around which to analyze historical developments at the intersection of sociology and educational policy. Similarly, the expansion of education is not a new topic, but current interest in globalization places the analysis of the transformation of education in developing countries at the center of the sub-discipline. Moreover, change in conceptual thinking within the field has moved the concept of community from geographically to functionally located (e.g., Coleman 1988), giving network analysis an important place in socio-logical research on education.

Schneider's additions to Dreeben's overview of the field highlight the importance of educational policy concerns within sociology of education. Dreeben did not ignore the inherent policy relevance of the field and noted that sociology of education has long struggled to serve the dual aims of con-tributing to theory and addressing problems in the practice of education. By identifying three substantive areas in which this tension is most evident, Schneider helps further the synthesis of sociology and policy analysis within the study of education.

CONCLUSIONS

Reflecting on the chapters in this book, we conclude that Dreeben's arguments from the 1960s, 1970s, 1980s, and 1990s hold up remarkably well today. Studies stimulated by *On What Is Learned in School* indicate that schools con-tinue to serve as the bridge between family and adult society, despite changes in family compositions and social norms. The structures of schools and class-rooms remain fundamental to student socialization and the creation of class-room goodwill remains essential to a teacher's success. School structure is also a central theme in studies stimulated by *How Schools Work*. Whereas Barr and Dreeben showed the importance of the hierarchical structure of school sys-tems for resource allocation in a loosely coupled system, today's era of tighter control makes the technology of schooling even more important than in times of looser coordination. The persistent difficulty of modifying technology—of changing what teachers and students do in classrooms—means that contem-porary reforms will continue to struggle to raise achievement.

The chapters on teaching reforms also resonate with Dreeben's views more than three decades after *The Nature of Teaching* appeared. Despite efforts to centralize control at the state and district levels, teachers remain substan-tially autonomous within their classrooms, moreso with regard to instruc-tional methods than curriculum content. Thus instructional change is extremely difficult to bring about through the exercise of hierarchical control.

Finally, Dreeben's overview of progress in sociology of education remains current, although recent concerns with policy and reform among sociologists—including Robert Dreeben himself—have broadened the field in a positive way.

REFERENCES

Barr, Rebecca. 1973–74. "Instructional Pace Differences and their Effect on Reading Acquisition." *Reading Research Quarterly* 9:526–54.

Barr, Rebecca and Robert Dreeben. 1983. *How Schools Work*. Chicago: University of Chicago Press.

Coleman, James S. 1988. "Social Capital in the Creation of Human Capital." *American Journal of Sociology* 94:95–120.

Dreeben, Robert. [1968] 2002. *On What Is Learned in School*. Clinton Corners, NY: Percheron Press/Eliot Werner Publications.

Dreeben, Robert. 1970. *The Nature of Teaching: Schools and the Work of Teachers*. Glenview, IL: Scott, Foresman.

Dreeben, Robert. 1994. "The Sociology of Education: Its Development in the United States." Pp. 7-52 in *Research in Sociology of Education and Socialization,* vol. 10, edited by Aaron M. Pallas. Greenwich, CT: JAI Press.

Gamoran, Adam. 1986. "Instructional and Institutional Effects of Ability Grouping." *Sociology of Education* 59:185–98.

Gamoran, Adam. 1987. "The Stratification of High School Learning Opportunities." *Sociology of Education* 60:135–55.

Gamoran, Adam, Martin Nystrand, Mark Berends, and Paul C. LePore. 1995. "An Organizational Analysis of the Effects of Ability Grouping." *American Educational Research Journal* 32:687–715.

Goffman, Erving. [1974] 1986. *Frame Analysis: An Essay on the Organization of Experience*. Boston: Northeastern University Press.

McFarland, Daniel A. 2001. "Student Resistance: How the Formal and Informal Organization of Classrooms Facilitates Student Defiance." *American Journal of Sociology* 107:612–78.

Parsons, Talcott. 1959. "The School Class as a Social System: Some of Its Functions in American Society." *Harvard Educational Review* 29:297–318.

Parsons, Talcott. 1960. *Structure and Process in Modern Societies*. Glencoe, IL: Free Press.

Perrow, Charles. 1984. *Normal Accidents: Living with High-Risk Technologies*. New York: Basic Books.

II

Schooling and Socialization

2

On What is Learned in School: A Verstehen Approach

Aaron M. Pallas
Matthew Boulay
Melinda Mechur Karp

On What Is Learned in School (Dreeben [1968] 2002) is widely recognized as a classic account of how the organization of schooling can facilitate young people's learning of norms. Building on Dreeben's analysis, we expand the consideration of schooling effects to encompass a broadened conception of what is learned in school. Through an interpretive analysis of life history interviews of adults, we strive to understand the meaning of schooling through individuals' accounts of what they learned in school. Our analyses suggest that adults recall the social psychological aspects of schooling much more so than the cognitive dimensions.

THE EFFECTS OF SCHOOLING

Since Durkheim ([1922] 1956) initiated the sociological study of educational institutions, two major issues have guided sociological research on education: "How do schools and schooling contribute to the maintenance of the social order?" and "What is the relationship between schooling and social stratification?" These questions have grown progressively more complex over the years as new empirical data and theoretical perspectives have been brought to bear on them. The first question draws attention to schools as socializing institutions and the ways in which schools develop the knowledge, skills, and dispositions that enable individuals to become competent members of society. The second question examines how education is related to social hierarchies defined in terms of social goods such as economic class, power, and prestige.

Aaron M. Pallas, Matthew Boulay, and Melinda Mechur Karp • Teachers College, Columbia University, New York, New York 10027.

Stability and Change in American Education: Structure, Process, and Outcomes edited by Maureen T. Hallinan, Adam Gamoran, Warren Kubitschek, and Tom Loveless. Eliot Werner Publications, Clinton Corners, New York, 2003.

Social scientists have struggled for decades to understand schooling's role in the lives of individuals as a window to the twin phenomena of socialization and stratification. Many studies have conceptualized the effects of schooling as changes in the qualities of the individuals exposed to different amounts of schooling, especially qualities such as knowledge, skills, and values (see Pallas [2000] for a review). Numerous researchers have designed projects that look across the lives of many different individuals who have had different schooling experiences. Often these studies use quasi-experimental designs to contrast the experiences and achievements of individuals who had some form of schooling with the experiences and achievements of comparable individuals who had not. In this tradition are studies on the effects of attending school on student achievement, including those that contrast learning when school is in session with summer learning (e.g., Heyns 1978, 1987; Entwisle and Alexander 1992, 1994), as well as studies on the effects of dropping out of school on learning (e.g., Alexander, Natriello, and Pallas 1985). Other researchers have relied on weaker designs for assessing the influence of schooling on individuals' values and knowledge (Hyman, Wright, and Reed 1975; Hyman and Wright 1979).

Studies on the effects of schooling have also emerged from the literature on social stratification and social mobility. Blau and Duncan (1967), for example, emphasized the process of stratification and used U.S. Census data to examine the extent to which occupational achievements depended on social origins, the extent to which education mediated the effects of social background on adult attainments, and the independent contribution of education to the prediction of socioeconomic achievement over and above the effects of social origins. This pioneering work—the beginning of the status attainment tradition in sociology—was extended by Sewell and his colleagues at the University of Wisconsin (Sewell, Haller, and Portes 1969; Sewell, Haller, and Ohlendorf 1970) who incorporated social psychological factors in adolescence into the model of the stratification process, and by Duncan, Featherman, and Duncan (1972) who added background variables, intervening variables (e.g., intelligence, motivation, and social influences), and career contingencies (e.g., marital status, fertility, age at first job, and residential migration). Over the years the status attainment literature has expanded to include organizational allocation mechanisms in school and the workplace, such as curriculum tracking and firm and labor market characteristics. The capacity of this research tradition to incorporate both socialization and allocation mechanisms has made it the primary framework for understanding the relationship between education and social stratification.

These literatures have paid little attention to the interiors of educational institutions. Beyond organizational structures, such as classroom ability grouping and tracking (e.g., Oakes 1985) and the occasional attention to how teachers teach (Bossert 1979; Plank 2000), just how educational institutions transform the qualities of individual students has not been explored thoroughly. Elsewhere (Pallas 2000) one of us has suggested that these transformative effects seem so rational to social scientists that they do not require empirical verification.

ON WHAT IS LEARNED IN SCHOOL

Even if there is evidence of such effects, the existing literature has not been very effective in articulating a theory of how the organization of schools affects the learning of individuals who attend them. In *On What Is Learned in School* ([1968] 2002), Dreeben attempted to link the social organization of schools to the socialization of children and youth. The argument, which Dreeben modestly called a "speculative essay," hinged on the claim that the social organization of schools differs from the social organization of other institutions in which children and youth participate, particularly the family. The distinctive ways in which schools are organized (he suggested) shape what is learned in school, particularly norms specifying how one ought to behave.

Dreeben's argument has often been linked to a functionalist account of the relationship between education and society. Such accounts typically associate the rise of mass education with the transition from an agricultural to an industrial economy. The shift of the locus of production from the family to the factory, coupled with growing urbanization and cosmopolitanism, taxed the capacity of the family to provide children with what they needed to know in order to function as competent adults in an industrial society. Parents could no longer count on their children to inherit their jobs directly and learn those jobs through in-home observation and apprenticeship. Schools sprang up, therefore, to provide the skills that young people would need as adults—skills that they could no longer obtain at home.

This is the technical side to technical-functionalism. However, Dreeben was not concerned with the technical knowledge gained in schools. Instead, he focused on what he referred to as some of the psychological outcomes of schooling, particularly the acquisition of norms or principles of conduct. By learning to cope with the tasks and demands implicit in the school setting, individuals come to accept the legitimacy of principles such as achievement, independence, universalism, and specificity and apply these principles to their own conduct. Although these principles are developed in the context of specific task situations, he argued, they become psychological dispositions relied on in other circumstances.

More than thirty years have passed since the publication of *On What Is Learned in School*, and the book is still read and discussed in sociology of education courses across the United States. It remains among the most provocative accounts of the relationship between the social organization of schooling and student learning. Davis (1971) once published a paper that explored what makes a theory interesting. Davis wrote that "interesting theories are those that deny certain assumptions of their audience." In contrast, uninteresting theories are those that simply affirm the assumptions of their audience. He went on to say:

Those who carefully and exhaustively verify trivial theories are soon forgotten; whereas those who cursorily and expediently verify interesting theories are long remembered. In fact, the truth of a theory has very little to do with its impact, for a theory can continue to be found interesting even though its truth is disputed—even refuted! (p. 309)

By this standard *On What Is Learned in School* is an interesting theory—not because its truth is disputed or refuted, but rather because it reorients the questions that educational researchers typically ask. Contrary to the typical assumption that what is learned in school is driven by curriculum and instruction, Dreeben argued that the structure of the school itself, particularly in relation to the structure of the family, affects learning outcomes. Moreover, the learning outcomes at issue (he suggested) were not the internalization of the manifest curriculum appearing in textbooks and on chalkboards, but rather the learning of social norms.

EMPIRICAL STUDIES OF SCHOOL LEARNING

Despite the power of Dreeben's ideas, relatively little empirical research assessing and enlarging on them has ensued. Instead, the field of sociology of education has drawn strength from large-scale prospective longitudinal surveys that have traced the experiences of cohorts of youth as they move through middle and high school into college and the world of work. But there are limits to what can be learned about schooling and the lives of individuals from large-scale social surveys. Though extremely useful for describing fundamental patterns of social stratification, and for estimating the correlation between educational attainment and adult socioeconomic success or failure, these surveys are unable to portray the dynamics and complexities of the processes by which education shapes lives and life experiences—including what is learned within such experiences. Sample surveys cannot tell us much about what being a student feels like; nor can they tell us how adults make sense of their schooling experiences and how they connect schooling to family, work, religion, and other social institutions. They cannot tell us what (if anything) students make of the content of their learning, especially as they move into adulthood. The meanings that adults draw from their schooling experiences are, in and of themselves, a new way of thinking about how schooling affects the lives of individuals. They are also a window to how schooling fits into a complex web of social institutions. The study of narratives of what individuals have learned in school provides a fresh (albeit partial) look at some of Dreeben's central ideas.

Although some social scientists have examined schooling in the life course, we know very little about how students—particularly children and adolescents—experience schooling and its social context in the immediacy of their everyday lives, how children and adolescents make sense of and feel about diverse facets of their schooling in the moments of their occurrence.

Nor do we know how adults, looking back at their childhood and adolescence, make sense of their schooling, including whether they even recall their schooling and how they live with their remembered experience in adulthood. The prevailing methodological approach, the quantitative analysis of longitudinal surveys, has not been well suited to addressing such questions. Because we are particularly interested in the latter question, we adopt a phenomenological approach to studying the role of schooling in the life course.

THE PHENOMENOLOGY OF THE LIFE COURSE

Phenomenological perspectives on the life course (Schutz [1932] 1967; Gubrium, Holstein, and Buckholdt 1994) suggest that social phenomena gain personal meaning—that is, they are converted into personal experience—when they are seen, thought through, and defined, often in retrospect and rarely if ever in their immediate occurrence. Phenomenologists typically view experience as knowable in retrospect more so than in immediacy (Schutz [1932] 1967). If schooling viewed as experience is indeed knowable to those being schooled after its occurrence in their lives, then individuals' retrospective thought and talk about their schooling experiences represent personal and heretofore untapped sources of data on schooling effects. Such data may provide insights on how it is that young people becoming adults come to know and live with the schooling of their childhood, adolescence, and adulthood.

A phenomenological conceptualization of schooling effects has only rarely been articulated or explored in the literature on schooling and the effects of schooling on children and society in general (see, e.g., Antikainen et al. 1996). The aim of recall—in a phenomenological sense—is less to reconstruct an event or situation in terms of some definition of accuracy than it is to evoke experience constructed in retrospect, and thereby reveal how schooling comes to manifest itself in adult lives. In this view memory is the adult's possession of knowledge garnered through past experience. The content of that memory represents effects of the past learning. Our study does not focus on children's schooling per se but rather on adults' memories, experiences, and understandings of schooling in childhood, adolescence, and adulthood.

Interpretive Methods

In relying on interpretive methods, we seek to expand the ways that social scientists have attempted to understand the effects of schooling on socialization and stratification. Most studies of schooling effects have located the effects of schooling in changes in the levels of various socialization and stratification outcomes (e.g., aspirations, academic achievement, occupational status) reported by individuals in prospective longitudinal studies, particularly large-scale social surveys. Although they represent a well-respected genre of sociological research, such studies treat these changes as actual or objective effects.

However, these surveys are not able to consider these changes in the levels of various socialization and stratification outcomes in relation to how individuals experience them and make sense of them. Our study relies on interpretive analyses of personal accounts of these effects, drawing on the responses that adults construct while being interviewed specifically about the perceived effects of schooling, as well as less direct accounts in the form of narratives of educational experiences in relation to subsequent life events.

In focusing on subjective experience and meaning, we are relying on an interpretive method akin to Weber's conception of sociology as a science seeking interpretive understanding (*Verstehen*). Though there are many strands of interpretivism, both within and across the humanities and social sciences, we believe it is fair to say that all take as their goal apprehending the meaning of social life—its events, experiences, and institutions—from the standpoints of individuals situated in local social, cultural, and historical contexts. No researcher can ever apprehend these meanings directly since they are always mediated by the gap between the experiences, consciousness, and language of the researcher and the experiences, consciousness, and language of those whom he or she seeks to study. There is, then, a conscious process of interpretation that occurs as the researcher strives to understand the meanings of events and experiences from the standpoint of the actor/interviewee.

The Nature of Life Histories

Runyan (1982) draws an important distinction between life history as method, a way of eliciting and recording a personal account of one's experience, and life history as object of study in which a researcher is interested in understanding the sequence of events and experiences in a person's life. He notes:

> Controversy about the value of the study of life histories stems in part from a lack of clarity about whether life histories are to be considered as a method of data collection or as a subject matter that can be investigated with an array of different methods. (p. 6)

We are using life histories as a method for gaining insight into the personal meanings that individuals ascribe to their schooling experiences, particularly the ways in which their narratives portray the role of schooling in socialization and stratification processes. We do not study narratives of schooling and subsequent life events qua narratives, but rather as a window to the meaning of schooling.

It is critical to understand how such narratives are produced and what they can tell us. First, a narrative of experience emerging from an interview is socially constructed, in fact, jointly constructed by the individual providing an account and the interviewer. Mishler (1986) notes:

> The interviewer's presence as a coparticipant is an unavoidable and essential

component of the discourse, and an interviewer's mode of questioning influences a story's production. Differences in whether and how an interviewer
encourages, acknowledges, facilitates, or interrupts a respondent's flow of
talk have marked effects on the story that appears. Finally, interviewers and
interviewees are both aware of and responsive to the cultural and research
contexts within which a particular interview is located. (p. 105)

A narrative life history is a fiction in the sense that Geertz (1973)
describes all anthropological writing—indeed all interpretation—as a *fictio*,
something that is made. This is because a narrative cannot capture or reproduce life as it is lived, or even as it is experienced. As Freeman (1993) and others have pointed out, no narrative of life experience can be complete or
exhaustive. Rather, even a narrative that is intended to convey only factual
material must interpret the past in selecting which past events are to be
described, and in what way. Even determining what is an event, whether
selected for a narrative or not, is an interpretive act. Such interpretive acts represent attempts to organize one's past in the terms of not only the past, but also
the present and even looking forward into the future. That is, a life history
narrative represents an attempt to make sense of the past in terms of the meanings conferred on the past in light of present experience. Beyond the effort to
make sense of events, a life history narrative also is an attempt to make sense
of the self (Freeman 1993). Thus as the self evolves over time and the meanings of past events are continually reinterpreted in light of ongoing experience, narratives that interpret the past also will change.

If we acknowledge that a narrative is of necessity an interpretation, then
the very question of the validity of a narrative as an account of past events
becomes problematic. Is it meaningful to interrogate a life history narrative as
a true account of events in the past? That depends on one's conception of
truth. Freeman (1993) argues:

> If we think of "truth" in this context only in terms of its faithful correspon-
> dence to what was, then autobiographical texts must indeed be deemed illu-
> sory and fictional; in relying on the vantage point of the present for their very
> sense, it could be held that truth is, of necessity, out of the question. But there
> is little reason, I will suggest, to think of truth in this limited and simplistic
> way. . . . In relegating autobiographical texts to the status of mere fictions, we
> not only cut ourselves off from the possibility of attaining those insights that
> can accrue from the process of rewriting the self; we cut ourselves off from
> the possibility of thinking about historical truth itself in a deeper and more
> comprehensive way than is often allowed. (pp. 32–33)

There are two important points to be made here. First, there is no inherent reason to conclude that there is a disjuncture between a life history narrative and reality. As Antikainen and his associates (1996:29) point out, "It is
wrong to say that life-stories have nothing to do with reality just as it is wrong
to say that it would be possible to reach some absolute conception about the

past reality." Second, the truth of a life history narrative must be evaluated in terms of the specific ways in which the narrative is being used. Bertaux and Kohli (1984:219) note, "The question of the validity of retrospective data becomes much more important for those sociologists looking for patterns of historically given sociostructural relations than for those studying perceptions, values, definitions of situations, personal goals, and the like." As sociologists we cannot deny our interest in social structure and social change, but in this particular study our interests lie mainly in understanding how people make sense of their schooling experiences. We are, therefore, less interested in what the lens of memory reveals about events and even experiences occurring in the past than in the content and form of past experience relayed into—and lived—in the present tense. That reflects effects, effects known and felt deeply in individual adult lives today.

There is one more point we wish to make in addressing the issue of our use of narrative life histories as a source of data on the meanings that individuals ascribe to schooling in their lives. The validity of narrative accounts for this purpose is clearly a function of the skill of the researcher as interviewer and data analyst, as well as of the researcher's knowledge of the subject being studied. The ability of the interviewer to adopt a reflexive stance toward his or her role in the interview (Hammersley and Atkinson 1997) and also to interpret an interviewee's narration in real time—making judgments about what is important and what is not, what needs to be probed, what is internally coherent, and what is inconsistent with other sources of evidence—is a critical determinant of the narrative that the interviewer and interviewee coproduce. Beyond the interview setting itself, however, a researcher's capacity to interpret the various elements of a life story as an individual's own interpretation also requires analytic skills, including detailed knowledge about the subject of study.

Thus our intent was to rely on life history interviews about the role of schooling in the life course as a source of empirical data that we could juxtapose with some of the arguments posed in *On What Is Learned in School*. In particular, we sought to understand what adults had to say about what they had learned in school, including the balance between the cognitive/curriculum and social dimensions of schooling. We were equally interested in what adults might say about what they did not learn in school and the locus (such as family, work, church, or community) of out-of-school learning. In this chapter, however, we limit ourselves to adults' accounts of school learning.

METHOD

In the mid-1990s we conducted 51 interviews with adults aged 25 to 65 in the Lansing, Michigan, area. The original design for the study called for a sample of forty adults stratified by race (black or white), sex (male or female), and age (25–44 or 45–64). Respondents were randomly sampled from listed residential telephone numbers in U.S. Census tracts with high concentrations of minorities. Initial phone calls were followed by a letter and a subsequent phone call attempting to recruit participants. Participants were paid $25.00 for completing the face-to-face interviews, which averaged approximately one and one-half hours in length. The resulting sample of 39 interviewees is approximately evenly divided by race, sex, and age, although younger African American males and females are underrepresented.

We subsequently supplemented the original sample of 39 participants with an additional sample of Latino adults in mid-Michigan, sampling randomly from individuals with Spanish surnames in the residential telephone directory. We completed one dozen supplemental interviews with Latino participants.

The interview protocol was designed to elicit a roughly chronological account of individuals' educational careers and adult lives, thereby allowing the interviewee to construct a narrative tracing his or her school transitions and experiences to subsequent events in adult life. But the interview process does not impose a linearity on that process. Rather, the interviewer must attend to the narrative that the interviewee is constructing and probe to fill in gaps as necessary or appropriate.

During the interview we asked participants how far they had gone in school. More important, we asked about their school experiences. We asked why they had or had not continued in school and about their best and worst memories of school. Most important, we asked participants to tell us what they had learned in school and the effect this had on their lives. A list of some of these questions is included in the Appendix.

We analyzed the transcripts of the interviews in multiple ways. For some interviews we have written detailed case reports, treating the cases holistically. For others we coded for particular forms of school and out-of-school learning and looked across the transcripts to identify recurring patterns in the data. The analyses we report reflect this two-pronged approach. The analytic question we pose is "What kinds of school learning do adults report?" We begin by summarizing the types of learning in school that our respondents reported, including curriculum and social learning. We then report a specific case in greater detail to illuminate some analytic issues that are observed more easily in the context of a particular case.

REPORTS OF SCHOOL-BASED LEARNING

We begin to address the question of the kinds of school learning reported by our interviewees by enumerating the categories of learning. Our categories are not exhaustive but the most salient—based on their frequency in the data and prior research and theory—are curriculum learning, the learning of norms, learning about the self, and learning about difference.

Curriculum Learning

Some, but by no means all, respondents mentioned learning the formal curriculum of the school. The question often seemed to surprise people, perhaps because it seems so obvious that one learns basic literacy and numeracy skills in the early years in school. When prompted interviewees were more likely to describe academic learning. One woman said that she learned "just the basics, you know, reading, writing, arithmetic, and stuff like that." A middle-aged African American man who had dropped out of high school tied basic numeracy skills to handling currency. "You know, [to] do money, you need to know how to count," he said. Janelle (all names are pseudonyms, to protect the confidentiality of the respondents), a 34-year-old white nurse, stated, "Well, I learned how to read and write and I think that's real important. I was a very good speller. I have a pretty good vocabulary."

More often the respondents discussed academic knowledge garnered in secondary school. Interestingly, history and social studies were often cited as the most salient subjects learned in school. Accounts of history and social studies were frequently tied to imagining or envisioning differences, whether temporally or spatially. Ida, a 45-year-old African American inspector at Oldsmobile, liked learning about history.

> I always wanted to know what it would be like if [I] could live back in history—I really did. I always wanted to live back when the witches and stuff—back there in Salem. I really wanted to know how, what that was all about. How it felt to be, not be a witch, but just livin' in that time, you know.

Phil, a 62-year-old African American labor negotiator, was fascinated by geography.

> Just learning about, oh, history, geography, look at different places and people and, oh, different cultures and, oh just, different things, just about the world, what it was all about and the different areas of the world and the different people. . . . How they interacted, even to the point of what their diet was and this sort of thing, you know, the kind of things that were relevant, germane to the people of the area and how that differed from us here.

Geography was of similar interest to Paulo, a Greek immigrant who completed ninth grade. "See, my kids right now they don't know where, I don't know, France is," he said. "They don't know where South America is; Mexico is maybe," he laughed.

> We used to know every country's capital. Supposed to know the capital, supposed to know about their population, basic things. What kind of, how big it is, and their neighbors . . . is it agricultural, is it, you know, what kind of economy they do have, is it a poor country, is, and also if they're democracy or, you know, socialism country, or whatever. . . . It helped me a lot and I can talk with you if you, let's say, I can socialize with people who knows [sic] about geography.

Language skills also were a frequent point of reference. "[My junior high school English teacher] taught me how to structure, how to write extemporaneously, too," said Miranda, a 48-year-old music teacher. "Impromptu writing. . . . Just that one class—she taught me grammar, we diagramed sentences. And because I got that training in grammar—I took the language and it was no problem for me. Because I understood grammar."

The interviewees rarely linked the curriculum knowledge that they learned in elementary and secondary school to their experiences in the workplace. The few exceptions were classes that had a vocational cast to them. Harriet, a 34-year-old white dispatcher, mentioned learning to drive. "We learned to drive in school," she said. "That's where they had drivers' training. That was a whole set of new freedom—learning to drive . . . I remember almost running the car in a ditch! . . . Driver's Ed car almost in the ditch, in the snow!" she laughed. Some students mentioned home economics classes or shop classes, whereas others pointed to bookkeeping or typing classes. Mitch, a 52-year-old white director of a social service agency, said, "I used [to] think, 'What would a guy need typing for?' . . . and that, perhaps, my high school and grade school, was the most beneficial topic, was typing, 'cause I've used it."

Among those respondents who attended college, and particularly those who obtained graduate education, there were frequent references to learning curriculum content. Music teachers described what they had learned in music classes; accountants and engineers discussed accounting and engineering classes; and even liberal arts majors mentioned philosophy, sociology, government, and theology classes. Not surprisingly, many linked professional education to the practice of their profession.

However, respondents usually drew a distinction between the technical knowledge that they garnered in school and the technical knowledge employed on the job. A civil servant with a degree in accounting noted, "So, you use those accounting tools, but it's not like *public* accounting. . . . So yeah, I use my accounting degree, but not like someone who wears a green eyeshade and keeps T-accounts and stuff—it's not like that." Stuart, a 32-year-old African American engineer, was even more pointed. "In school, they teach you a certain way—when you get to the job, they teach you another way," he said. "And you have to do it the way the job taught you." Perhaps least surprising, a classroom teacher was particularly ambivalent about school learning as preparation for her career as a teacher. "I didn't learn a lot that I could use in my career," she said. "I think what I had when I first started work. I didn't have a lot that I had learned that I could use with the type of work that I was doing . . . the things that helped me in my career, I learned that through experience."

Far more common than references to subject-matter learning were claims about "learning how to learn." Carleton, a 44-year-old program coordinator for a school district, said, "If I don't know something, I know how to find out, and I'm not afraid to ask questions or to go try. I'm not afraid to, to take risks along those lines. The old adage of, the only bad question is the one you don't ask." Another respondent, speaking of his undergraduate days, reported, "You learn certain skills or you begin, I'd say I learned a lot, but I would define it as learning how to learn, or learning how to begin a process of teaching and learning."

Others spoke of learning to value or love learning itself. Susan, a 44-year-old composer, stated that she "learned to value learning," attributing this jointly to her family and particular teachers she encountered in high school. Carleton marveled at

> realizing that learning was not a destination, was not a goal, it was a process, you know, and it was something that you did continuously. And I think that more than anything else that idea, that philosophy, that it's not just to get to the end of the book or the end of the chapter, it's an ongoing process, that stuck with me more than anything else.

In sum, adults reported learning simple intellectual tasks, facts and figures, and complex and abstract ideas. These types of learning correspond roughly to what Broudy (1977) referred to as "knowing that" and "knowing how." However, the learning described by our respondents went beyond these forms of learning to include learning how to learn, which approaches Broudy's notion of "knowing with."

The Learning of Norms

Schools regulate behavior and our interviewees described a remarkable variety of rules of conduct. One said:

> [In high school] we had four hundred kids always millin' around on one floor of a long, narrow school. And so, to kinda manage that, we had floor monitors and you always go out a room, to the right. And you could cross over here, and you could cross over there, and you could cross over at each end. And, of course, if you tried to cross over in-between there, you'd get nailed—OK? So there were a lot of rules.

Some rules—such as dress codes and the like—seemed arbitrary, but even such rules could be viewed as contributing to preparation for work and adult society. Dressing properly and looking clean were seen as having long-term benefits, but more in hindsight than at the time. Paulo, for example, described his run-ins with his junior high school principal.

> Used to go with a tie. If we didn't have a tie, our principal was in the door. We didn't like, some things we didn't like, but, you know, we had it in our pocket. Put the tie, go in, and take it [off] again. But that taught me when I started working, I had to do that. . . . This is the way of life. . . . If I didn't know, learn at the school, those kind of things, to be a little bit clean, whatever, probably I wouldn't fit into society, I'm thinking.

Perhaps the most vivid account of the regimentation of school life is that of Susan.

> When I have a school bus dream, oh, my God, what's happening in my life because it's where I'm trapped in something where I can't say I don't belong here and it's uniformity and being stuck in a glove that doesn't fit. You must eat at this time. You must eat this food no matter what color it is or what it tastes like. You have to eat off of these plates and they're ugly and there's a feeling like you're in the belly of a slave ship or something.

Students who broke the school's conduct rules were typically punished, which often evoked feelings of shame or embarrassment that were memorable even decades later. A woman in her late forties recalled, "First grade, I did have one bad memory. But, it was because I disobeyed the teacher. And I got punished—I remember that. Had to put my head down for recess time, you know." Sighing, she said, "So I learned, you know."

Although some respondents recall flouting the rules of the school with fondness, more often learning these rules of conduct was characterized as just something one did. Miranda said:

> You learn how to be responsible for things that the teacher tells you to be responsible for. You learn how to take a test. You learn how to give a teacher the answers that they want—whether you think they're right or not. What you learn is to spit back information that you're given by a teacher.

Other social norms were more comfortable. "If you work hard, you will get a good grade," said Carleton. "If you understand and not always need to be understood, you know, you'll find that you get along better in most situations and with most people. So school provided the framework where all of these things were confirmed." The word "confirmed" here suggests that many norms and values originated in the family, but then were validated or extended in school settings.

Perhaps the most common account of learning in school involved learning to get along with other people. Ida described high school as teaching her "how to live in the real world. That's what I call it. 'Real world.' Bein' able to deal with people, you know? . . . You learn how to socialize. You learn how to go out. You learn about boys." Similarly, Paulo pointed to how middle school "helped me out to, you know, socialize with people." Harriet even described "[learning] how kids get along" as "the social rules, if you wanna call 'em that."

The adults in this study were quick to point to life in schools as dictated by rules, both written and unwritten, some imposed by the school and some imposed by the youth culture on students. As with learning the formal curriculum, it may be that the learning of norms is so taken for granted that it is not worthy of mention. Even so, adults pointed to the social features of schooling as a source of learning far more than the cognitive features.

Learning about the Self

Many interviewees described schooling as a site for learning about themselves, particularly their abilities and competencies. Through elementary and secondary schooling, they reported, they came to understand what they were good at—in a sense, the self as performer or, perhaps, as learner. Stuart allowed that "through my schooling, I learned that I had a lot more talent than I knew—that I was a commercial artist." Sylvia, a middle-aged Chicana, recalls "my peers, walking home from school one day, talking about how difficult [a high school English] class was, and I didn't find it difficult at all. And it was then that I realized, oh, okay, well, this may be a talent of mine." It is unlikely that Sylvia could have learned about her academic proficiency at home, because in the family individuals usually are compared to their siblings—who may be older or younger and thus not really comparable—and usually not along academic dimensions. Harriet explicitly compared herself to her brothers and took great pride in besting them. "That was always nice, to come home with a good grade," she said. "I was the only daughter with three brothers, so it was kinda nice—come home and say, 'Look what I did and you guys didn't!'"

For Carleton it took going to community college to see what he was capable of academically.

> I found out . . . that I was a more competent, a better student than I had ever given myself credit for. . . . You know, that through elementary school and freshman and sophomore year, I acquired a, I learned quite a bit of knowledge. More so than that, I learned how to learn, learned how to do research, how to put together papers, and so forth.

Part of learning about the self is learning about the self in the context of, or in relation to, others. Several respondents mentioned the ways in which schooling helped them be more self-confident in group settings. One respondent said, "I know I used to be a very shy person, timid person, and some of my going, going to some of these classes and things that I had to learn in the classes that I have attended have helped me to deal with the people out in the real world where I couldn't do that before." Another interviewee recalls "being *afraid* of people, or afraid to offend people, or things like that. And yet, to run for class office, I had to give a speech in front of the whole school, and I had to, you know, create posters that said what a great guy I was, and things like that." Communications and speech classes were particularly beneficial. "I think speech class really helped me to be . . . more comfortable in front of people," Miranda told us, "'cause I was very shy. And so that was a good thing for me."

Learning about the self, then, took many forms, some of which (self as learner) were directly related to the student role and others of which (self as performer or self as a social creature) were not. Learning about the self was frequently cast as the transformation, or unveiling, of psychological dispositions: introversion, extroversion, and openness, for example.

Learning about Difference

Schools are larger than families, and as students progress through school, they are likely to encounter more and more individuals who are different from their family members in complex ways: in social class background, skin color, religion, ethnicity, and language, just to name a few social characteristics. Respondents routinely described school as the place where they learned about the diversity and differences that exist in the world outside of their kin relations and neighborhoods. Harriet said:

> [School] taught me to deal with people, a diversified people. My neighborhood was primary middle-class white, not much exposure to a colored person or Hispanic. And it helped me with dealing with that culture and that ethnic—yeah, I think it did. Different kinds of people. Exposure to different people—different temperaments—different ideas.

For minority students, though, learning about difference often meant learning about prejudice. Phil saw the ugly side of race relations in high school.

> When the folks started interacting, proms and one thing or another, then that's when some lines got drawn. . . . Also in my high school, and this is kind of hanging dirty linen, but in my high school the black kids in my high school were not allowed to take swimming. We had to take gym. There was no rhyme or reason to it but we weren't allowed. My entire high school career, I had never, never ever got into that pool.

Sylvia recalled a more particularistic experience of prejudice.

> I remember in second grade a nun accusing me of cheating on a test, because I got the highest score. And I remember remarking to her, "Well, how is it possible that I could have cheated if I got the highest score, who could I have copied from?' And got in a lot of trouble over that. And she made it quite clear, that her next sentence in front of the class was, 'Well, you couldn't have gotten the highest score because you're a Mexican, and everyone knows that Mexicans are stupid.' And I carry that lesson with me through life. And understand that people have prejudices that you just have to be able to understand. It's difficult to understand them, but not all people come from the same place and the same experiences.

Even individuals who had little formal contact with the schooling system managed to learn about prejudice and intolerance in school. Roberto, a Mexican American man in his forties, was raised in a family of migrant farmworkers. His family moved so frequently during the picking season that he was never in school in one place long enough to learn to read. When he did alight briefly in a school in Florida, he recalls

> kids laughing because here's a guy that—everybody else could read, and this guy can't read. . . . I remember getting mad a lot. . . . A lot of arguments, a lot of fights, as a young kid in school because of that. You know? I didn't like anybody making fun of me; and to me, I didn't think I was what they say I was. I forgot what names they used to call me, but I was called different names.

Summary

From the evidence we have presented, one might conclude that the adults in our sample felt that they had learned a great deal in school. Many did proclaim this, although others found school to be a complete waste of time and far less valuable than the "street sense" that others held dear. What is apparent, though, is that even those individuals who felt they learned a lot in school frequently were talking about learning different things. Some emphasized the formal academic curriculum, others the social psychological dimensions of schooling, and still others the social rules necessary to function effectively in the workplace and adult society generally.

Our presentation to this point does not delve deeply into the conditions under which various forms of learning might have taken place. In the next section, we present the case of Rich Dalton, an adult reflecting on his learning in a particular time and place. In doing so we hope to further elaborate our understanding of the conditions that are associated with recollections of particular kinds of learning.

GOING TO COLLEGE DURING THE VIETNAM WAR

We interviewed Rich Dalton, a real estate broker, when he was 48 years old. He grew up in a working-class white suburb of Detroit, Michigan, and has spent virtually his entire life in the state. He describes his family as blue collar. His father, who was "very uneducated, although very bright," was a pipefitter. His mother went to business college but he did not mention whether she was employed while he was growing up. He has a twin sister with a master's degree in music who is a professional accompanist. His brother, who is five years older, is also a real estate broker.

Rich graduated from high school and attended a private liberal arts college, graduating with a degree in business in 1969. He drew number one in the draft lottery and refused induction, fleeing to Canada. On returning to Michigan, he chose military service over jail and received a medical discharge. Thereafter he worked for a defense industry firm, and after a few years went into real estate management.

Rich describes his high school as a "tough" working-class school in which perhaps 40 percent of the students dropped out of high school and perhaps 10-15 percent went on to college. He was heavily involved in the concert band, orchestra, and pep band. "It's funny," he says, "educationally, as far as academics are concerned, high school—I think high school for me was, band and orchestra was there, and you had to go to classes in order to participate in band and orchestra."

Rich describes himself as a "mediocre" student in high school, with an occasional "D" in mathematics. His favorite subject in high school was "history, without a doubt." He also liked English a great deal. He remembers more bad teaching than good teaching in high school but, he says, "My best memories are centered around band and orchestra. I don't know what I would've done without band and orchestra."

Rich's memories of high school are vague; "I didn't learn a thing," he says. Perhaps this is because his experiences in college have been so influential in his life. Going to college was "almost an afterthought," says Rich. "I didn't have the foggiest notion [what to do with my life]. I wasn't even sure if I wanted to go to college." Rich's minister "pushed" him to go to college and helped him submit applications to a number of schools, each of which accepted him. Rich recalls thinking, "'I don't think I wanna do this,' you know, 'I just—I'm not ready for this.' And then all of a sudden, halfway through the summer, I said, 'Oh, maybe I do.'"

It is at this point that the Vietnam War began to loom as a context for Rich's life, and for his college years in particular.

> [I was] always shadowed, even then, at the beginning, by the Selective Service, OK? The draft. And that plays very, very heavily in my life. OK? I mean, it was extremely important, the war years. And that was the thought, that if you didn't go to school, they're gonna throw an M-16 in your hand and go tell you to kill people. So that was an extreme motivator for people of my immediate generation, of my age group. . . . I know that's what kept me in school after I got there.

College was different from high school in many ways. It was a small school in a small town, quite liberal, and far more diverse than his white, blue-collar upbringing. Rich recalls:

> It was a very, very relaxed atmosphere, and lots of, you know, diverse people—I mean, I was thrilled, I made a point of meeting people there that I would not have met in my lower-class white home, you know, upbringing, so I was thrilled to meet black kids, you know—I'd never really talked to a black kid in my life, and I was made an honorary 'Seoul Brother'—not from the black kids, but from the Korean kids who were all from Seoul, Korea.

Rich mentioned two important ways in which the social organization of college enabled him to learn things that he otherwise would not have learned. The first was the exposure to a more diverse social and cultural world than the family and community in which he grew up. College made Rich "stop and look at different things" and made him "more aware of different people." He said, "I came from a household that was very racist. And my parents are good people, but they're from a different era, you know? . . . It was the idea of going to a place like [this college] that . . . gave me the opportunity to meet people of different backgrounds," ranging from students from Southeast Asia to blacks from the South Side of Chicago. Rich was "absolutely in awe of meeting all these people. And it—that has never left me . . . I've been blessed [to have] the ability to go talk to and meet and enjoy people from all different backgrounds."

Rich learned about different cultural traditions and many of his memories are of the distinctive traditions of the Korean students, some of whom had fought in Vietnam. He joked about the drinking habits of the Koreans and how they would be offended if you stopped drinking while socializing. He also was shocked to learn that the sister of a Korean student was party to an arranged marriage with a Korean professor teaching in the United States. But he was equally excited to learn about black culture, recounting a game that two black students from Chicago and Detroit played involving cutting buttons off clothes with a knife. "That was very important for me to meet all these people, from various cultural backgrounds," Rich says. "'Cause it was just, it was just so exciting, and to realize that different people—I mean, they're just different."

The second way in which Rich's college experience enabled him to learn was through the informal ways in which he developed his antiwar views.

> Everything at [college], educationally, was shrouded by Vietnam. When I was in school, people didn't talk, necessarily—if the guys sat around the dorm, you know, they talk about sure—they talk about girls, they talk about sports—then, the conversations always, and I mean always, wound up, at least, with my circle of friends, wound up political. OK? Talkin' about the Vietnam issue . . . this was all unfolding, you know, as I entered college.

Rich drew on many sources of information about the war from outside the classroom. He spoke to Vietnam veterans returning to college after completing their service. "We were meeting, constantly meeting," Rich says, "and I was a person that I was always talking to them. You know, 'What's goin' on? Tell me what's goin' on." Although Rich describes himself as "very political," he

> never carried a placard, or I never did any of that sort of stuff. I was much more interested in readin' the Constitution and trying to develop an idea— try to understand how they could have the draft, when involuntary servitude is directly and indirectly forbidden . . . we were talking to people, we were reading, you know, we knew about all the resolutions, we knew about that sort of stuff.

The war reached deeply into the social lives of the students because the stakes were so high. "People would fail their draft physical, or whatever," Rich recalls, "and, and it was—it was party time. Because if you didn't fail the draft physical, if something didn't happen, you were gonna go."

"I never participated with the antiwar effort because it was campy, or anything," Rich asserts, noting that he is not against defending one's country.

> I was participating because they were killing my friends. They were killing, you know, people that I went to high school with. And then, of course, it didn't take you long to realize that they were killing Vietnamese. Because as my experience at college increased, all of a sudden I met people that had different color skin, and spoke different languages, and ate things that were ungodly, and they were all good people. And that's, then, I could associate with the Vietnamese—be it South Vietnamese or North Vietnamese—doesn't make any difference.

Rich summarizes:

> [College] did play a big role. But not necessarily—that's funny, not necessarily class work but it was the whole, you know, the whole experience of some of the teachers I had; of the different ethnic backgrounds; and then assimilating those with what was going on nationally—you know, or internationally, I should say, with the war in Vietnam, and the killing and the, you know, and all that sort of stuff. So that's what affected me.

One of the interesting features of this case is the way in which historical time interacts with educational experience to produce a distinctive conception of what is learned in school. Rich attended college during a period of substantial social upheaval, with the dark shadow of the Vietnam War looming over all aspects of his college years—and even beyond—as he resisted the draft, fled to Canada, and returned for a brief period of military service. He is aware of just how different his experience was from the experiences of other generations of collegians. Rich said:

> [The] Vietnam War was incredible, you know, on how it affected, not me, but everyone. You know, especially during those, that particular time in history. It was a great time to be in college, because things were changing so quickly—I mean, the civil rights movement was just exploding.

In another sense going to college during the war years was a consciousness-raising experience. Certainly this was true for Rich, who acknowledges the ways in which going to college gave him access to information about the war, and to people who he believed were knowledgeable about the war effort. Interestingly, these were rarely his professors, but rather other students and campus visitors. Colleges and universities were the primary settings in the United States for these kinds of discussions and debates to take place.

However, we want to focus here on Rich Dalton's account of how he came to apprehend difference in college. He notes that his parents were "very racist" and that his high school was overwhelmingly white and working class. The structure of college created opportunities for learning about cultural differences and similarities that simply did not exist in Dalton's family, nor in his prior schooling. The family of origin, of course, is typically culturally homogeneous, and residential segregation can lead to relatively homogeneous elementary and secondary schools.

In contrast, the structure of the residential college creates more opportunities for engaging with differences among students. The physical separation of the school from the family, coupled with the application of relatively meritocratic admissions criteria, is likely to result in a student body that is more diverse culturally than are the elementary and secondary schools that most students previously attended. Moreover, the structure of college life provides opportunities for sustained contact with individuals of differing backgrounds outside the classroom. College students have a schedule of classes that allows substantially more freedom of association than do high school or elementary school students. When one is at college, relatively few hours are spent in the classroom.

Now suppose that these same structural features of the residential college were present in the elementary school. Could elementary school students have come to apprehend the nature of cultural difference and similarity in the way that Rich Dalton did? That is, would these same structural features lead to similar learning outcomes among youngsters as they seem to among the college aged? Our contention is that they would not.

We conjecture that there are cognitive and developmental constraints on the ability to classify individuals into categories of similarity and difference. For example, Hirschfeld (1996) has argued that American and European children begin to organize the world on the basis of race as early as age three—not because they are modeling their parents' beliefs, but rather due to innate mental structures that have been adaptive over time. If this is so, then school structures that might allow for learning about universalism and specificity may simply not be very effective in applying these ideas to racial and cultural diversity.

On the other hand, it is clear that many adults (such as Rich Dalton) have been able to develop a more nuanced understanding of race and culture. Dalton attributes this to the interplay of school structure and culture in the form of the civil rights and antiwar movements. School structure alone does not seem an adequate explanation for Dalton's learning about universalism and specificity. Apparently the effects of structure are contingent on both individual psychosocial development and cultural context.

CONCLUSION

One of the great strengths of *On What Is Learned in School* is the way in which it straddles the micro-macro divide that bedevils so much of sociology.

Dreeben uses a microanalysis of how individuals learn norms in school to build a macrolevel argument about the relationship between education and society. If at the microlevel schooling contributes to the learning of norms, then at the macrolevel schooling creates individuals who can adapt to the demands of modern life, especially those imposed by the complex economy of the industrialized state and the political system such as American democracy. Although schools are not the only institution that can produce the requisite psychological capacities—that is, the learning of norms such as independence, achievement, universalism, and specificity—they are, Dreeben argues, better suited than the family to do so.

This is a great argument for the ways in which the massification of education at the elementary and secondary level functioned to support stable political and occupational structures. However, Dreeben did not extend his argument to tertiary education, which of course has a different set of school structures than does elementary and secondary education. We would like to suggest that the processes of industrialization and globalization have created a world in which the polity and the economy are infused with cultural diversity. The stability of these institutions may depend on a citizenry with a growing understanding of cultural differences and similarities. Perhaps the expansion of higher education can contribute to this stability through its effects on what is learned in school.

One of the challenges of this project is disentangling the experience of going to school from other experiences in the lives of our respondents. Schooling does not take place in isolation from social life. Rather, it is intertwined with family, work, and peer relations in fundamental ways. We continue to puzzle over how to judge what our respondents report as learning in school: whether it is attributable to the distinctive social relations of schooling, or whether it is simply that individuals locate their learning in school. High school, for example, coincides with adolescence. In the absence of schooling, would teenagers still learn about how to get along with their peers, including socially acceptable ways to relate to the other sex? Casual observation at any mall suggests that they would. Similarly, how much of Rich Dalton's political awakening stemmed specifically from being on a college campus, and how much from conversations with peers, watching the nightly news, and seeing demonstrations on the street? Antiwar activism was surely not limited to college campuses, although clearly they were a key site for protest.

What is at issue here is whether young people can, and frequently do, learn social norms in institutional settings other than schools. We do not doubt the declining ability of the family by itself to prepare the young to become adults in a complex, modern society. Other social institutions must bear much of the burden of socialization and the American public holds schools accountable for teaching values as well as facts. But it is not evident that schooling is the only such institution that might contribute to the learning of norms.

In suggesting the exchangeability of socializing institutions, we do not intend to detract from Dreeben's ([1968] 2002) analysis. Whereas he carefully documented how the social organization of schooling might contribute to the learning of norms, there are no parallel analyses of other socializing institutions. Moreover, the structures of schooling are highly stable (Tyack and Cuban 1995) such that virtually all children who enter the school are subjected to fundamentally similar experiences. It is not evident that the same is true of other socializing institutions that provide individuals with more customized experiences. As in so many other features of social life, it may be that middle-class origins confer advantages that lessen a child's dependence on the school as a site for learning norms. For children whose lives lack other stable social institutions, though, schooling may assume an even greater importance to their lives. Young people might encounter such institutions, perhaps serendipitously, and a great deal of social learning might take place. We ought not leave this up to chance.

Our analysis leads us to propose some additional lines of research. First, the norms that our adults articulated were far more specific than the norms of achievement, independence, universalism, and specificity discussed by Dreeben ([1968] 2002). Moreover, we discovered other forms of nonacademic learning in school reported by adults reflecting on their schooling experiences. Of course some of this learning took place in high school and college, whereas Dreeben focused his attention on the elementary years. Perhaps Dreeben's argument about the socializing effects of the social organization of schooling can be extended to these other forms of nonacademic learning.

Second, our analysis suggests that the learning of norms in school, as well as other forms of nonacademic learning in school, is framed by time and space—that is, by historical time and social space in the form of one's position in the social structure. Race, ethnicity, gender, and social class all surfaced as important contingencies in individuals' accounts of what they learned in school. Perhaps future research can incorporate these social categories more explicitly into the study of these nontraditional schooling effects.

Acknowledgments

This study was supported by the Institute for Children, Youth, and Families and the Institute for Research on Teaching and Learning across the Life Span at Michigan State University. We thank Anna Neumann, the editors, and the participants at the conference for their comments on earlier versions of this manuscript.

REFERENCES

Alexander, Karl, L. Gary Natriello, and Aaron M. Pallas. 1985. "For Whom the School Bell Tolls: The Effects of Dropping Out of High School on Cognitive Performance." *American Sociological Review* 50:409–20.

Antikainen, Ari, Jarmo Houtsonen, Juha Kauppila, and Hannu Huotelin. 1996. *Living in a Learning Society: Life Histories, Identities and Education.* London: Falmer Press.

Bertaux, Daniel and Martin Kohli. 1984. "The Life Story Approach: A Continental View." *Annual Review of Sociology* 10:215–37.

Blau, Peter M. and Otis Dudley Duncan. 1967. *The American Occupational Structure.* New York: Wiley.

Bossert, Stephen T. 1979. *Tasks and Social Relationships in Classrooms: A Study of Instructional Organization and Its Consequences.* Cambridge, UK: Cambridge University Press.

Broudy, Harry S. 1977. "Types of Knowledge and Purposes of Education." Pp. 1–17 in *Schooling and the Acquisition of Knowledge,* edited by Richard C. Anderson, Rand J. Spiro, and William E. Montague. Hillsdale, NJ: Erlbaum.

Davis, Murray S. 1971. "That's Interesting! Towards a Phenomenology of Sociology and a Sociology of Phenomenology." *Philosophy of the Social Sciences* 1:309–44.

Dreeben, Robert. [1968] 2002. *On What Is Learned in School.* Clinton Corners, NY: Percheron Press/Eliot Werner Publications.

Duncan, Otis Dudley, David L. Featherman, and Beverly Duncan. 1972. *Socioeconomic Background and Achievement.* New York: Seminar Press.

Durkheim, Emile [1922] 1956. *Education and Sociology* (Sherwood D. Fox, trans.). Glencoe, IL: Free Press.

Entwisle, Doris R. and Karl L. Alexander. 1992. "Summer Setback: Race, Poverty, School Composition, and Mathematics Achievement in the First Two Years of School." *American Sociological Review* 57:72–84.

Entwisle, Doris R. and Karl L. Alexander. 1994. "Winter Setback: The Racial Composition of Schools and Learning to Read." *American Sociological Review* 59:446–60.

Freeman, Mark. 1993. *Rewriting the Self: History, Memory, Narrative.* New York: Routledge.

Geertz, Clifford. 1973. "Thick Description: Toward an Interpretive Theory of Culture." Pp. 3–30 in *The Interpretation of Cultures: Selected Essays,* edited by Clifford Geertz. New York: Basic Books.

Gubrium, Jaber F., James A. Holstein, and David R. Buckholdt. 1994. *Constructing the Life Course.* Dix Hills, NY: General Hall.

Hammersley, Martyn and Paul Atkinson. 1997. *Ethnography: Principles in Practice,* 2nd ed. London: Routledge.

Heyns, Barbara L. 1978. *Summer Learning and the Effects of Schooling.* New York: Academic Press.

Heyns, Barbara L. 1987. "Schooling and Cognitive Development: Is There a Season for Learning?" *Child Development* 58:1151–60.

Hirschfeld, Lawrence A. 1996. *Race in the Making: Cognition, Culture, and the Child's Construction of Human Kinds.* Cambridge, MA: MIT Press.

Hyman, Herbert H. and Charles R. Wright. 1979. *Education's Lasting Influence on Values.* Chicago: University of Chicago Press.

Hyman, Herbert H., Charles R. Wright, and John S. Reed. 1975. *The Enduring Effects of Education.* Chicago: University of Chicago Press.

Mishler, Eliott G. 1986. *Research Interviewing: Context and Narrative.* Cambridge, MA: Harvard University Press.

Oakes, Jeannie. 1985. *Keeping Track: How Schools Structure Inequality.* New Haven, CT: Yale University Press.

Pallas, Aaron M. 2000. "The Effect of Schooling on Individual Lives." Pp. 499–525 in *Handbook of the Sociology of Education,* edited by Maureen T. Hallinan. New York: Kluwer Academic/Plenum.

Plank, Stephen. 2000. *Finding One's Place: Teaching Styles and Peer Relations in Diverse Classrooms.* New York: Teachers College Press.

Runyan, William McKinley. 1982. *Life Histories and Psychobiography: Explorations in Theory and Method.* New York: Oxford University Press.

Schutz, Alfred [1932] 1967. *The Phenomenology of the Social World* (George Walsh and Frederick Lehnert, trans.). Evanston, IL: Northwestern University Press.

Sewell, William H., Archibald O. Haller, and George W. Ohlendorf. 1970. "The Educational and Early Occupational Status Attainment Process: Replication and Revision." *American Sociological Review* 35:1014–27.

Sewell, William H., Archibald O. Haller, and Alejandro Portes. 1969. "The Educational and Early Occupational Attainment Process." *American Sociological Review* 34:82–92.

Tyack, David and Larry Cuban. 1995. *Tinkering toward Utopia: A Century of Public School Reform.* Cambridge, MA: Harvard University Press.

APPENDIX

Questions asked of the survey participants include:

• What was going to high school like for you?

• Sometimes people make conscious decisions about staying in school or leaving school. Other times they just wind up staying in school or leaving school without thinking about it that much. How did it happen that you [left high school] [stayed in high school through graduation]?

• If the respondent was a high school graduate: How did it happen that you [stopped with high school] [went to school after high school]?

• If the respondent continued his or her education after high school: What kind of student were you in [college] [other PSE]? What was that school like?

• What are your best memories of school, at any level?

• What are your worst memories of school, at any level?

• Everyone has times in school that are particularly tough. What do you consider to be the toughest time for you personally when you were in school?

• Some people say they learned a lot in school, and others say they didn't learn very much. Can you think of an example when you learned something really important in school?

• Some people think that going to school made them better workers, better citizens, or just plain better people. Other people don't feel that way. In your opinion, what sort of effect has your schooling had on your life?

3

The Problem of Classroom Goodwill

Charles E. Bidwell

In his classic book *On What Is Learned in School* ([1968] 2002), Robert Dreeben reflects on the meaning of goodwill and its manifestation in the classroom. He writes that "[t]eaching involves a classic problem in the creation of goodwill; finding in the classroom some equivalent to affection and support in the family, those forms of gratuitous pleasure not tied to *specific* acts in a relationship of exchange" ([1968] 2002:37). He goes on to observe that

> a general relationship of friendliness between teacher and pupils may . . . affect the terms of exchange [here referring to such exchanges as grades for performance] even if it is not such a term itself. . . . Conditions for the creation of goodwill . . . probably include associations between persons that endure beyond each social transaction as well as the successful use of *generalized* resources such as the expression of positive emotion. ([1968] 2002:37)

Dreeben raises the question of goodwill in his analysis of the resources that teachers can use to institute a classroom regime in which such instructional sanctions as grades, criticism, and praise "exchanged for specific manifestations of discrete skills and conduct" ([1968] 2002:37) are accepted as legitimate by the students. He notes that this problem differs between elementary and secondary schools. In the former it is a question of initially inducing students to "like school, accept the prevailing rules of the game, find gratification in doing school work, and learn to accept as rewarding the symbolic expressions that teachers intend them to experience as rewarding" ([1968] 2002:37). In the latter it becomes a problem if this work of socializing students to studentship has not been done properly.

Although Dreeben's discussion of goodwill is set within a theory of schooling as norm learning, he makes clear his belief that understanding

Charles E. Bidwell • Department of Sociology (Emeritus), University of Chicago, Chicago, Illinois 60637.

Stability and Change in American Education: Structure, Process, and Outcomes edited by Maureen T. Hallinan, Adam Gamoran, Warren Kubitschek, and Tom Loveless. Eliot Werner Publications, Clinton Corners, New York, 2003.

classroom goodwill is of broad importance for understanding how school social organization affects students' learning. I share his belief. I assume that goodwill in relationships between teachers and students is a condition of effective instruction, and the social organizational sources of goodwill in classrooms is my topic. First, I will define classroom goodwill and consider its relationship to the probability that a classroom operates as a common enterprise, with collective engagement in its academic tasks and common observance of norms of decorum. Second, I will discuss the bases of goodwill in classrooms and their variation among different kinds of schools. Third, I will ask how the institutional character of schools affects the emergence of goodwill in classrooms, sketching implications for students' individual academic effort and for the collective orderliness of the classroom.

GOODWILL DEFINED

Goodwill in classrooms is a principal condition for the legitimacy of classroom social and moral order. It can be defined as the willingness of students to accept the teacher's academic goals as their own. As a result of this acceptance, they commit substantial effort to the tasks that the teacher sets for them, accept the teacher's authority, and take the rules of classroom conduct and the rewards and punishments entailed in classroom tasks as right and proper.

Consider this definition in light of Portes and Sensenbrenner (1993:1322–27) on social capital. They specify four mechanisms by which individuals can be induced to participate in a common enterprise: value introjection, bounded solidarity, reciprocity transactions, and enforceable trust. Value introjection denotes the internalization of goals and norms of conduct. Once it has occurred, the individual is committed to the goals and rules and will act accordingly without external constraint or incentives. Goodwill certainly will occur when students have internalized classroom goals and norms. From a teacher's point of view, this is an ideal classroom situation.

Bounded solidarity refers to situations in which group boundaries are strong and well defined, so that group membership constitutes a distinctive identity and a focus of common interest such as a street gang, elite club, or selective high school. Goodwill may emerge when a classroom acquires bounded solidarity because all of its members find a desirably distinctive collective identity in their membership.

However, because students below the school-leaving age are to some degree coerced into attendance, value introjection cannot be assumed and it is usually unevenly distributed among the students even in the more academically selective schools and classrooms. Moreover, in this situation the sheer fact of classroom membership is not likely to provide a desirably distinctive identity of any sort.

As Dreeben argued, in the absence of goodwill, the specific rewards and punishments in a classroom economy of incentives are not likely to have much meaning. Thus neither of the two remaining mechanisms, reciprocal exchange and enforceable trust, is likely to be an effective means of ensuring effort or good conduct. Reciprocal exchange denotes face-to-face interaction in which actor A provides something valuable to actor B, and B in return provides something valuable to A. Each self-interestedly will tend to comply with the terms of their relationship in the expectation of further benefits. Potentially, a student and teacher might exchange academic performance or conduct for grades, but for a series of such exchanges to affect the student's performance or behavior requires that the grade have real value for the student.

In a situation of enforceable trust, each person can be confident that every other person will follow the rules, because group membership provides a sufficient flow of benefits to make it worthwhile to orient one's conduct to the group's goals and to comply with group norms. As in reciprocal exchange, a calculus of self-interest is central, but the expected benefits require some sort of good standing in the whole group rather than in any specific face-to-face relationship. In contrast to situations of bounded solidarity, expected utility—rather than commitment to the group—motivates compliance.

If a classroom were a situation of enforceable trust, the teacher could be confident that effort would be made and conduct would be orderly, while the students could be no less confident that rewards and punishments would be appropriate. However, unless the students believe that being in good standing in the class will lead to real benefits, enforceable trust cannot occur. Thus we are back to the question of inducing the goodwill, not simply in any one student but among the entire class, so that all accept the idea that making effort and following the classroom rules will yield equitably distributed benefits.

Consequently, goodwill is potentially a central problem for all teachers in the elementary and secondary grades. It may be no less a problem beyond the secondary level for students who do not have a strong positive reason to attend—for example, students who continue into college or vocational training as a path of least resistance.

SOME MECHANISMS OF GOODWILL

Now consider mechanisms that may create goodwill and their variation across schools of different levels and organizational forms, beginning with the contrasting situations of the primary grades and the college and university. Dreeben is principally concerned with the early years of schooling. Therefore he centers on the teacher's expression of positive affect in a way that substantially reproduces the affective climate of the family. That is, the warmth of the teacher's response to each student does not center on specific performances or acts, but is characteristic of their relationship throughout the daily round of class activity.

He sees this diffuse affectivity as a mechanism that induces pupils to accept praise or blame when it is a specific response to given performances or conduct. By strong implication, classroom goodwill in the early grades can occur because the affective climate of the classroom reproduces the diffusely positive affective climate of the family (see Parsons [1959] on the importance of nurturing behavior by teachers in the primary grades). Indeed, in an important sense goodwill can be induced among these pupils not only when relationships with the teacher reproduce the affective tone of relationships with the parents, but because the parents themselves—to the degree that they administer praise or blame for work or conduct in school—contribute to their children's socialization to the world of the classroom.

By the time students reach college and university (and perhaps the later grades in academically selective high schools and schools that prepare for advanced technical occupations), goodwill has little to do with diffuse affect in students' relationships with instructors. Now goodwill arises in part from the students' prior successful socialization to the student role, as Dreeben argued, and in part from personal commitment—whether instrumental or consummatory—to the substance of the work at hand. Moreover, although the goodwill of primary grade pupils (once induced) is not contingent, the goodwill of the college and university student is to some degree contingent. At the more advanced levels, it is roughly proportional to the perceived competence of the instructor chiefly in the subject matter; and at the less advanced levels, it is more dependent on instructional competence. This contingency corresponds to the disciplinary specialization of instruction in these settings, in contrast to the generalist subject matter of the early grades. However, the students' prior socialization and substantive commitment more often than not prevent a total loss of goodwill—even when the instructor is thought to be incompetent—unless the students have the option of voice or exit rather than grudging loyalty.

In schools with some degree of curriculum complexity and differentiation (and, therefore, less often in the lower grades than elsewhere), classroom goodwill may occur, as I have suggested, as a correlate of bounded solidarity. This outcome should be found primarily when the school's student body presents a heterogeneous mix of academic performance or other student attributes believed locally to be associated with academic capacity. This effect should be more pronounced when the heterogeneity is socially ordered into a stratified curriculum than when it is not (see Sørensen [1970] on the demography and social psychology of stratified and otherwise differentiated curricula).

Under these conditions the school class may form a cohesive unit, embracing both the teacher and students and centered on a common fate and identity associated with status as either top dogs or underdogs in the school's achievement order. No doubt this effect is more likely to occur near the top of the achievement pecking order than near the bottom—that is, where the putative identity is positive rather than negative. Nonetheless, the teacher of a basic track or special education class, for example, might use its underdog status as a basis for building fighting-group solidarity.

Although I have limited this discussion to the case of the classroom, certain schools may themselves display bounded solidarity, in particular when their missions are clear and provide highly desirable outcomes for students and when they are sufficiently small for relatively dense networks of social ties among students and staff (see Meyer [1977] on the chartering of schools). When bounded solidarity characterizes the school itself, students' identification with the school should devolve on individual classrooms, creating goodwill.

Goodwill also can be secured through what Swidler (1977) calls charismatic teaching. Charismatic teaching refers to the manipulation of the particularistic in relationships with students—for example, the teacher who tries to become the "pal" of the students by revealing aspects of his or her personal life or in other ways attempting to reduce social distance in these relationships. However, as Waller (1932) argued with classic clarity, such efforts result in at best a very unstable condition of goodwill, and Dreeben has shown us a prime reason for this instability. Specific exchanges of performance or conduct for grades, praise, or blame must be detached from the particularistic in relationships with the classroom group but nonetheless have palpable consequences for students' work and conduct. Therefore their strength of effect must have a source other than the particularistic in classroom relationships.

THE INSTITUTIONAL BASIS OF CLASSROOM GOODWILL

The foregoing mechanisms for inducing classroom goodwill represent somewhat exceptional cases: the primary grades, schools at advanced levels, academically heterogeneous schools, and the unstable case of classroom particularism. Across the broader range, however, most school classrooms operate at some level of instructional adequacy, so that we must look elsewhere for more generalized bases of classroom goodwill. Stating that the goodwill-building work of teachers in the higher grades is primarily remedial, Dreeben implies that—with the exception of failures—early socialization to the sanctioning regime of classrooms is effective. That is, it is sufficiently thorough and gains sufficient intrinsic reinforcement in later specific classroom transactions to create a fund of potential goodwill on which teachers can draw.

Without doubt such a fund exists and provides the basis for some degree of instructional adequacy. This effect on instruction should be stronger the more closely aligned are parental values and support with what teachers expect of their students and the closer the classroom comes to a condition of bounded solidarity. However, there is reason to doubt that early socialization can have such strong and uniform effects without later reinforcement. Indeed, in the absence of secure early socialization, later sanctioning exchanges could perhaps more easily lead to a downward than an upward spiral of reinforcement.

Consistent and strong reinforcement can scarcely be expected in most school settings from the intrinsic pleasures of schoolwork and decorous classroom conduct. To a degree in middle and high schools, this reinforcement may be provided by such instrumental incentives as grade requirements for participation in athletics or such desirable extracurricular activities as newspapers or yearbooks. Nevertheless, such incentives are not often widely available or salient among a student body.

The more ubiquitous mechanisms of reinforcement are to be found in attributes that schools possess by virtue of their status as institutional organizations. As Meyer and his colleagues (e.g., Meyer and Rowan 1978) have taught us, schools (like hospitals and mainline churches) embody core values of their societies (see Shils [1975] on core values and their institutional manifestations). In schools core values are institutionalized most centrally in the curriculum. The curriculum expresses broadly accepted understandings of the nature of citizenship—that is, the commitments, knowledge, and technical skills that are basic to participation in our society and contribute to the distribution and individual realization of economic, political, and social responsibility.

Associated with this normatively potent curriculum (and deriving their own normative force by virtue of the association) are conventional understandings that are no less powerful and are shared by teachers, students, and parents in company with most of the society. These understandings include conceptions of appropriate modes of classroom presentation such as lecturing and projects, and the scope and speed of coverage. Of particular importance here, they include understandings about what it is fair for teachers to expect by way of levels of effort, accomplishment, and decorum and about the right balance and intensity of praise and blame that the students should receive.

These understandings, of course, vary with the age of the students, the academic selectivity of the school, and a variety of other local circumstances. Understandings about levels of effort and attainment are more often than not the upshot of a history of negotiation between students and teachers, embedded in general beliefs about fairness that parents and teachers have come to share. These understandings, I propose, reinforce and specify earlier socialization to the sanctioning regime of school and make possible a persisting equilibrium in specific exchanges of sanctions for performance or conduct.

Consider a school that experiences strong, nonrandom shocks that alter the composition of its student body, its effective instructional goals, or the resources available to pursue them. The very institutionalization of conventional understandings grounding goodwill means that disparities between these beliefs and the realities of the emerging, altered situation may deplete the fund of goodwill on which instructional effectiveness depends. A critical turn of events of this kind, one might think, would stimulate organizational learning (March 1999; Brown and Duguid 2000)—that is, sustained efforts by teachers individually and collectively to diagnose the problem; alter the sanctioning regime; and try to move toward new and more locally appropriate understandings of fairness, effort, accomplishment, and conduct. However, the fact that the school is an institutional organization sets strong limits on its capacity for local instructional problem solving, including solving the key problem of the loss of classroom goodwill. Even in dynamic local environments, schools' curricula and teaching methods will be very slow to change.

In the broader sense, this striking level of stability at the technical core of schools can be explained in part by the normative force of the curriculum itself, in part by a cultural authority derived from the disciplines from which the school subjects derive, and in part by the integration of the school into the complex of organized education. The limited capacity of school faculties for organizational learning also derives from the commitment of teachers themselves to locally institutionalized practices. Moreover and ironically, departures from the institutionalized template are likely to arouse suspicion or more active opposition among a school's constituents, including parents and students as well.

AN EXAMPLE OF STABILITY AND AN EXAMPLE OF CHANGE

In the course of a long-standing program of fieldwork in American high schools, I have been struck by a socially stratified correspondence between the behavioral styles and expectations of students and the putative work styles and expectations of their parents. Although these matters were not the prime objects of my observations and were not investigated systematically, the consistency nonetheless seems striking.

In academically selective high schools, which primarily enroll upper middle-class students, attendance on Mondays and Fridays was no lower than in the middle of the week. In these schools students came early and left late, occupied with both academic and extracurricular activities well beyond class hours. When they left school, they left burdened by heavy backpacks filled with materials for a long evening of homework. In this they looked very much like school-specific clones of their professional and managerial parents. Teachers in these schools typically said that their students expected to be pushed and challenged and were disappointed and sometimes disengaged if they thought that their teachers were easy. In these classrooms fairness meant consistent academic toughness.

In less selective schools that enroll working-class student bodies, attendance was lower on Mondays and Fridays than on other weekdays. Aside from the athletes, students tended to arrive just before the first bell and leave soon after their last period class, taking home few books or papers. Their level of engagement with school looked rather like the engagement with the workplace that would have characterized many of their parents. In one of these schools, located in a thoroughly working-class Chicago suburb, achievement tests were always scheduled for mid-week to ensure reasonable attendance and the teachers tended to follow the same practice with their own exams. In all of these schools, fairness meant limited academic demands, recognition for modest accomplishments, in many instances muted classroom recognition of academic rate busters, and an even (though fairly heavy) hand in discipline.

The consequences of institutionalized understandings for classroom goodwill are directly implicated in these examples of stability. They are also clearly implicated in the events at "Merriwether Lewis," an example of changes in a high school that I have described in more detail elsewhere (Bidwell 2000). This school had been founded and continued for many years to serve an academically select, college-bound student population, and its teachers during all that time had held their students to high performance standards, finding—by the retrospective accounts of current faculty—a ready student response. However, the student body had undergone recent and rapid change, so that this very senior faculty found itself teaching students with at best modest academic expectations. These students reacted with obvious resentment and alienation to the continuing demands of their teachers for strenuous effort and substantial accomplishment in an academically oriented curriculum. There was no evidence that these teachers, either individually or collectively, were making efforts to solve the obvious problems of student motivation and (I think) goodwill that confronted them.

ENVOI

Several of the chapters in this volume—including those by Pallas, Boulay, and Karp; McFarland; and Gamoran and Kelly—document the resistance of established (and often much less than optimal) modes of instruction to improvement, with adverse consequences for students' learning. If my argument is cogent, then these adverse consequences must be attributed in some measure to failures to induce or sustain goodwill in classrooms. If so, we are required to search not only for the sources of such goodwill, but also for the impediments in schools to organizational learning about classroom goodwill.

I have argued elsewhere (Bidwell 2001) for the importance of understanding the sources and specific mechanisms involved in faculties' capacity for collective problem solving as a key part of our understanding of the classroom processes that affect what and how much students learn. In my view the sources of this capacity, which is at the root of effective organizational learning, are in the social organization of the faculty workplace. It is formed out of local relationships among faculty colleagues, but relationships of a very particular kind. These are relationships that constitute bounded solidarity among the teachers in a school, focused not on defense against the incursions of administrators or parents or the students themselves but on local professionalism. In these faculties or faculty groups, what is at issue is the productive solution of everyday instructional problems that occur in the school to block effective teaching, and then inducing the consistent implementation of the solutions.

Whether bounded solidarity of this order characterizes a whole faculty or subgroups within it, such as the subject matter departments of a high school, will be affected substantially by the degree to which the faculty is specialized as well as the sheer size of the faculty. When it is faculty subgroups rather than whole faculties that constitute such problem-solving collectivities, it may on the surface appear problematic for the welfare of the school as a whole. However, I believe that the more critical issues have to do with the degree to which a school's administrative leadership creates a cooperative rather than adversarial relationship with the faculty. Of particular importance is the degree to which the faculty subgroups are knit together by collegial ties that span boundaries, not only within the school but to broader professional communities and organizations, providing ties that lead into the flow of ideas in wider, more cosmopolitan pedagogical circles. To come to a better understanding of the conditions under which such faculty groupings form, the ways in which they work as problem-solving agents, and the consequences for the welfare of students and schools strike me as interesting and potentially valuable directions for sociology of education.

Acknowledgments

I am grateful to the conference participants, and in particular Maureen Hallinan, for helpful comments on this essay.

REFERENCES

Bidwell, Charles E. 2000. "School as Context and Construction: A Social Psychological Approach to the Study of Schooling." Pp. 15–36 in *Handbook of the Sociology of Education,* edited by Maureen T. Hallinan. New York: Kluwer Academic/Plenum.

Bidwell, Charles E. 2001. "Analyzing Schools as Organizations: Long-Term Permanence and Short-Term Change." *Sociology of Education* 74:100–14.

Brown, John Seely and Paul Duguid. 2000. *The Social Life of Information.* Cambridge, MA: Harvard Business School Press.

Dreeben, Robert. [1968] 2002. *On What Is Learned in School.* Clinton Corners, NY: Percheron Press/Eliot Werner Publications.

March, James G. 1999. *The Pursuit of Organizational Intelligence.* Malden, MA: Blackwell Business.

Meyer, John W. 1977. "The Effects of Education as an Institution." *American Journal of Sociology* 83:55–77.

Meyer, John W. and Brian Rowan. 1978. "The Structure of Educational Organizations." Pp. 78–109 in *Environments and Organizations,* edited by Marshall W. Meyer and W. Richard Scott. San Francisco: Jossey-Bass.

Parsons, Talcott. 1959. "The School Class as a Social System: Some of Its Functions in American Society." *Harvard Educational Review* 29:297–318.

Portes, Alejandro and Julia Sensenbrenner. 1993. "Embeddedness and Immigration." *American Journal of Sociology* 98:1320–50.

Shils, Edward. 1975. *Center and Periphery: Essays in Macrosociology.* Chicago: University of Chicago Press.

Sørensen, Aage B. 1970. "Organizational Differentiation of Students and Educational Opportunity." *Sociology of Education* 43:355–76.

Swidler, Ann. 1977. *Organizations without Authority: Dilemmas of Social Control in Free Schools.* Cambridge, MA: Harvard University Press.

Waller, Willard. 1932. *The Sociology of Teaching.* New York: Wiley.

4

Social Status versus Psychosocial Maturity as Predictors of School Outcomes in Japan and the United States

Alex Inkeles
P. Herbert Leiderman

In all modern industrial societies, performing well in secondary school is a critical determinant of a young person's later chances in life, playing a key role in whether he or she can get into college—and if so, to what kind of college. Those first steps, in turn, play a major role in shaping later career opportunities and other aspects of success in life. For sociologists the key to explaining these outcomes is the social background of the pupil including his or her religion, ethnicity, and (above all) social class. For social psychologists the key to success in school is presumed to lie in personal qualities such as intelligence; in conative aspects of personality such as being persistent, organized, and task oriented; or in having values that give importance to such qualities as achievement and social conformity. Whether the sociological or the psychological factors explain more about, and in particular how well they explain different elements of, the many outcomes shaped by schooling are questions of long-standing interest.

Our contribution to this debate comes from representative national samples of youths between the ages of thirteen and eighteen in Japan and the United States. We focus in particular on two outcomes: first, the grades that pupils earn in their schoolwork; and second, their expectations of going on to higher education. To predict these outcomes, we especially stress both the separate and the joint, interconnected influence of two contrasting causal variables: social class background and a distinctive measure developed to assess any student's *psychosocial maturity*. However, our explanatory models also take into consideration other frequently cited influences on school perfor-

Alex Inkeles • Department of Sociology (Emeritus), Stanford University, Stanford, California 94305.
P. Herbert Leiderman • Department of Psychiatry and Behavioral Sciences (Emeritus), Stanford University, Stanford, California 94305.

Stability and Change in American Education: Structure, Process, and Outcomes edited by Maureen T. Hallinan, Adam Gamoran, Warren Kubitschek, and Tom Loveless. Eliot Werner Publications, Clinton Corners, New York, 2003.

mance such as religion, race or ethnicity, and the experience of private as opposed to public schooling. Moreover, to take into account the earlier and different paths to maturation followed by girls, we conducted our basic analyses separately for each gender.

To anticipate the main outcomes of our investigation, we found the following results. First, the psychosocial maturity of adolescents is clearly the major explanation for the grades that they receive in school, with the general correlation approximately twice as large as that for social status in predicting the school grades earned by both boys and girls in both the United States and Japan. With a few exceptions, other theoretically relevant explanatory variables play a minor or even insignificant role. However, there are interesting variations in the pattern of prediction depending on the subject matter (such as mathematics or language studies), the gender of the students, and their national homeland.

Second, the expectation that one will reach college presents a contrasting picture, with social status the more powerful predictor—although psychosocial maturity is only moderately weaker as an influence on the expectation that one will attend college or beyond. This pattern holds for both boys and girls and applies in both Japan and the United States, with some interesting variation. Other variables play a lesser (although sometimes statistically significant) role in the United States but have virtually no influence in Japan.

Our third set of results indicates that the interaction between social status and psychosocial factors is complex, but clearly supports the primacy of psychosocial maturity as a predictor of the grades that pupils earn. While such interactions do not contradict the finding that social status is the leading factor in encouraging the expectation that one will get to college or beyond, they strengthen the case for the relative importance of psychosocial maturity in shaping expectations for postsecondary education.

In what follows we present the detailed evidence to support these general conclusions, along with additional information about how the explanatory patterns vary depending on the school subject under review (e.g., mathematics or language studies). In the body of the chapter, we will give details on how the outcomes of schooling are influenced by forces other than status and maturity such as the nature of the school subject under review, the gender of the pupil, and the national origins of the sample.

THEORETICAL AND RESEARCH BACKGROUND

This article is the latest report from a research program that began in the early 1990s. A detailed discussion of the origin and development of the concept of "adolescent psychosocial maturity," and of the scale to measure that quality, is presented in our first published report on the project (Inkeles and Leiderman 1998). That source also reviewed related studies to highlight similarities and differences between our concept and other ways of thinking about adolescent psychosocial development. We therefore limit ourselves here to a brief summary of the essential facts about the project, which was stimulated initially by Leiderman's experience as consulting psychiatrist to the California Youth Authority. In that capacity he observed marked differences in the attitudes and values of boys who were deemed more ready for discharge, and those the staff judged to have made less progress toward a potentially successful adjustment to the outside world. On an informal basis, he collected evidence concerning the relative success or failure to stay out of trouble experienced by these boys once they were discharged. His observation further reinforced the impression that there was a definable set of psychosocial characteristics of adolescents that made for more or less successful adaptation to and performance in the social roles defined for them in contemporary modern societies.

Leiderman identified the main elements of this syndrome as cooperativeness, efficacy, individualism, perseverance, planfulness, and responsibility. Generalizing from his experience, he developed the hypothesis that the greater the degree to which any adolescent (boy or girl) manifested these qualities, the greater would be his or her success in performing the roles typically assigned to youths in modern societies. In particular, the more they manifested these qualities, the better would be their performance as students in school and the more focused and relevant would be their readiness to advance their education and move toward adopting stable, socially approved, and rewarding adult roles.

To test these ideas required the development of a statistically reliable scale to measure objectively the personal qualities that the earlier clinical experience identified as important. To that end the research team, now augmented by the collaboration of Inkeles, developed and pretested a large battery of questions that it assumed could measure the qualities identified by the theory. The preliminary questionnaire given to small exploratory samples from Chile and the United States provided clear evidence. The data revealed a coherent syndrome of psychological qualities with content common to both countries, yielding in each case a statistically reliable summary score to reflect a general quality of adolescent maturity, with a robust alpha for the United States of .90 and for Chile of .92 (Inkeles and Leiderman 1998). Subsequent studies with as many as six additional exploratory samples drawn from populations differing in ethnicity and national citizenship consistently documented the existence of the same underlying syndrome of qualities reliably measured by the items used in different versions of our scale.

The early experimental versions of the maturity scale proved not only to be highly reliable, but also to have notable validity. For example, in Chile the scale showed that rural village girls attending an experimental agricultural school with a unique curriculum were evidently enabled by this experience to earn psychosocial maturity scores equal to those obtained by girls attending an elite urban school in the capital city of Santiago. Further evidence indicating the validity of the maturity scale came from a large sample of Mexican American youths in Pueblo, Colorado. A comparison of the adolescents who dropped out of high school with those who stayed in showed that a version of our psychosocial maturity scale was the single best predictor of dropout behavior.

Taken together, the evidence from the samples we collected convinced us about the reliability and validity of our measure of adolescent maturity. This conclusion was reinforced by the fact that the samples were very diverse in social composition and in the regional and national settings in which they were collected. We also felt that our case was strengthened by the fact that our samples were selected as opportunity presented itself, and certainly not in a way that might artificially support our assumptions. However, we realized that some critics would argue that the eclectic nature of the samples assembled—and in particular the very small size of some of those exploratory samples—gave reason to question our more sanguine assessment of the reliability and validity of our scale. Fortunately, we can now assuage such doubts since we were able to secure representative national samples of adolescents between the ages of thirteen and eighteen for both the United States and Japan.

DATA AND METHODS

Masamichi Sasaki of Kyogo-Kyoiku University collected the data as part of a study on national character as manifested by adolescents in Japan and the United States. He surveyed a representative national sample of approximately one thousand youngsters in each country. One adjustment, which we consider minor in this context, was due to the fact that limits on the budget required the use of quota sampling rather than the more desirable but much more costly random sampling method. Two other requirements were more profound in their effect. We had to limit ourselves to adding no more than 28 questions to the set already included in the questionnaire by Sasaki, and the questions we used had to potentially take the least amount of time in the interviewing process. This was a severe restriction, but one with which we coped because our earlier exploratory work in the United States, Chile, and elsewhere identified a large pool of items whose reliability was indicated by statistically significant item-to-scale correlations. For example, even using the stringent requirement that an item have at least a .3 item-to-scale correlation, we could select from a pool of 74 items from our initial American study and 53 items from our exploratory work in Chile (Inkeles and Leiderman 1998).

Maturity Scale Construction

Given the constraints, we decided to limit ourselves to the four basic dimensions (or the most central elements) of maturity as indicated by previous work with the scale. This permitted us to increase the reliability of the subscales by allowing up to seven questions to assess each of the four qualities—*cooperativeness, efficacy, perseverance/planfulness*, and *responsibility*. This set of four qualities was one less than the set we previously used, but analysis of the data from earlier samples indicated that our separate subscales to measure perseverance and planfulness overlapped considerably. Hence they could properly be collapsed to measure a single quality.

As required by our theoretical model, the questions meant to assess each quality were selected to represent action and feeling in four different domains of life: *school, family, peer group,* and *community.* Although in earlier studies we also included a domain of *work,* we found that usually not enough of our high school students had worked to warrant taking up critical space in the questionnaire to explore that experience. Therefore, for the study reported here, we eliminated questions relating to work experience.

In response to the constraint on the time available to us, we decided to use only questions couched in the familiar and easily understood Likert scale format, requiring the interviewee to express only degrees of agreement or disagreement. To forestall the risk of acquiescence bias that comes with using this format, we put our questions in both positive and negative form. To be scored as more mature, therefore, a respondent had to disagree with some statements while agreeing with others. The following examples—each chosen to tap a different quality in a different domain, some couched in positive and some in negative terms—will give some sense of both the variety of the questions and the consistency of the framework. We indicate in parentheses the domain and the quality to which we presume the question is related.

> *When I have schoolwork to do, I usually do not plan out how I am going to get it done.* (School/Planfulness)

> *I just don't know how to deal with problems in my neighborhood.* (Community/Efficacy)

> *I take responsibility for how I get along with my friends.* (Peers/ Responsibility)

> *Even when I strongly disagree with my family about some things, I still believe we should work together.* (Family/Cooperation)

In response to each question, the interviewee was asked to choose among five responses ranging from strong or mild agreement through neutrality to two degrees of disagreement. The full set of 28 questions used to construct the scale scores is reproduced in the Appendix.

Any perceptive reader, to say nothing of an expert in public opinion research, can surely find fault with one or another of these questions. We say in their defense that they were used with a great variety of audiences who seemed to have no trouble understanding them. Moreover, they all stood the further test of achieving high item-to-scale correlation in the course of our preliminary testing of scale items with the many samples mentioned previously. But of course the ultimate test of their utility and appropriateness lies in whether the use of these items in the present study yielded a statistically reliable scale that in turn proved itself valid by its relationship to various key outcomes. The next section of the chapter addresses these two challenges.

Maturity Scale Reliability

Since the key element in our analysis is the score that each pupil received on our scale to measure maturity, it is important to establish the reliability of that measure. We took two approaches to calculating the maturity score of each individual. To assure that the strength of any single quality would not bias the outcome, we assigned scores to each individual by summing his or her scores across the four subscales measuring each of the qualities. We also computed maturity scores by weighing equally the responses to all 28 items in our questionnaire. The results were very similar and gave assurance that we were measuring what was indeed a coherent syndrome of attitudes and values constituting a relatively seamless web.

Due to the fact that using all 28 items rather than the subscales yielded a measure with modestly better statistical characteristics, we elected to use that version in this analysis. That version of the scale yielded an alpha of .82 in the United States and .78 in Japan. These numbers indicate very satisfactory levels of reliability for the measure of maturity, which we refer to as the Psychosocial Maturity Scale.

MATURITY AND THE OUTCOMES OF SCHOOLING

To assess the importance of psychosocial maturity as a determinant of student performance, we selected two outcomes: the grades earned by the student in coursework, and his or her expectation of going beyond high school to college or graduate study. Our explanatory model featured two key variables: socioeconomic status and psychosocial maturity. Maturity was expressed as a score on our 28-item maturity scale. Socioeconomic status (SES) was represented by a factor analysis score, taking into account the education and occupation of both father and mother as well as the interviewer's assessment of the social class of the family. Also taken into account was the possible influence of four additional variables that earlier experience or theoretical considerations indicated might be important. These included the student's own assessment of whether he or she was religious, grade level (year in the standard sequence of schooling), and whether the school was public or private including religious. In the United States, we also recorded the apparent race of the respondent as judged by the interviewer, but our Japanese colleagues—stressing the homogeneity of the country—did not take into account such distinctions.

School Grades

Because we did not have access to the students' school records, we were obliged to rely on each respondent's self-report to judge the quality of his or her academic performance. Since numerous studies show that students generally report their grades fairly accurately, we have no hesitation in using these reports as an indicator of how those in our samples were performing academically.

In the United States, we used five categories ranging from "mostly A's" down to "mostly below D." In Japan the students reported their grades at four levels, ranging from "good" through "average" to "not good at all." We inquired about grades in math and science as a set and, separately, in social studies for Japan and in the set social studies and English in the United States. For purposes of this report, the two categories were combined into a single-grade summary measure.

In Table 1 we provide the main facts needed to predict whether a student, viewed separately in each country, would receive good or poor grades. We first present the zero-order correlations, separately for boys and girls, for our key variables of maturity and social status. We then test the robustness of those results through a regression analysis that takes into account those key variables along with others that might be relevant. Details about the content and construction of those variables may be found in Inkeles and Leiderman (2000).

In our view the results are clear and unambiguous, and surely must be surprising to many: in the case of both boys and girls, and in both Japan and the United States, the psychosocial maturity of the students—rather than their socioeconomic background—proved to be a much more powerful predictor of the grades that they earned in school. This held true even when other factors were taken into account.

Table 1. Predicting Grades: Summary by Gender in the United States and Japan

Zero-order Correlations	United States		Japan	
	Girl	Boy	Girl	Boy
Maturity	.46	.32	.28	.25
Social Status	.27	.24	.16	.11

Regression	United States		Japan	
	Girl	Boy	Girl	Boy
Maturity	.40 ***	.24 ***	.27 ***	.24 ***
Social Status	.14 ***	.17 ***	.13 **	.10 *
Religious	.11 **	.21 ***	–a	—
School Type	.12 **	—	—	—
"Race"	—	—	—	—
Year in School	—	—	—	—
Multiple R	.51	.44	.31	.28
R^2	.26	.19	.10	.08
N	460	489	499	501

Significance levels:
* $p < .05$
** $p < .01$
*** $p < .001$
a Coefficients not significant at .05 are not shown.

Looking first at the zero-order correlations, we see that in all four comparisons the basic coefficient of association between the outcome of good grades and what we interpret as the causal variables is much stronger for the Psychosocial Maturity Score than it is for the SES measure. Indeed, the correlation coefficient linking maturity and grades is usually about twice as large as the correlation of social status and grades. Thus, for example, for girls in Japan school marks correlate at .28 with the maturity score but at only .16 with the measure of social status.

Another way of looking at these relationships, and one which is perhaps more transparent, is to think of them as a kind of life chances lottery where each child at birth was asked to choose some combination of the extremes of psychosocial maturity and socioeconomic status. At these extremes, if this newborn wanted to maximize the chances of getting good grades in school, she would be best advised to select the combination "Highest Maturity Score combined with Lowest SES." In the case of a Japanese girl, that combination would give a 25 percent chance of getting top grades. By comparison, if she chose the opposite extreme combination of "Highest Status combined with Lowest Maturity," her chances of being a top student would be a mere 7 percent. The pattern was the same for boys, and it held in the United States as well as in Japan. The High Maturity combination was at least twice as likely as the High SES combination to result in good grades in all four comparisons involving these extreme profiles.

Our impression that psychosocial maturity is by far the most powerful predictor of the marks that a student earns in school is strengthened by the regression analysis presented in the second part of Table 1. This way of looking at the outcome is especially important because the two key independent variables we used, Psychosocial Maturity and SES, were substantially correlated with each other. In the United States, for example, the coefficient linking the maturity measure to status was at the highly significant level of .24. That fact makes especially clear the importance of disentangling the separate influence of each causal variable on the dependent variable, such as school grades, which can be done by a regression analysis.

Even taking into account the simultaneous influence of the other variables, maturity remains clearly the most powerful explanatory force. Indeed, in this context three of the four pairs of coefficients show the figure for maturity to be at least twice as large as that for status. In the extreme case, that of girls in the United States, the regression coefficient linking school marks to the measure of psychosocial maturity is almost three times as large as the coefficient linking grades to socioeconomic status.

We should also note that the influence of maturity on the marks earned by students is much greater than that of any of the other variables considered in our model. Indeed, in Japan none of the other influences we measured yielded a statistically significant correlation. In the regressions for the U.S. samples, five of eight were also not significant.

In the United States, however, being religious proved to be a quite significant independent factor in explaining the school marks that our adolescents received. We interpret the student's report that he or she is religious as also being essentially a psychosocial factor. Therefore we conclude that this finding in no way weakens the argument that in explaining what accounts for getting good grades in school, the attitudes and values of the students are more important than their social status. By contrast, in Japan religion is well known to be a much less important influence in the daily life of people of all ages. Therefore we would not expect the measure of religiosity to be significantly correlated with the grades that a Japanese student earned.

The fact that the students' year in school was not statistically significant in either country is of particular importance. As the name we assigned our measure (the Psychosocial Maturity Scale) would suggest, our initial assumption was that our instrument would most likely reflect development over time, whether because of biological maturation over time or because of the cumulative impact of more years of schooling. However, our analysis of the several small samples that we collected as we experimented with the instrument failed to support that assumption. The year in school generally failed to qualify as a statistically significant influence on our measure of psychosocial maturity. We tentatively assumed that this outcome might be due to the small size of most of our exploratory samples. However, now that we have the larger and more representative samples reported here, we are obliged to accept the conclusion that there is no clear evidence that the average adolescent becomes psychosocially more mature year by year—at least as measured by our instrument. One might claim that the fault lies with our instrument. But we feel that both the manifest content of our questionnaire and the many significant connections between the scale scores and important attitudes, values, and behaviors argue strongly against such a cavalier dismissal.

We suggest instead several other explanations. First, it may be that some adolescents do indeed become more mature in our sense, but that others move backward and thus cancel any evident effect of age or grade level. Since we were not able to follow the same individuals over several years, we cannot test this assumption. We can only record our belief that it is unlikely that such a neat and near perfect cancellation process occurred.

A more plausible explanation would focus on the particular age range that we studied. Considerable maturation of the kind potentially tested by our instrument does perhaps take place over time, but at an earlier stage in the life cycle of the adolescent. If that type of change occurred before the age of fourteen, and the psychosocial maturation process was substantially completed by that point, our samples would indeed be giving us the evidence of stability that we recorded. This possibility can be tested only if we can in the future study youngsters who range in age from approximately six through thirteen.

A more radical assumption is that the qualities we measure and express as a score on the Psychosocial Maturity Scale are in substantial degree shaped by a genetic disposition. If maturity (as we measure it) is indeed largely an expression of genetic disposition or inborn temperament, then it would not be at all surprising that the maturity scores failed to increase as youngsters passed through successive stages of physical development—and simultaneously moved to higher grades in school—between the ages of fourteen and eighteen.

Expectation of College Attendance and Beyond

Obtaining reasonably good grades may be a prerequisite for getting into college but in itself provides no guarantee that one will be able to get an education beyond secondary school. For many economically disadvantaged youngsters, tuition fees and the cost of books—even at public institutions of higher learning—present a barrier not easily overcome. In addition, such students may well experience strong pressure from their families to start earning money in order to support the parental household. Given these conditions, many who were good students in secondary school will nevertheless decide that they must give up the hope of securing a college education. Others, coming from families with more means, may count on getting a college education despite having a less impressive grade average. Such harsh facts of life evidently played their expected role in our samples.

Our questionnaire did not ask adolescents whether they would like to go to college, but rather asked them whether or not they expected to do so. In other words, we were asking them to take into account the reality of their personal situation—both scholastic and financial. Under the circumstances some youngsters with a mature disposition and good grades nevertheless told us that they did not expect to secure a higher education. Others, having the support of wealthier parents, expressed confidence that they would get to college despite the fact that they scored as less mature and had poorer grades. The interaction of these competing forces was expressed statistically in a different pattern from that which characterized the model for explaining school marks. In predicting the expectation that one would go on to higher education, it was the socioeconomic status of the students—and not their maturity scores—that explained the greater amount of variance. However, as we shall see, even in this realm the psychosocial maturity of the student played a notably strong role.

To assess educational expectations, we adapted our measures to certain cultural differences distinguishing Japan from the United States. In Japan very few students expressed the expectation of going beyond college. For all practical purposes, getting a college education could be interpreted as the ceiling beyond which most students could not think of going. By contrast, in the United States finishing college was evidently not thought of as a ceiling by large portions of the population. Instead, getting some graduate or professional education was perceived as the goal to be attained. Accepting these facts in the respective national patterns of educational expectations, we used getting to college as the outcome to be explained in Japan and getting some post-college education as the outcome to be explained in the United States.

Looking first at the zero-order correlations in Table 2, it is clear that in explaining expectations for higher education, the socioeconomic status of the student was consistently a stronger predictor then the measure of maturity— although always by only a modest margin. In the typical case, which we may take as that for girls in the United States, the correlation between the expectation of higher education and socioeconomic status was .35, while that linking the maturity score to the same outcome was .29. The same pattern was observed in Japan, and in both countries it held true for both boys and girls.

As was true in the analysis of school grades, the zero-order correlations were not greatly altered by the regression analysis applied to expectations for postsecondary education. The regressions took into account the simultaneous action of the two main explanatory variables and other variables that might be expected to play some role in shaping expectations concerning advanced education. Thus we see in Table 2 that the socioeconomic background of the adolescents continues to be the prime factor explaining the expectation that one will obtain a higher education, with a regression coefficient of about .3, whereas the coefficient for the maturity score was generally in the vicinity of .2.

Given that school grades and the expectation of higher schooling are con-

Table 2. Predicting Education Expected by Gender in the United States and Japan[a]

Zero-order Correlations	United States		Japan	
	Girl	Boy	Girl	Boy
Maturity	.29	.32	.22	.20
Social Status	.35	.38	.31	.31
Regression	United States		Japan	
	Girl	Boy	Girl	Boy
Maturity	.21 ***	.24 ***	.19 ***	.18 ***
Social Status	.31 ***	.32 ***	.28 ***	.29 ***
Religious	_[b]	.15 ***	—	—
School Type	.15 ***	.12 **	—	—
"Race"	-.13 **	—		
Year in School	—	—	.10 *	.08 *
Multiple R	.45	.51	.37	.38
R^2	.20	.26	.14	.14
N	460	489	499	501

[a] In Japan the analysis applies to those expecting to go only as far as a four-year college or university. In the United States, it applies to those expecting to get as far as some form of postgraduate education.

Significance levels:

* $p < .05$

** $p < .01$

*** $p < .001$

[b] Coefficients not significant at .05 are not shown.

ceptually quite distinct, it is no surprise that the other variables we considered in the standard regression model play a somewhat different role in explaining educational expectations. For example, in Japan the student's year in school is in this case statistically significant, even if only at a modest level. We interpret this fact as reflecting the impact of the ubiquitous entrance examinations, the tension over which increasingly preoccupies Japanese high school students as they move into their third and fourth year of study in secondary school.

In the American sample, the regressions indicate that being religious has lost some of its strength among the boys and for girls no longer has a significant influence when college expectations are the outcome predicted. It is easy to understand that having a religious disposition would lead a youngster to stress the qualities measured by the maturity scale, but would not necessarily affect an adolescent's estimate as to whether he or she advanced to a higher education.

Given that the socioeconomic status of the parents is the main variable predicting the expectation of higher education, we are not surprised that in the United States the school type was a quite significant factor. The significance of this finding is derived from the way in which this variable was coded, with public schools at the lower end followed by private (including Catholic) schools. Economically advantaged children could be expected to enroll more often at the latter type of school, and equally would more often expect to continue their education to the postgraduate level. Hence school type has a positive and significant association for both boys and girls in the United States.

In Japan whether a school is private or public, or religious or nonreligious, is not a significant factor in shaping expectations about the chances for a college education. There the key to college admission is performance on the exceedingly competitive entrance examinations, and if any secondary school characteristic were important, it would probably be the cram school that virtually all college-bound Japanese high school students attend as a supplement to their regular schooling.

Once other factors were taken into account, it is notable that the classification of students by race was not a predictor of psychosocial maturity. Presumably the home environment and character of the parents could compensate for a lack of financial resources in stimulating the psychosocial maturity of the child. However, when it comes to meeting the cost of college, some harsh economic realities may interact with cultural factors to produce special effects. We see those factors as explaining why, at least in the case of girls, our racial classification yielded a significant negative correlation with the expectation for higher schooling. We arranged this variable in the order Hispanic, African American, Asian American, and white. In the United States, youngsters from some minority communities often overestimate their objective chances of getting to college and beyond. If that were true of our sample, it would explain the negative correlation. However, it will require additional—and more detailed—study to determine whether the observed negative correlation resulted from the fact that Hispanics and African Americans, in contrast with Asian Americans and whites, reported exceedingly sanguine estimates of their prospects for higher education.

Alternative Analysis

The regression analysis utilized in the immediately preceding section may be usefully supplemented by a different, and generally more transparent, mode for analyzing our data and presenting the results. In this mode we feature the percentage of those with different combinations of characteristics expecting to go on to given levels of higher education. For this purpose and to keep things simple, we decided to use the same definition of expected postsecondary education for both the Japanese and the American samples. The outcome that we assess is the percentage of our national samples who expect to go to college plus those who expect to go on to some form of postgraduate training. To predict the outcome, we use combinations of the Psychosocial Maturity Score and the SES score, with each of those divided into quartiles. The data are presented in Table 3.

In general and as would be expected, this form for expressing the relationship that we are studying confirms the impression gained by examining the correlations and regressions, although it does so in another mode. Thus the extreme combination "Highest SES combined with Lowest Maturity" consistently yields a percentage expecting to go to college and beyond, which is higher than that yielded by the other extreme of "Highest Maturity combined with Lowest SES." However, with the exception of the much greater contrast in the case of girls from the United States, these extreme combinations give only a modest advantage to socioeconomic status as opposed to psychosocial maturity. In three of the four relevant comparisons, the combination featuring high status yields percentages of students expecting advanced education that are only about 10 percentage points higher than the combination featuring high-maturity scores. Girls in the United States are the exception, with high status giving them a very large boost in the percentage expecting an education at the college level or higher.

Table 3. Percentage Expecting to Attain Higher Education by Contrasting Socioeconomic Status and Psychosocial Maturity Profile

	SES + Maturity Profile	Girls	Boys
United States	Hi SES + Lo Maturity	88% (8)	85% (26)
	Lo SES + Hi Maturity	59% (22)	75% (16)
Japan	Hi SES + Lo Maturity	60% (15)	58% (31)
	Lo SES + Hi Maturity	50% (12)	44% (9)

Base number of cases in each cell given in parentheses.

A different way of looking at the pattern of results presented in Table 3 urges us to reason as follows. It is not exactly news that being economically advantaged tends to encourage a youngster into believing that he or she will surely get into college and indeed into some professional school later, and to further assume that those benefits will come even if he or she does not demonstrate habits such as perseverance in studies and responsibility in the communal life of the school. The prime example is the student from an old Boston Brahmin family who is confident that he will enter Harvard even if he is an indifferent student at some elite private secondary academy. Therefore the critical question to raise concerning these measures is "What influence does psychosocial maturity have on educational expectations among those high school students who, being most disadvantaged economically, might otherwise be expected to have the lowest expectation of securing a higher education?" The answer, which can be read from Table 4, is notable.

Among those least advantaged economically, in three of four relevant instances, the percentage of those expecting to go on to higher education doubles as one moves from the cell with the lowest score in maturity to that with the highest average maturity score. For example, within the set of Japanese boys coming from the families lowest in socioeconomic status, the proportion expecting to go on to higher education rose from only 21 percent of those with the lowest maturity scores to reach 44 percent among those with the highest maturity scores. This was the typical pattern, although it will be seen in Table 4 that at times the contrast was even more marked (as in the case of boys in the United States) or somewhat less marked (as in the case of girls in the United States).

SUMMARY AND CONCLUSION

Using representative national samples of adolescents between the ages of fourteen and eighteen in Japan and the United States, we sought to explain two important school outcomes: the grades that students earned and their expectations about postsecondary education. Sociologists may surely take some comfort from our analysis since the factor that they assume will generally be

Table 4. Percentage Expecting Higher Education among the Economically Least Advantaged by Contrasting Levels of Maturity

	Lowest SES and	Girls	Boys
United States	Lowest Maturity	43% (35)	25% (44)
	Highest Maturity	59% (22)	75% (16)
Japan	Lowest Maturity	16% (19)	21% (19)
	Highest Maturity	50% (12)	44% (9)

Base number of cases in each cell given in parentheses.

stronger than all others (socioeconomic status) did indeed prove to be a major determinant of the outcomes under study. However, the comfort they may take in the results can only be small, because social status proved to be the prime explanatory variable only in the case of expectations for postsecondary education. In predicting the grades that pupils received in their classroom work, a quite different factor, the psychosocial maturity of the student—as measured by our scale—proved to be unambiguously the primary cause, while social status was a decidedly secondary factor. Taken together, these two pieces of evidence highlight the critical role of psychosocial factors in explaining the differential success that adolescents have in meeting the demands that the secondary school places on them, and in the process establish the validity of our newly developed measure of psychosocial maturity.

Our claim that psychosocial maturity, as measured by our scale, is a fundamental determinant of the adolescent's success in school is reinforced by the fact that the patterns we observed were basically the same for boys and girls and were manifested in both Japan and the United States. However, in some respects our outcomes did·vary by gender and nation in ways that it seems important to note.

Whether we were predicting school marks or educational expectations, the power of the causal variables to explain those outcomes was consistently greater in the United States than in Japan. We attribute this to the much greater diversity in ethnicity that characterizes the United States. In addition, there is a fundamental difference between the two countries in the importance of social class factors in influencing what schools are like, and in shaping what goes on in the classroom. In virtually every respect, Japan is a much more homogeneous society than is the United States. Beyond that fact, Japan is often cited as outstanding in the degree to which it provides a uniform school experience for its youngsters despite differences in their socioeconomic status. Moreover, Japanese teachers are professionally strongly oriented toward assuring that even the seemingly weakest students are brought up to the standard.

As to the similarities and differences between boy and girls, our analysis indicates that in general the same factors—and in roughly the same proportions—explain the responses of the two genders. However, a more fine-grained analysis gives some support to the widespread assumption that girls will be socially more mature than boys at any given age in the adolescent years. For example, in both Japan and the United States, we can more fully explain the grades earned when we consider the performance of girls rather than boys. Moreover, in all cases it is the maturity score of the girls, reflecting behavior likely to be rewarded in school, that sets them apart. Even in the study of mathematics and science, in which some would assume that boys have the advantage of stronger interest, the girls held their own. For example, in the United States the proportion getting "mostly A's" was 32 percent for girls as opposed to 27 percent for boys. And at the other end of the scale, "D" grades were reported by only 5 percent of both boys and girls. Whether girls are intrinsically more intelligent than boys raises an issue that our data cannot resolve. However, it does speak clearly to another issue. Going beyond the well-known fact that at any age in the adolescent period girls are physically more mature than boys, our data tell us that at any age in the adolescent years girls are also more mature psychosocially. This finding clearly has implications for public policy, and the information should enter into the decision-making process when educators weigh the case for educating boys and girls in either separate schools or separate classrooms.

Acknowledgments

The authors gratefully acknowledge the generous assistance of Professor Masamichi Sasaki of Kyogo-Kyoiku University, who included a set of our maturity questions in a sample survey in Japan and the United States. The survey provided the data for the current study, which would not be possible otherwise. The opinions and conclusions of this study are those of the authors and not of Professor Sasaki.

REFERENCES

Inkeles, Alex and Herbert Leiderman. 1998. "An Approach to the Study of Psychosocial Maturity: The Development of a Cross-National Scale for Adolescents." *International Journal of Comparative Sociology* 39:52–76.
Inkeles, Alex and Herbert Leiderman. 2000. "Being Cooperative as a Form of Social Capital: Evidence from a Sample of Japanese Adolescents." *World Studies in Education* 1:25–54.

APPENDIX

The Short Form of the Psychosocial Maturity Scale

We would like your opinions on different issues about school and other aspects of your life. For each statement I read, please tell me if you agree strongly, agree somewhat, disagree somewhat, disagree strongly, or have mixed feelings.

The first questions are about school.
- Even when things get tough at school, I can get my schoolwork done.
- When I have schoolwork to do, I usually do not plan out how I'm going to get it done.
- I take responsibility for the grades I get, good or bad.
- I try to get others to work together in order to make school a better place.
- When things get hard at school, I don't give up, I just work harder.
- I don't think it's that important to get my homework done on time.
- It is up to my teachers to make school interesting and fun; I just do my own thing.

The next questions are about your community.
- I prefer when everyone works together in my neighborhood.
- I just don't know how to deal with problems in my neighborhood.
- If people in my neighborhood don't want to make it a better place, I just do not give up on them.
- If nobody else in my neighborhood will help, I don't see why I should.
- I know how to get people to cooperate when something has got to be done in my neighborhood.
- When I see something wrong in my neighborhood, I can't just walk away from it.
- It's not much use to plan for your neighborhood when you don't know who else will be living there next year.

The next questions are about friends.
- It's important to me to keep promises I make to my friends.
- I prefer to take my friends' ideas into account when deciding what we do together.
- I can't deal with the social pressures other teenagers put on me.
- It is more important to me to have the support of my friends than to do my own thing.
- I am not very successful in getting my classmates to overcome their differences.
- Even if I don't get along with my friend, I don't avoid him or her.
- I take responsibility for how I get along with my friends.

The next questions are about your family.
- I am not very good at communicating my thoughts and feelings to my family.
- Even when I strongly disagree with my family about some things, I still believe we should work together.
- I'm not good at handling the problems I face at home.
- Even when I have trouble with my family, I keep working at the problem.
- It's not up to me to help my family get along with each other.
- In order for us to make it as a family, it's not all that important we pull together and support each other.
- I just give up on my family when we can't seem to get along.

III

How Schools Work:
Organization and Effects

5

How School Governance Works: The Implementation of Integrated Reform in the Chicago Public Schools

Kenneth K. Wong

DREEBEN'S CONTRIBUTION TO THE STUDY OF SCHOOL GOVERNANCE

Robert Dreeben's research has called into question the assumption that school governance reform can improve teaching and learning in the classroom. This skepticism poses a challenge to school system reformers and political scientists who value the notion that policy consequences of school system organization are closely connected to leadership at the top and its policy priorities. Despite this difference in disciplinary orientation, Dreeben's sociological approach to the study of districts, schools, and instructional units is highly relevant to the current debate on educational reform. His body of research is not intended to support a particular type of reform initiative. Yet Dreeben's work provides a conceptual basis for assessing the fundamental nature and the politics of the current educational reform models. In this chapter I will discuss how Dreeben's analytical perspective has influenced the conceptualization of the politics and governance of school reform in urban systems. Designers, implementers, and evaluators of school governance reform have much to gain from Dreeben's systematic inquiry.

Dreeben's research suggests the need for a more differentiated understanding of school system organization and practices. Decisions and activities about school systems can be differentiated by levels of analysis, institutional roles and functions, and the kinds of constraints that personnel face and the resources that they command at a given level. Such a differentiated understanding enables us to fully appreciate the constraints, nature of resource allocation, and proper role of a given unit in the organizational system. Clearly,

Kenneth K. Wong • Department of Leadership, Policy, and Organizations and Department of Political Science, Vanderbilt University, Nashville, Tennessee 37203.

Stability and Change in American Education: Structure, Process, and Outcomes edited by Maureen T. Hallinan, Adam Gamoran, Warren Kubitschek, and Tom Loveless. Eliot Werner Publications, Clinton Corners, New York, 2003.

these specifications direct our attention to the nature of production in school systems. While student achievement may be an important measure of organizational performance, Dreeben's research suggests that school system organization influences choices and the allocation of resources that accomplish central goals. A framework of accountability may be a matrix that takes into consideration these productive processes.

Drawing on Dreeben's multilayered, differentiated understanding of how the school system organization works, I focus on three related aspects of how school governance operates. First, what are the institutional features of school governance reform at the systemwide level, the connection between schools and other institutions in terms of governing public schools, and the patterns of interplay among institutional actors? Political analysts are particularly interested in the role of other governing institutions at the systemwide level— the mayor's office, media, governor, state legislature, and other organized interest groups. For example, Peterson's *School Politics, Chicago Style* (1976) provides a systematic analysis of how Mayor Daley balanced the interests between his political machine and the reform faction on the Chicago school board during the 1960s and early 1970s. Peterson's discussion of pluralist versus ideological bargaining remains an original contribution to the politics of education. Likewise, Grimshaw's (1979) notion of the teachers' union as a group with veto power in school matters remains relevant in many urban districts. These and other studies draw our attention to the distribution of authority and power between school and other governing institutions. One may consider how a particular school reform shapes the authority boundary in terms of a continuum between a unitary or integrated system of control versus a dispersed or fragmentary system (Fuhrman 1993; Wong, Jain, and Clark 1997; Wong and Sunderman 2000).

Second, what are the managerial aspects of governance reform at the systemwide level? Dreeben's research suggests that a core productive agenda exists at each layer of the school system organization. This is certainly the case at the districtwide level. Even in a decentralized climate, the central school board and the superintendent maintain crucial functions: selecting top administrators, disbursing funds according to various formulas, implementing federal and state guidelines on equal educational opportunity, and evaluating students. From a political scientist's perspective, I focus on decision rules that explain how priorities are set, how resources and personnel are allocated, and how sanctions and support are distributed to achieve systemwide goals. While some decision rules are universalistic in nature, others are designed to target supplementary resources on categories of disadvantaged and low-performing students and schools (see Levy, Meltsner, and Wildavsky 1974; Wong 1999). The political basis of these rules needs to be further examined.

Third, what are the technical aspects that transcend school system organizational layers in the delivery of schooling services? Concerns about the macro-micro linkages call for a more systematic understanding of the nature of resource allocation and utilization in a multilevel, complex organization such as the school system. As Barr and Dreeben (1983) suggest, managerial functions performed at the districtwide level tend to define the kinds of fiscal and personnel resources that have a substantial bearing on school and classroom activities. Indeed, how the school operates is directly affected by such systemwide decisions as staff development, assessment standards, administrative promotion, interpretation of and compliance with federal and state mandates, and integration of school and other social services in the city. The top of the system, for example, exercises direct influence over the quality of middle-level administrators in charge of curriculum development, program operation, and the application of assessment standards to schools. Districtwide curriculum framework and board decisions on attendance may create constraints on practices at the school and classroom levels. At the classroom level, Barr and Dreeben (1983) argue that the organizational arrangement of grouping students can be differentiated from the amount of coverage in instructional practices. In addressing the macro-micro linkages and the instructional decisions made by teachers, policy analysts often take into consideration two political science perspectives—the implementation literature (Pressman and Wildavsky 1973; Wong 1992) and the notion of the "street level bureaucrat" (Lipsky 1980). The former offers insights into how the interactions between actors at various organizational levels constrain and facilitate change, whereas the latter focuses on how the nature of the teaching task influences the success or failure of systemwide accountability policies (Wong and Anagnostopoulos 1998). In short, the macro-micro linkage needs to be mapped out in a systematic, detailed manner.

In this chapter I will apply these analytical concerns to examine one type of urban reform, mayor-led reform of urban school systems. I will draw on some of the findings from our research on high schools in the Chicago public schools during the first five years of Mayor Daley's takeover. Dreeben was a collaborator on the project and was listed as a coauthor on three of the project's reports prepared between 1994 and 2001. By differentiating the various aspects of the 1995 governance reform in Chicago, I hope to begin to address Dreeben's concerns on the effects of governance reform.

REDEFINING THE INSTITUTIONAL BOUNDARY OF SCHOOLS AND POLITICS

City government and the urban school system have traditionally existed as two separate, independent jurisdictions. An insulated school system has been facilitated by both institutional and structural factors over time. Historically, the American public has endorsed the authority of the school board due in part to its belief in strong local control over schools. This creed of local control is frequently equated with an independent, nonpartisan school board. Moreover, due to the progressive tradition of taking politics out of schools, school districts are largely isolated from other lateral institutions (such as health care agencies) in various areas that affect children within the same locale. Finally, powerful constituencies and corporate actors such as teachers'

unions have been successful in dominating resource allocation within the educational enterprise. Consequently, big city school politics generally fit the
image of bureaucratic insulation where the school system resembles a complex, self-contained, hierarchical structure with centralized authority in the
office of a professional superintendent.

Since the 1990s, however, the institutional boundary of schools and the
political system has changed. Big city mayors have become more interested in
managing their local schools. The changing relationship between the mayor
and the schools gained national attention in 1995 when Chicago's Mayor
Daley gained complete control over managing the Chicago public schools. In
1987 William Bennett, Ronald Reagan's secretary of education, characterized
the Chicago public schools as "the worst system in the nation" (*Chicago
Tribune* Staff, 1988). A few years after Daley assumed leadership, President
Clinton mentioned the Chicago schools as a model of school improvement in
two State of the Union messages.

To be sure, Chicago was not the first system where the mayor has taken
over in recent years. With less national attention, Mayor Menino of Boston
assumed authority over the school district in 1992. In Baltimore the school
system has long been a department of city hall and the superintendent a cab-
inet member of the mayor's team (Wong 1990). Daley's control over the
Chicago schools, however, has generated broader policy implications. Daley
not only focused on improving education as an important revitalization strategy in Chicago itself (Wong and Jain 1999), but as chair of the U.S.
Conference of Mayors, he also brought greater nationwide attention to the role
that mayors can play in improving their city school systems. Prior to Daley's
term as its chair, the U.S. Conference of Mayors lacked a division on education. Under Daley's leadership the conference issued a major report *Best
Practices in Education* (1996), held a joint conference of mayors and big city
school superintendents, and created a task force on public schools that was
chaired by Daley and Boston's Menino. Clearly, the conference activities
endorsed the notion of mayoral leadership in public schools.

Why Mayoral Involvement?

An increase in mayoral involvement in schools is closely related to the politics
and functions that public schools serve at the local level. From a fiscal perspective, public schools constitute one of the largest local employers. For
example, the Chicago public schools rank as the second largest public employ-
er in the state. Although it is not a part of the budget in most cities in a technical sense, education dominates most local budgets and accounts for any-
where from 25 to 35 percent of total city expenses. Schools' heavy reliance on
local property taxes impacts highly on a city's taxing and spending capacity.

From the perspective of the city as a service provider, education remains
one of the most important issues that voters want their local leaders to
address. While preferring to receive more federal and state funds, the public

continues to define education as primarily a local responsibility. In the 1990s mayors demonstrated their fiscal prudence and initiated administrative reforms to improve city government performance. Consequently, mayors see the bureaucratized school system as their next key challenge for service improvement (Wong, Jain, and Clark 1997). Nonetheless, mayoral interest in education can be frustrated by existing structural barriers such as a nonpartisan, elected school board that stops politics at the schoolhouse door.

Local schools remain an important neighborhood institution. For high-poverty neighborhoods, schools serve as social buffers that create opportunities for children and parents of low-income backgrounds to connect to the social and economic mainstream (Wilson 1987). In neighborhoods that are marred by constant warfare among rival gangs, schools offer signs of stability and provide an accessible safe haven for the local students. Increasingly, urban politicians are willing to allocate funds to build up schools as community centers for local activities such as after school and summer recreational programs.

Public support for school improvement can be seen as an indication of increasing citizen concern for quality of life issues. In an analysis of agenda setting in Congress during the last thirty years, Berry (1999) found that citizen-based organized actions have rivaled those of traditional groups that are based on the economic interests of labor and industry. Political parties, institutional actors that are hierarchically organized, no longer play a key role in mobilizing voter turnout. Instead, organized interests are realigned in several ways. They have become more focused on quality of life issues, less hierarchically organized, and more pragmatic about governmental and market solutions to educational and social problems. In short, this recent reconfiguration of interest group politics is likely to shape our understanding of group-based influence on public education.

In the context of intercity competition for economic gains, city leaders find schools an important developmental tool (Peterson 1981). A major task for mayors is to retain middle-class families. It is commonly known that young professional couples stay in the city until they have to raise school-age children. Concerns about the quality of education and crime often contribute to the outmigration of the urban middle class. In order to maintain a taxpaying labor force in the cities, public schools must improve to attract middle-class students. Similarly, businesses also choose cities that have a good record of school performance so that they can attract a pool of talented employees. These related factors in today's urban economic reality suggest that the pressure is building on mayors to tackle the problems of their cities' educational systems. Mayors, in other words, can no longer afford an educational system that is largely isolated from the economic future of their cities.

The emergence of mayoral involvement in education can also be seen as an institutional response to the decline in public confidence over the current state of urban school leadership. Based on a 1998 survey, the National School Boards Foundation (NSBF) found that "there is a consistent, significant difference in perception between urban school board members and the urban public on a number of key issues" (1999:12). While 67 percent of the urban board members rated schools in A and B categories, only 49 percent of the urban public did. Whereas three out of four board members rated the teachers as excellent and good, only 54 percent of the public agreed. The public seemed half as likely as the board members to agree that the schools were doing a good job in the following areas: preparing students for college, keeping violence and drugs out of schools, maintaining discipline among students, and teaching children who do not speak English. Subsequently, the NSBF called on urban leaders to sharpen the focus on student performance.

Mayoral involvement in education represents an institutional effort to fill the confidence gap by addressing the performance challenge. In this regard mayoral leadership in education occurs in a policy context where years of decentralized reform alone have not produced systemwide improvements in student performance in big city schools. Reform advocates who promote site-based strategies may overestimate the capacity of the school community to raise academic standards. Decentralized reforms are directed at reallocating power between the systemwide authority and the schools within the public school system. However, decentralized initiatives often fail to take into full consideration powerful quasi-formal actors such as teachers' unions and other organized interests. Decisions made at the school site are constrained by collective bargaining agreements. In addition, decentralization may widen the resource gap between schools that have access to external capital—such as parental organizational skills and grants from foundations—and those that receive limited support from nongovernmental sources. For example, the 1988 Chicago reform was guided by the belief that parent and citizen empowerment through Local School Councils (LSCs) would improve educational performance. The law specifically linked LSCs to better academic outcomes, including a significant reduction in dropout rates and an increase in test scores. However, several years of LSC reform did not produce satisfactory improvements in student performance. The school-by-school trends in reading on standardized tests showed sharp declines, although math and writing performance did not worsen between 1989 and 1995. Whereas one-third of the elementary schools experienced improvement, most elementary and high schools fell behind in the decentralized reform. With bipartisan support the state legislature granted mayoral authority over the Chicago schools in July 1995.

INTEGRATED GOVERNANCE AS A COMPONENT OF MAYORAL INVOLVEMENT

A new framework of educational governance is gaining prominence in urban districts across the nation. "Integrated governance under mayoral leadership," as we have labeled this framework (Wong et al. 1997; Wong 1999), maintains a proper balance between site-based decision making and systemwide performance-based accountability.

Integrated governance in mayor-led systems focuses on district-level capacity to reduce institutional fragmentation and raise academic accountability. This kind of systemwide restructuring is based on a clear vision of educational accountability that focuses on academic standards and performance outcomes. It includes strong political support to improve the operation of the school system and district-level capacity to intervene in failing schools. It utilizes a mix of direct intervention and support strategies to meet the challenges faced by urban schools.

This emerging model is likely to spread as an increasing number of mayors gain control over the public schools. Among the major mayor-led districts are Chicago, Cleveland, Boston, Oakland, Baltimore, and Detroit. Mayors in many more cities—such as Indianapolis, San Francisco, Birmingham, New Orleans, and Buffalo—have expressed strong interest in governing schools. According to an analysis of the mayor's state of the city addresses in 23 cities across the nation, over 90 percent showed a distinct interest in public education even though most mayors currently do not hold a formal role in the school system (Wong and Jain 1999).

To be sure, mayoral control may not necessarily turn into integrated governance reform. In some instances mayors may be reluctant to play an active role even though they are granted the legislative authority; in others mayoral control may be constrained by state legislative compromise. Some mayors may treat the public school sector as a patronage base for short-term partisan gains. In yet other instances such as Houston, civic leadership may be the driving force behind a more focused, performance-based accountability framework (McAdams 2000).

More important, integrated governance reform is not simply a recentralization of authority nor can it be fully understood by focusing only on the issue of city takeover. Instead, integrated governance redefines the responsibilities and enhances the capacity of the districtwide leadership. Given its strong focus on raising student performance, integrated governance legitimizes systemwide standards and policies that identify and target intervention at low-performing schools. In effect, integrated governance creates institutional pressure and support that are necessary to address a key limitation of decentralization: that organizational change at the school site is not a sufficient condition for academic improvement systemwide. While decentralization may produce successful reform in some schools, systemwide improvement is not likely to occur unless districtwide leadership has the political will and capacity to implement outcome-based accountability.

School reform in Chicago represents a clear example of the shift from a fragmentary, decentralized paradigm to integrated governance. During the last decade, Chicago has undergone two major phases of reform, each promoting a particular set of policy strategies. While the 1988 reform empowered the parents and community representatives at the school sites with the establishment of Local School Councils, the 1995 reform substantially strengthened the authority at the districtwide level. The 1995 legislation did not completely dismantle the major provisions in the 1988 reform. The parent-dominated local council, for example, remained in operation in each school and continues to enjoy the power to hire and fire school principals. However, the decentralized arrangements are properly defined within the overarching framework of integrated governance, thereby enhancing accountability. In the following discussion, I will illuminate what we learned about the nature of integrated governance using data collected from the Chicago public schools that pertain to the system's institutional, managerial, and technical functions.

INSTITUTIONAL ASPECTS OF INTEGRATED GOVERNANCE

As public dissatisfaction grew over the 1988 decentralized reform, the Republican governor and the Republican-controlled state legislature declared that an "educational crisis" existed in the Chicago public schools and passed the Chicago School Reform Amendatory Act in July 1995. This law integrated school governance by placing authority for the public schools under the control of the mayor and providing the district with enhanced powers over financial, managerial, and educational matters. The act expanded the district's power to control and reorganize financial and management policies. It also directed the newly established Reform Board of Trustees and chief executive officer (CEO) to increase the quality of educational services within the system by giving the latter authority to place poorly performing schools on remediation, probation, and intervention.

The legitimacy of the public school system was enhanced following mayoral control over the Chicago schools. The 1995 reform put the mayor in charge of appointing the five-member school board without having to select from slates put forward by the nominating commission and the CEO in charge of the schools. Since the board appoints the top administrative officers, these changes facilitate an effective link between the mayor's office and the central office. Under this arrangement education becomes a part of the mayor's policy agenda and gives the mayor the option to decide the amount of political capital he or she is willing to invest in improving the schools.

Public confidence over the mayor-controlled school board is indicated by our analysis of 114 editorials on educational issues in the city's two major newspapers, the *Chicago Tribune* and the *Sun Times,* between August 1995 and March 1997 (Wong and Jain 1999). In both newspapers 75 percent of the editorials endorsed school board control over policy issues and only 25 percent suggested a more pluralist approach. Further, our analysis of about one thousand news articles during this period found positive coverage of the role of the central administration. CEO Paul Vallas managed the district affairs in an open fashion and the top administrators seemed to move swiftly to respond to public concerns about waste and inefficiency. The central administration preempted external investigation by setting up its own Office of Investigations, under the guidance of a former newspaper reporter, to uncover administrative fraud.

The effectiveness of efforts to restore public confidence in public schools ultimately lies with mayoral leadership, governing style, and decisions about how much political capital the mayor wants to allocate to the school sector. In other words, the political will of the mayor plays a critical role. In this regard Mayor Daley has been instrumental in projecting the image of an effective school district to the public. Daley prefers to be seen as an efficient manager rather than a ward politician (Johnson 1997). Positive editorials and reports on the central administration have endorsed the mayor, who has enjoyed strong backing from both newspapers. When a mayor is highly popular and witnesses overwhelming support in his most recent reelection campaign, newspapers are not likely to go in the opposite direction. After all, newspaper reports that ignore Daley's accomplishments or call into question his initiatives to improve city services make neither good political nor sound business sense. Since Daley declared education to be his top priority, business and the media readily rallied behind him. In short, mayoral control made the school system an integral part of the citywide agenda.

The mayor-appointed school board and the CEO took highly visible steps to address the public's concerns about poor performance. In spring 1996 the district declared that it would end social promotion and announced a new academic promotion policy. Third, sixth, eighth, and ninth graders could be retained a grade if they failed to score at the district benchmark on nationally normed tests, the Iowa Test of Basic Skills (ITBS) or the Test of Achievement and Proficiency (TAP) for ninth graders. The district generally set the benchmark at approximately one grade level below the national norm. Students who failed to post adequate scores attended a Summer Bridge Program. In addition, the policy also required third, sixth, and eighth graders to receive passing grades in reading and mathematics and to have no more than twenty unexcused absences. Ninth graders had to earn at least five course credits their freshman year and have no more than twenty unexcused absences. The academic promotion policy has received broad public support, although it has been revised slightly in recent years.

Seeing the legislation as an institutional response to declining public confidence (Hirschman 1970), Mayor Daley acted swiftly to demonstrate his commitment to school improvement. The two top positions, the president of the Board of Trustees and the chief executive officer, came from the mayor's office: board President Gery Chico served as the mayor's chief of staff and CEO Vallas reigned as the city budget director. These key appointments illuminate a significant shift in leadership recruitment in the Chicago public schools. Drawing on corporate management practices, the 1995 reform created the position of chief executive officer to oversee the top administrative team, including the chief education officer. Our analysis of the 111 top administrative appointments made in various units of the central office between July 1995 and February 1998 shows a diversity of expertise among administrators, with 8.1 percent from the private sector, 6.3 percent from nonprofit organizations, 27.9 percent from city and other public agencies, and 57.6 percent from the professional ranks within the Chicago public schools. These numbers underestimate the fluid nature of shifting assignments between the schools and other city agencies. For example, a former chief of staff for Paul Vallas was promoted to head the Chicago Housing Authority, the leader of which in turn moved back to become deputy mayor of education. This pattern of permeability among top administrators may constitute a broader issue network that cuts across agencies and school system domains but whose members find common ground to collaborate on educational issues.

Integrated governance is designed to facilitate policy coherence and improve organizational effectiveness. Not only was the mayor given the responsibility for overseeing schools, but the 1995 reform also eliminated competing sources of district-level authority—such as the School Board Nominating Commission—and suspended the functions of the School Finance Authority. Powers were granted to the citywide Board of Trustees to hold LSCs accountable to systemwide standards. The district acted on these powers to reallocate financial and managerial resources toward an accountability focus through downsizing the central office; privatizing several district functions; and monitoring poorly performing schools, principals, and teachers.

By strengthening the districtwide authority of the system, the 1995 reform shifted the balance of power between the central office and the LSCs. Prior to 1995 the LSCs had broad authority, but there was little direct accountability or oversight. For example, state Chapter 1 funds went directly to the schools, but the board remained accountable if the money was misused. The organized constituencies in the broader school community often influenced selection of principals by the LSCs. The new administration has signaled the LSCs that they can no longer operate with complete independence and has incorporated the LSCs into the overall system by defining the standards and responsibilities to which they must adhere in such key decisions as hiring and firing of principals.

THE MANAGEMENT OF INTEGRATED GOVERNANCE REFORM

The 1995 integrated governance reform has encouraged the adoption of business management strategies. The management and maintenance of school buildings, for example, were reorganized to stress customer service and contracting out. The board eliminated the Bureau of Facilities Planning in the central office (resulting in the elimination of ten jobs), reduced the number of positions in the Department of Facilities Central Service Center by half (26 out of 50 positions were eliminated), and reduced the citywide facilities administration from 441 positions to 34. Contracts for these services are now with private companies. To oversee the management and maintenance of school property, the board negotiated contracts with several firms to provide property advisory services for each region. Under this arrangement the firms advise principals and the Department of Operations on property management and provide custodial, engineering, and construction-related services to the schools. In addition, the board prequalified a number of general construction contractors from which schools can select.

The 1995 law increased school board discretion over revenue allocation, allowing the board to prepare a balanced budget. The board was granted new authority that expanded its financial powers. A number of funded programs—including K-6 reading improvement, substance abuse prevention, Hispanic programs, gifted education, and categorical funds—were collapsed into a general education block grant and an education services block grant, respectively. Although total revenues available to the board declined by 8 percent in fiscal year 1996 from the previous year, revenues going into the general fund increased by about 2 percent (approximately $28.5 million). Additionally, the board acquired greater flexibility over the use of pension funds and state Chapter 1 funds not allocated to the schools. Finally, there were no longer separate tax levies earmarked for specific purposes.

The school board successfully negotiated two four-year contracts with the teachers' union, including substantial raises for teachers. These actions brought both financial and labor stability to the system. In light of these financial and management improvements, bond companies upgraded the Chicago public schools' bond rating several times. In March 1996 Standard and Poor's raised the rating from a BBB- to BBB, and Moody's did likewise from a Ba to Baa, allowing the board to issue bonds for the construction of new buildings under lower interest rates than before. By summer 1997 the bond ratings were A- from Standard and Poor's and Baa1 from Moody's. Consequently, the board was able to issue $2 billion in bonds to fund a decade-long capital improvement campaign.

TECHNICAL CHALLENGES TO INTEGRATED GOVERNANCE

The 1995 reform sharpened its focus on low-performing schools and their students. Beginning in 1996 the CEO and School Reform Board of Trustees launched an educational accountability agenda focused on raising standards and improving student performance. This agenda included various types of policy levers aimed at directing and supporting improvements in school and student performance. We have identified three key types: formal regulations against low performance applied to students and schools; support for low-performing students and schools; and professional discretion for school-level control over the design and implementation of improvement programs (Wong et al., in press).

To illustrate how the district uses a mix of pressure, support, and professional incentives to improve school performance, we focus on four sets of key initiatives: probation and reconstitution, academic promotion, curriculum standards and assessments, and junior and senior academies. Each initiative entails varying degrees of sanctions, support, and professional discretion (see Table 1).

Probation, reconstitution, and academic promotion are examples of formal regulatory intervention, although they also involve some support and limited professional discretion. Under probation and reconstitution policies, the district can intervene in schools with less than 15 percent of their students

Table 1. District Policies Classified by Degree of Central Direction

Type of Policy Leverage	Probation/Reconstitution	Academic Promotion	Academies	Curriculum Standards & Assessments
Regulation	Threat of Restaffing	Grade Retention	Certificate of Mastery; CASE Promotion Requirement	Use CASE to Identify Low-Performing Schools for District Intervention
Support	External Partners; Probation Managers	Summer Bridge Program; Developmental Math and Reading Courses; Structured Curriculum	Funds for Common Teacher; Planning Time; Textbooks; Science Labs; Academy Resource Teacher	Curriculum Frameworks; Programs of Study; Structured Curriculum; Sample Exams and Questions; Staff Development
Professional Discretion	Principal Selection of External Partners; Teacher Instructional and Curriculum Choice	Promotion Waivers; Hiring Teachers for Summer Bridge Program; Teacher Instructional Choice	School Choice of Organizational Model	Teachers' Instructional Choice

Source: Wong et al. (in press).

scoring at national norms on either the reading test of the ITBS for elementary schools or the TAP for high schools. The district provides schools with a probation manager to help direct school improvement efforts. In addition, schools must hire one of several external partners with whom the district has contracted to assist schools in improving instruction and student achievement. The district pays for the external partners during the first year of probation. The schools must pay for one-fourth of the expense each consecutive year of probation. A similar support system exists for schools under reconstitution, which have less than 10 percent of their students scoring at national norms. In addition, the district can remove a principal from a reconstituted school and all teachers must reapply for their positions.

Prior to 1995 the subdistrict superintendent, not the citywide school board, had primary responsibility for monitoring the performance of the schools and identifying nonperforming schools. In the past, intervening in low-performing schools required the approval of the subdistrict council, which was made up of parent or community members from each LSC within the subdistrict. Rarely did the council endorse district intervention. In contrast, enabled by the 1995 legislation, the board and CEO placed 21 schools on remediation in January 1996 for failing to meet state standards for three consecutive years. In September 1996 the CEO placed 109 schools—that is, 20 percent of all the schools—under probation since 15 percent or less of their students scored at the national norm. In addition, seven high schools were reconstituted as a result of chronically low test scores. None of the reconstituted schools had more than 7 percent of their students reading at or above grade level. Five of the seven schools had their principals replaced and about 30 percent of the teachers were not rehired. Our classroom observation in four high schools showed that schools and teachers accommodated to policies that entail formal sanctions by allocating instructional time and activities to fulfill district policy objectives (see Table 2). On the average, English teachers allocated 7 percent of their teaching time to test practice and 29 percent of their time to test skills development activities. Math teachers on the average allocated 8 percent of their time to test practice and 7 percent to test skills development (Wong et al., in press).

Consistent with the focus on raising student performance, the Board of Trustees ended social promotion of students in third, sixth, and eighth grades who did not meet set levels on standardized tests. These students were required to participate in a systemwide summer school called the Summer Bridge Program. The central office provided bridge teachers with structured lesson plans that identified lesson objectives and materials, the order of activities, how the teachers should present the materials, and the instructional format that the teachers should use. At the end of the seven-week program, students took the ITBS again. If they met or exceeded the district benchmark, they were promoted to the next grade. If they failed, they were retained and placed in a class with no more than fifteen students. Eighth graders aged fifteen or over were placed in district transition schools. In recent years about

60 percent of eighth graders who participated in the program met the cut-off scores after the seven weeks. Considering those who passed the spring test, nine out of ten eighth graders had met the school system's new promotion standards by the end of the summer.

Unlike the regulatory probation/reconstitution policy, the district's junior/senior academy initiative allows for organizational discretion at the school sites. This initiative is central to the district's High School Redesign Plan and seeks to change how students progress through high schools, the nature of the curriculum that they receive, and how teachers work with one another and with students. The district has provided schools with support to implement the junior/senior academies in terms of funding for common teacher planning time and academy resource teachers to oversee the academies. The district allows the schools considerable discretion in how they organize the junior/senior academies. We found that some schools instituted a small-schools type of organization that arranged students and teachers into "pods" in order to personalize the relationship between them and keep better track of student attendance and discipline, while other schools maintained the traditional subject-matter high school structure (Wong et al., in press).

While schools enjoy flexibility in determining how teachers work with one another and students, the junior/senior academy initiative has its regulatory aspects as well. It entails district efforts to standardize curriculum and introduce formal sanctions to hold teachers and students accountable for achieving academic standards. Students in the junior academy (ninth and tenth graders) receive a core curriculum centered on four key subjects: math, English, social studies, and science. The district reduced the number of electives that a student could take in the junior academy. In order to graduate from the junior to the senior academy, students must earn credit in all core subjects; score at least a 9.8 on reading and math TAP tests; and pass the Chicago Academic Standards Exam (CASE), the district's standards-based assessment. The district's High School Redesign Plan states that students can remain in the junior academy for as long as it takes them to fulfill promotion requirements. Our 1998 survey of high school principals suggests that the academy has had a greater effect on students' social behavior and test performance than on curriculum and instructional practices (Wong et al., in press). Further evaluation is needed to determine whether these new initiatives will promote student learning in the longer run.

Like its other core policies, the district's use of the curriculum standards and assessments entails a combination of regulation, support, and professional discretion. Clearly the intent of the Chicago Academic Standards (CAS) and the CASE exam by the district and its implementation by teachers is complex. Based on interviews with teachers and 62 hours of classroom observations in tenth grade English in four Chicago schools, our project generated several findings about the implementation of the Chicago Academic Standards and Frameworks and its related assessment, the CASE (Wong et al. 2001).

First, districtwide standards in English represent multiple curriculum and instructional goals. District goals stated in the CAS document serve not only to regulate curriculum and instructional decisions, but also to support teachers by clarifying key instructional goals and objectives. A close analysis of Chicago's standards reveals that their scope represents a cross-section of different approaches to teaching English. Standards include a multicultural and historical approach to English instruction as well as constructivist, and conventional, text-centered approaches.

Second, the district's stated goals are displaced as standards and translated into the Programs of Study and CASE. A funneling process occurs as the standards and frameworks are translated into documents intended to guide teachers' instruction and assessment. While a broad array of goals is reflected in the CAS, these are not represented in the Programs of Study and the CASE. Those goals that remain tend to be ones that are easily measured and assessed.

This funneling process encompasses several stages. As mentioned above, the broadest range of goals exists at the abstract level of the standards themselves. At this point the funnel is widest because no single curriculum model is employed: the CAS incorporates numerous approaches to teaching. This variety of approaches is in part programmatic and in part attributable to the wide range of participants involved in developing the CAS; the latter includes teachers, local university partners, a Washington-based think-tank, and the Chicago Teachers' Union. Additionally, various models were used as guides, including professional standards like those of the National Council of Teachers of English and the National Council of Teachers of Mathematics as well as the Illinois state standards and standards developed by other states. Given this wide range of input, the CAS proposes a variety of sound—and at times innovative—approaches to teaching. At the same time, it is not easy to encompass such a variety of directives within a single practical teaching guide and assessment tool.

It is in this move toward practicality that the funneling process begins. The Programs of Study seek to extract key goals from the CAS and offer suggestions that would render such goals tangible to teachers. The Program of Study, however, does not merely aim to serve as a professional support tool for Chicago public school teachers. It also serves as the blueprint from which the CASE exam is formulated and, therefore, represents the primary CASE-preparation resource for teachers. Thus although the CASE exam is meant to assess the skills outlined in the CAS, in effect it is measuring those skills that were funneled from the CAS into the Program of Study. The Program of Study, then, became the de facto determinant of which skills teachers should be teaching.

Third, teachers' curriculum decisions and instructional choices are remarkably similar across the four high schools in our study. For example, the teachers' reported objectives for the instructional unit *To Kill a Mockingbird* were to have students understand the plot and main themes of the novel. In terms of classroom activities, teachers devoted most of their time to literal comprehension of the novel. This is reflected in their choice of activities, such as having students read silently or orally and reviewing the chosen selection, and in an analysis of the types of questions posed to their classes. No time was spent on discussion (see Tables 2–3).

Fourth, teachers respond most to the regulatory aspect of the standards and assessments. The CASE exam is the dominant mechanism guiding teachers' curriculum and instructional decisions. Teachers are allocating time to the curriculum tested in the CASE. Coverage of material is their priority; their instructional practices reflect a focus on literal comprehension rather than more complex thinking skills. They are practicing writing as modeled by the exam, which primarily focuses on basic proficiency. Our analysis of the sample questions in the multiple choice component of the exam, for example, showed that the questions were evenly divided between basic knowledge and items that emphasized understanding or reasoning. Similarly, in the constructed response section of the sample exam, we found that the reading rubric did not require students to show interpretive and implied reasoning skills in order to pass the test.

Fifth, the district and the schools have provided teachers with limited support in the form of professional development related to the standards and assessments. As a consequence teachers' ideas about how to respond are developed to meet curriculum alignment; professional development does not lead to teachers experimenting with different instructional approaches. In our analysis of instructional activities, we observed very little cooperative learning or student-centered activities. Even games aimed at greater student participation were veiled recitations with teachers asking students literal questions.

CONCLUSIONS

Dreeben's research has sharpened our understanding of how governance works in one type of current school reform, the mayor-led integrated governance model. Because of Dreeben's research, we are keenly aware of the institutional, managerial, and technical aspects of school governance reform. Equally important is the need to pay close attention to mechanisms that connect or fail to connect layers within the school system. Dreeben's work provides a set of criteria in assessing the implementation of mayor-led governance reform. Clearly, these criteria are applicable to study other school reforms. In other words, Dreeben's constructive skepticism about school reform has yielded a research agenda for school system analysts.

The leading questions that Dreeben's scholarship has raised can be framed as follows. First, from an institutional perspective, does the reform improve organizational coherence and integrate governance accountability? Second, in terms of management practices, does the reform allocate resources in ways that support the core goals of the system as a whole? Third, in considering technical aspects, does the reform support a core agenda directed at improving instruction and learning? Fourth, in terms of supporting instructional activities in the classroom, does the reform create the proper mix of sanctions, standards, support, and professional incentives?

These four criteria can be helpful for understanding both the accom-

Table 2. Percentage of Time Teachers Allocate to Instructional Activities, 1998–99

School	Teacher	Management	Discussion	Groups	Student Report	Recitation	Lecture	Seatwork	Reading Aloud	Silent Reading	Movie/ Audio	Test	Stand. Test	Diversion
A	1	11.0%	0.0%	0.0%	0.0%	8.0%	0.0%	37.0%	17.0%	0.0%	13.0%	12.0%	0.0%	2.0%
	2	23.0%	0.0%	0.0%	0.0%	16.0%	1.0%	10.0%	32.0%	0.0%	0.0%	11.0%	0.0%	8.0%
	Total	*16.0%*	*0.0%*	*0.0%*	*0.0%*	*11.0%*	*0.0%*	*26.0%*	*23.0%*	*0.0%*	*8.0%*	*11.0%*	*0.0%*	*4.0%*
B	3	17.0%	0.0%	0.0%	0.0%	14.0%	3.0%	0.0%	35.0%	7.0%	6.0%	15.0%	0.0%	2.0%
	4	20.0%	0.0%	3.0%	0.0%	23.0%	0.0%	16.0%	21.0%	3.0%	0.0%	1.0%	11.0%	1.0%
	Total	*18.0%*	*0.0%*	*2.0%*	*0.0%*	*18.0%*	*2.0%*	*8.0%*	*29.0%*	*6.0%*	*3.0%*	*9.0%*	*5.0%*	*1.0%*
C	5	10.0%	0.0%	13.0%	0.0%	35.0%	1.0%	4.0%	0.0%	0.0%	38.0%	0.0%	0.0%	0.0%
	·6	22.0%	0.0%	11.0%	3.0%	26.0%	0.0%	8.0%	5.0%	0.0%	0.0%	7.0%	16.0%	1.0%
	Total	*16.0%*	*0.0%*	*12.0%*	*1.0%*	*31.0%*	*0.0%*	*6.0%*	*2.0%*	*0.0%*	*20.0%*	*3.0%*	*8.0%*	*1.0%*
D	7	16.0%	0.0%	0.0%	0.0%	40.0%	3.0%	25.0%	8.0%	1.0%	0.0%	3.0%	0.0%	3.0%
	8	9.0%	0.0%	11.0%	0.0%	17.0%	2.0%	7.0%	3.0%	1.0%	30.0%	17.0%	0.0%	2.0%
	Total	*13.0%*	*0.0%*	*4.0%*	*0.0%*	*31.0%*	*3.0%*	*18.0%*	*6.0%*	*1.0%*	*12.0%*	*8.0%*	*0.0%*	*3.0%*
	Total	**16.0%**	**0.0%**	**4.0%**	**0.0%**	**23.0%**	**1.0%**	**15.0%**	**14.0%**	**2.0%**	**10.0%**	**8.0%**	**3.0%**	**2.0%**

Source: Wong et al. (2001).

Table 3. Definition of Activity Types

Management
During management episodes teachers discuss issues relevant to the running of the classroom and/or a specific activity. Management activities include teachers giving instructions, talking about students' grades, the class agenda for the day or future days, placing students into small groups, disciplinary issues, and taking attendance and record keeping.

Discussion
Discussion involves students elaborating on ideas or interpretations of an individual text, across texts, or between texts and the larger world. It has two distinguishing features: uptake and authentic questions. Uptake occurs when teachers incorporate student responses into subsequent questions, and when teachers and students elaborate on student ideas and responses. Authentic questions do not have prespecified answers; they are open-ended questions that students have to provide evidence or support to answer. Both uptake and authentic questions have to be present at the same time for talk to be considered discussion.

Groups
Students work with one or more other students to engage in and/or complete an activity. We did not distinguish between cooperative learning and collaborative seatwork.

Student Report
Students present material, including their own writing, to the class.

Recitation
Recitation typically involves a pattern of the teacher asking a question, students providing a response, and the teacher either evaluating the response or simply taking the response and moving on to the next topic. Recitation is marked by questions that the teacher believes have a right or wrong answer. Recitation is also marked by teachers moving from one topic to another, or from one question to another question unconnected to the previous question.

Lecture
Teachers provide students with information or explain something without student comment.

Seatwork
Students work independently, typically with a worksheet.

Reading Aloud
The teacher reads aloud to students, students read aloud in turns or parts, and students read aloud in small groups.

Silent Reading
Students read assigned work by themselves.

Movie / Audio
Students watch a movie or videotape, or they read as they listen to an audiotaped version of a literary work.

Test
Students take teacher-created quiz or test in class.

Standardized Test
Students take practice tests that simulate the content or format of standardized tests.

Diversion
This includes time spent discussing issues not relevant to understanding the course content, time when a teacher is not in the room, and time when nothing instructional or management oriented is occurring.

Source: Wong et al. (2001).

plishments and challenges of urban school reform. Chicago provides a rich example of school reform in the last decade. A key lesson learned from the decentralization experiment is the need for systemwide standards and intervention to address the challenge of student performance. The LSC and its supportive network alone are not sufficient to promote educational improvement systemwide. Indeed, decentralized reform may have widened the capacity gap among schools to raise performance. Instead, districtwide leadership is needed both to apply pressure to and provide support for schools. Such a mix of intervention strategies did not occur during the period of LSC dominance because the reform ideology, with its strong antibureaucratic sentiments, did not allow for the proper functioning of the central office.

The 1995 reform constituted a major effort to reduce organizational fragmentation with integrated governance. Mayor Daley assumed responsibility for improving education and has demonstrated his ability to use his political capital to bring about coherent policy. Because of integrated governance reform, the Chicago public schools are no longer complacent with their performance. The top leadership has engaged in ongoing self-learning and has made serious efforts to fine-tune many of its reform initiatives. The recent replacement of the CEO and the school board president further signals mayoral priority on educational performance.

The technical challenge remains enormous. What we learned from our classroom analysis at the high school is an urgent need to raise the level of instruction across the entire school system in Chicago. Findings from our study on CAS/CASE implementation indicate that teachers focus primarily on literal comprehension and use a limited number of activities in their classrooms. No differentiation in instructional coverage is found among classrooms comprised of students with varying literacy skills in schools ranging from a college preparatory magnet to a reconstituted school. Our classroom observation suggests a basic proficiency on the part of the teachers and the Program of Study provided by the district. If the district wants to raise the bar of instructional activity, it needs to provide sustained professional development—either through district programs or in the schools—aligned with district goals modeling an array of approaches. If the goal of the CAS and CASE is indeed to set basic proficiency levels, then it is consistent with current practice. If, however, the district wants to raise the instructional bar, it needs to re-evaluate its current approach to presenting and preparing teachers for the CASE.

Taken as a whole, the post-1995 reform shows positive signs in addressing the institutional and managerial aspects of the reform. Its technical aspects remain somewhat mixed, even though its strategies of sanctions and support have created a climate of strong accountability that leads to better student performance across the system. Since 1996 better test scores have been seen not only in elementary schools, but also in some of the most problematic high schools. For the current pace of student gains to be sustained in the long run, the Chicago reform must devote more attention to the linkage between school system expectations at the macrolevel and instructional practices at the classroom level. To the extent that its macro-micro connection is strengthened, the Chicago version of integrated governance will provide useful lessons for transforming urban school systems.

Acknowledgments

I would like to thank Robert Dreeben, Larry Lynn, and Terry Clark for their comments on various ideas that were discussed in earlier research reports. I would also like to thank Dorothea Anagnostopoulos, Stacey Rutledge, Frances Shen, Claudia Edwards, and Pushpam Jain for their research assistance.

REFERENCES

Barr, Rebecca and Robert Dreeben. 1983. *How Schools Work*. Chicago: University of Chicago Press.

Berry, Jeffrey M. 1999. *The New Liberalism: The Rising Power of Citizen Groups*. Washington, DC: Brookings Institution Press.

Chicago Tribune Staff. 1988. "Chicago Schools: 'Worst in America'" [compilation of articles published in the *Chicago Tribune*].

Fuhrman, Susan H., ed. 1993. *Designing Coherent Education Policy: Improving the System*. San Francisco: Jossey-Bass.

Grimshaw, William J. 1979. *Union Rule in the Schools: Big-City Politics in Transformation*. Lexington, MA: D.C. Heath.

Hirschman, Albert O. 1970. *Exit, Voice, and Loyalty: Responses to Decline in Firms, Organizations, and States*. Cambridge, MA: Harvard University Press.

Johnson, Dirk. 1997. "Once Stolid and Big-Shouldered, Now a Cinderella on the Lake." *New York Times*, July 15, p. A–10.

Levy, Frank, Arnold J. Meltsner, and Aaron Wildavsky. 1974. *Urban Outcomes: Schools, Streets, and Libraries*. Berkeley: University of California Press.

Lipsky, Michael. 1980. *Street-Level Bureaucracy: Dilemmas of the Individual in Public Services*. New York: Russell Sage Foundation.

McAdams, Donald R. 2000. *Fighting to Save Our Urban Schools . . . and Winning! Lessons from Houston*. New York: Teachers College Press.

National School Boards Foundation. 1999. *Leadership Matters: Transforming Urban School Boards*. Alexandria, VA: National School Boards Foundation.

Peterson, Paul E. 1976. *School Politics, Chicago Style*. Chicago: University of Chicago Press.

Peterson, Paul E. 1981. *City Limits*. Chicago: University of Chicago Press.

Pressman, Jeffrey L. and Aaron Wildavsky. 1973. *Implementation: How Great Expectations in Washington Are Dashed in Oakland*. Berkeley: University of California Press.

U.S. Conference of Mayors. 1996. "Chicago Public Schools: A New Start." U.S. Conference of Mayors, Best Practices Database.

Wilson, William Julius. 1987. *The Truly Disadvantaged: The Inner City, the Underclass, and Public Policy*. Chicago: University of Chicago Press.

Wong, Kenneth K. 1990. *City Choices: Education and Housing*. Albany: State University of New York Press.

Wong, Kenneth K. 1992. "The Politics of Urban Education as a Field of Study: An Interpretive Analysis." Pp. 3–26 in *The Politics of Urban Education in the United States*, edited by James G. Cibulka, Rodney J. Reed, and Kenneth K. Wong. London: Falmer Press.

Wong, Kenneth K. 1999. *Funding Public Schools: Politics and Policy*. Lawrence: University Press of Kansas.

Wong, Kenneth K. and Dorothea Anagnostopoulos. 1998. "Can Integrated Governance Reconstruct Teaching? Lessons Learned from Two Low-Performing Chicago High Schools." *Educational Policy* 12:31–47.

Wong, Kenneth. K., Dorothea Anagnostopoulos, Stacey Rutledge, and Claudia Edwards. 2001. *The Challenge of Improving Instruction in Urban High Schools: Case Studies of the Implementation of the Chicago Academic Standards.* Report submitted to the U.S. Department of Education, Washington, DC.

Wong, Kenneth K., Dorothea Anagnostopoulos, Stacey Rutledge, Laurence Lynn, Jr., and Robert Dreeben. In press. "Implementation of an Educational Accountability Agenda: Integrated Governance in the Chicago Public Schools Enters Its Fourth Year." In *A Race Against Time: Responses to the Crisis in Urban Schooling,* edited by James G. Cibulka and William L. Boyd. Norwood, NJ: Ablex.

Wong, Kenneth K., Robert Dreeben, Laurence Lynn, Jr., and Gail L. Sunderman. 1997. *Integrated Governance as a Reform Strategy in the Chicago Public Schools.* Unpublished report, Department of Education and Irving B. Harris Graduate School of Public Policy Studies, University of Chicago.

Wong, Kenneth. K. and Pushpam Jain. 1999. "Newspapers as Policy Actors in Urban School Systems: The Chicago Story." *Urban Affairs Review* 35:210–46.

Wong, Kenneth. K., Pushpam Jain, and Terry Nichols Clark. 1997. "Mayoral Leadership in the 1990s and Beyond: Fiscally Responsible and Outcome Oriented." Paper presented at the annual meeting of the Association for Public Policy Analysis and Management, Washington, DC.

Wong, Kenneth. K. and Gail L. Sunderman. 2000. "Implementing Districtwide Reform in Schools with Title I Schoolwide Programs: The First 2 Years of Children Achieving in Philadelphia." *Journal of Education for Students Placed at Risk* 5:355–81.

6

School Organization and Response to Systemic Breakdown

Maureen T. Hallinan

Following the Three Mile Island accident in 1979, Charles Perrow wrote *Normal Accidents* (1984) in which he presented a sociological analysis of systemic failure in complex technological systems. Perrow focused on breakdowns in high-risk technological systems, which have the potential for catastrophic outcomes when they malfunction. Examples of these systems include nuclear power plants, space missions, genetic engineering, public transportation, and air traffic control systems. At risk from a systemic accident are the operators of these systems, persons who use the systems, those who are located near them, and even future generations.

A high-risk technological system has two defining characteristics that account for its vulnerability to accident: complex interactivity and tight coupling. An interactively complex system has feedback loops and branching paths and requires transference of processing from one linear sequence to another. In addition, its subsystems may perform different tasks at various points in the production process. A tightly coupled system is one in which no slack exists between units in the system. What happens in one unit has a direct impact on the functioning of other units.

A technological system that is both interactively complex and tightly connected operates according to rigid rules. First, the production process is time dependent and cannot tolerate delays or interruptions to production. Second, the sequencing of tasks is invariant and the overall design of the system allows only one way to perform each task. Finally, the system requires precision in terms of resources, supplies, and equipment; substitution of resources is not possible.

Perrow's premise is that accidents are normal in interactively complex and tightly connected technological systems. The structure and operational

Maureen T. Hallinan • Department of Sociology, University of Notre Dame, Notre Dame, Indiana 46556.

Stability and Change in American Education: Structure, Process, and Outcomes edited by Maureen T. Hallinan, Adam Gamoran, Warren Kubitschek, and Tom Loveless. Eliot Werner Publications, Clinton Corners, New York, 2003.

modality of these sophisticated systems increase the likelihood that they will malfunction. The number of interactions in the system increases exponentially with the number of units in the system and a breakdown can occur at each of these interaction points. Since the system has no buffers or redundancies to take the place of the malfunctioning unit, the potential for systemic collapse is considerable.

Failures in sophisticated technological systems are caused by either human error or random events. Human error occurs when an agent or operator exercises poor judgment or does not have access to information needed to avert a disaster. For example, a small electrical outage in one unit may prevent vital information from reaching an operator in time to influence a decision that affects the whole system. Random events trigger a calamity in a technological system less frequently than human error, but they do occur on occasion. At Three Mile Island, four small independent failures that were unknown to operators caused the accident. In this case the system itself, not those operating it, was responsible for the catastrophe.

Perrow's analysis of the collapse of sophisticated technological systems is timely in light of the terrorist attacks on the World Trade Center and the Pentagon on September 11, 2001. While the destruction of the World Trade Center and damage to the Pentagon are themselves not examples of the collapse of an interactively complex and tightly knit technological system, they alert us to the possibility that future terrorist acts could be directed at high-risk technological systems. In particular, nuclear power plants in the United States and abroad, air traffic control systems, satellite technology, the Internet, and countless other technologically based systems are at risk. Perrow's analysis can aid safety examinations of these systems. Perrow suggests that awareness of these points of vulnerability should reduce human error and provide some protection against shocks to the system.

In contrast to the complex structure of the technological systems that Perrow analyzed, many systems are characterized by simple linear interactions and/or a loosely coupled design. Examples can be found in communications systems, social networks, businesses, hospitals, religious organizations, nonprofit and service agencies, and schools. As with more complex systems, these simpler systems are also subject to human mistakes and random error. However, the likelihood of a systemic collapse resulting from these errors is smaller than in more complex systems.

In a simple linear system, each unit performs its single, dedicated function as one step in a linear sequence. The output of one step serves as the input for the next step. If one unit breaks down, it can be replaced, fixed, or bypassed without affecting the entire system. The predictable result is a temporary slowdown or even a brief shutdown in production, but the system will not collapse because the consequences of such interruptions are known and expected. In a loosely coupled system, the units are somewhat independent and to a certain extent act according to their own logic. Loosely coupled systems have greater flexibility in terms of the sequence of steps in production and the transferral of tasks from one unit to another. They can better tolerate waste of resources, loss of time, and other inefficiencies without damage to the overall system. The flexibility and redundancies built into a loosely coupled system suggest that the system should be better able to adapt to an error than a more tightly coupled one. As a result one might expect that loosely coupled systems would also be less likely to suffer a complete systemic collapse.

The great danger in the collapse of a complex technological system is the threat to human life. While the failure of a simpler system may be less threatening, it too may have serious consequences. For example, one reason that the United States was not better prepared for the terrorist attacks in New York and Washington is that its intelligence systems failed to function properly. The CIA and FBI now acknowledge that if a network of federal agencies had better coordinated their information and activities, the September 11th atrocities might have been averted. In other words, a breakdown in our communications systems facilitated the terrorist attacks.

More frequently, however, the immediate effects of a breakdown in a simple linear or loosely connected system involve loss of time, resources, and opportunities rather than human life. Consequently, an accident in such a system would not be as immediately threatening as the failure of a complex technological system. Nevertheless, the impact may cause harm. For example, the effect of a breakdown in production at an automotive factory (a simple system) would be a loss of revenue, which could be recouped over time. But if the factory were disabled for a long period of time, customers might switch to another product and ultimately drive the company out of business. The effect of a collapse in the functioning of a school (a loosely coupled system) would be the disruption of its students' education. If the school were unable to sustain instructional processes for a period of time, students might be deprived of educational opportunities and their academic achievement and educational attainment could suffer. Hence systemic collapse in simple linear or loosely coupled systems can have serious effects even when not endangering human life. Perrow's analysis of the collapse of high-risk technological systems has utility for an examination of systemic failure in simple linear and loosely coupled systems as well as high-risk, complex technological systems. The present study relies on Perrow's insights about complex technological systems to study the effects of a breakdown in a simpler, loosely coupled system—specifically, a case in which the process of scheduling high school classes and assigning students to those classes broke down. While the scheduling crisis had a negative impact on student learning, it did not cause a total collapse in the functioning of the school.

Several sociologists have conceptualized the school as a simple interactive and loosely coupled social system. Bidwell (1965) identified several features of a school that exemplify these characteristics. Schools are linked directly to the school district of which they are members but maintain considerable autonomy at the school level. They have only tenuous connections to other schools in the same district. The administrators and faculty in each school have discretion over how their school functions on a daily and an annual basis. They control the curriculum, pedagogical practices, and instructional organization of their schools. While teachers are hired at the district level, the principal of the school to which they are assigned must approve them. The hierarchical structure of a school isolates teachers in the classroom and separates them for most of the day from the principal and faculty colleagues. A teacher has almost complete authority over how the classroom runs and how the curriculum is taught. Interactions among teachers, counselors, and staff are limited and involve social as well as professional exchanges. Interactions between the principal and teachers or staff typically extend primarily to bureaucratic matters rather than substantive issues. Bidwell sees these features as typifying a loosely coupled organization characterized by simple linear interactions.

Barr and Dreeben (1983) described in detail the simple hierarchical structure and loosely connected organization of schools. In *How Schools Work*, they conceptualized a school as a hierarchy of structurally differentiated levels that form nested layers. The activities and events that occur at each level make a unique contribution to the overall functioning of the school. The levels are linearly interactive, with the output at one level serving as input to the next level. The independence of activities within levels and the loose linkages between levels reflect the structure of a loosely coupled organization.

Several researchers have extended Bidwell's and Barr and Dreeben's model of a school as a loosely coupled organization. Meyer and Rowan (1977, 1978) pointed out that the isolation of teachers in their classrooms contributes to the somewhat diffuse authority structure within the school. Weick (1976) saw attributes of a loosely coupled system in the decision-making structure of a school. Decisions made by the principal or teachers typically affect only some members of the faculty or student body and have little or no impact on others. Weick (1976) also pointed out that teacher pedagogy is based on how teachers are trained and socialized into the profession, not on organizational features of the school such as administrative leadership and school resources. Meyer (1977) went further to claim that the goal of schooling (which is student learning) is dependent on societal expectations rather than school properties such as climate, resources, or classroom instruction. In an empirical study of eight high schools, Powell, Farrar, and Cohen (1985) found that all of the schools adopted the same external structure and routines—such as the arrangement of the school day into class periods and the practice of grouping students by ability for instruction—but that student experiences within the schools differed significantly.

The aim of this chapter is to examine how the structure and organization of a school relates to its efficient functioning. Specifically, the study will analyze how the simple structure and loosely coupled organization of a school affect its propensity for a systemic breakdown. The research focuses on the process through which a school creates a master schedule of courses and assigns students to these courses for instruction. Based on data from a single comprehensive public high school in a midwestern city, the analysis examines how a single human error caused a breakdown in the scheduling process and how the loosely coupled organization of the school cushioned the impact of the breakdown on teacher instruction and student learning.

THE SCHEDULING PROCESS

Few studies examine the process of course scheduling. In a case study of scheduling in four high schools, DeLany (1991) described how the master schedule was developed and how students were matched to courses. His outline of the six steps involved in constructing the master schedule for the schools in his sample is illustrative of the procedures followed in most contemporary high schools. First, a list of course offerings is prepared as the basis for curriculum planning. Second, the course offerings are circulated to teachers, parents, and students. Third, students and teachers submit course preferences to the counselor and principal. Fourth, the principal negotiates with the district supervisor for courses, teachers, and other resources based on estimates of course needs and demands. Fifth, the counselors create a master schedule, taking into account the information gathered about course requirements, teacher and student preferences, and teacher availability. Sixth, the counselors adjust the schedule as new information becomes available before the beginning of the school year and as the school year progresses.

Despite the preparatory work done on the master schedule, some schedule changes still need to be made at the beginning of the school year for three reasons. First, schedule changes are necessitated by organizational constraints such as unpredicted changes in student enrollment, funding, staffing, and other resources. For example, an advanced-level mathematics course may be canceled due to low enrollment, or a new section of chemistry may be added due to teacher availability. Second, schedule changes result from errors in a student's initial course schedule or new circumstances regarding the student's schedule. For example, students may register for a course that they subsequently pass in summer school, fail to register for courses needed for graduation, or sign up for courses for which they have not met requirements. Third, parents and students may request schedule changes because the student's academic interests and preferences have changed, the student wishes to be in a class taught by a different teacher or in a class with friends, or the student prefers a more challenging or less difficult class. Of course counselors cannot make all requested schedule changes. Riehl, Pallas, and Natriello (1999) suggest that some requests for schedule changes made by parents and students reflect widely held beliefs about schools and students that are inconsistent with constraints on course scheduling.

Regardless of the reason for a schedule change, the process of assigning students to new classes after the school year has begun places considerable demands on school resources. Typically, a student with a schedule conflict meets with a counselor during the school day. The counselor examines available courses until a suitable schedule is found. This process is facilitated by the use of computers. If one of the goals of the counselors is to return students to classes as quickly as possible, as is likely, then they will not spend a great deal of time questioning why a student is requesting a change, assessing the ramifications of the change for student achievement, or ensuring that the student is taking sufficiently challenging courses. The most that counselors may be able to do, given the press of time, is to be sure that the students are meeting graduation requirements. As a result some students select courses that are inconsistent with their academic goals.

Schedule changes that occur after the school year has begun have a negative impact on the smooth functioning of the school and negative consequences for student learning. Pallas, Natriello, and Riehl (1993) examined rescheduling in four high schools serving poor minority students. Their study showed that the volume and intensity of schedule changes after the school year began was very high and that the changes that needed to be made were disruptive of both instructional and learning processes. The greater the number of students requiring schedule changes, the greater the disorder.

Schedule changes are disruptive both for the student who is being reassigned to a new class and the teachers and students in the class that the student joins. Changing classes requires that the student making the change adapt to a new classroom situation, teacher, and classmates. Students must make up work that was already covered in the class. The greater the number of classes changed, or the later in the semester that changes are made, the greater the burden of covering a backlog of material. Ultimately, the difficulty of adjusting to a new class is likely to have a negative effect on student achievement.

The instructional disruption caused by schedule changes affects not only the student making the change, but also the student's classmates. When a teacher must spend time helping a new student adjust to a class, the other students are deprived of the teacher's attention and instruction. The more students changing classes, the greater the impact of the disruption on instruction and learning. Moreover, if the new student adds to the class size (as opposed to replacing a student who leaves), the student-teacher ratio increases, leaving less time for the teacher to interact individually with each student.

AN EMPIRICAL STUDY OF SCHEDULE CHANGES

In spring 1997 we conducted a pilot study to prepare for an in-depth investigation of the causes and consequences of schedule changes in high school. We observed the process of creating a master schedule and assigning students to courses during the 1997–98 school year. Data were obtained from a single, racially and ethnically mixed, comprehensive public high school with about 1,200 students in a medium-sized midwestern city. The pilot study revealed a sufficiently large number of schedule changes at the beginning of the year to merit a detailed study of the scheduling process. As it turned out, the scheduling process for the 1999–2000 school year was an anomaly that resulted in a school crisis that had the potential for a systemic breakdown. For this reason it is the focus of the analysis reported here. The scheduling process was studied again in the 2000–01 school year to obtain a better understanding of the determinants and consequences of schedule changes in a more typical school year.

The process of developing a master schedule for the sample high school in 1999–2000 followed virtually the same sequence of events that DeLany outlined in his research. In the initial step, begun almost a year in advance, the district superintendent's office approved a list of courses designed to satisfy the needs of a diverse student population. The number and choice of courses on the list were influenced by accreditation demands and graduation and college entrance requirements, and were limited by teacher qualifications and the availability of funds for teachers' salaries.

In the second step of the scheduling process, the list of courses was disseminated to teachers, parents, and students. After this information became available, counselors met with students to obtain their course preferences for the following year. They guided the students' choices by noting graduation requirements, courses that must be taken in sequence, and college admissions requirements. The counselors also visited feeder schools to help eighth grade students who would enter high school in the fall select their courses.

The students' final course preferences were handed in to the school by the end of May. During June and July, the school principal finalized negotiations with the superintendent for the resources needed to offer the courses that the students had chosen. Budgetary constraints required modification of the preliminary list of course offerings. The principal then negotiated with teachers and counselors to decide the final list of instructional assignments.

When the negotiations were completed, the master schedule was prepared. It should be noted, however, that while the final schedule could not be prepared until the summer, much of the work on the schedule occurred in the spring. Most student course selections, most teacher hires and assignments, and even a relatively complete (though still preliminary) master schedule were set before the end of the school year.

Preparing a final master schedule is complicated. Meeting student course requests and teacher preferences while remaining within organizational and budgetary constraints requires processing a large amount of information. The school utilized a computer program to create a master schedule that took organizational restrictions into account while accommodating as many student and teacher course requests as possible.

The final step in the scheduling process involved adjusting the master schedule and student schedules. This process began toward the end of July. Schedules were mailed to students and those who had scheduling conflicts or desired a schedule change were asked to contact the school two weeks before it opened. Most students cooperated and were assigned a ten-minute slot with a counselor to resolve the student's conflicts. However, more students had

conflicts or desired schedule changes than could fit into the three days scheduled for these adjustments, so some conflicts were not resolved before the
school year began.

In the pilot study, approximately 27 percent of the students requested one
or more schedule changes at the beginning of the school year. Of these students about 75 percent asked either to switch sections of a required course, or
more likely to change an elective. In most cases this was easily and quickly
accomplished. The remaining students (25 percent) were forced to make a
schedule change due to an organizational constraint, such as the cancellation
of an English class when a teacher became unavailable. All of the schedule
changes were completed during the first two weeks of school.

The pilot study suggested that a similar volume of schedule changes
would be observed in 1999–2000. However, in that year a breakdown in the
scheduling process occurred that resulted in an unanticipated and overwhelming number of schedule conflicts at the beginning of the school year.
The problem began during the summer when the head counselor retired and
one of the assistant counselors replaced him. The new head counselor
assumed responsibility for the master schedule. Apparently, due to her inex-
perience and poor communication with the retired counselor, she repeatedly
made a computer error that had devastating effects on the scheduling process:
she adjusted the master schedule by moving a significant number of courses
to different time slots, and in so doing unwittingly moved all of the students
in those courses to a different time period. For example, if the counselor
moved a section of English from fifth to first period, all of the students
assigned to that English section were moved as well. Those who were already
enrolled in another first-period class suddenly had a schedule conflict.
Numerous students whose original schedules had been fine now needed to be
rescheduled.

When the students received their schedules two weeks prior to the opening of school, many called the school and set up ten-minute appointments
with a counselor to resolve their conflicts. However, a large number of students were unable to make appointments because there were not enough
counselor openings. In addition, a number of students with schedule conflicts
did not attempt to set up an appointment. The school seemed unaware that so
many schedule conflicts remained unresolved. When school opened at the
end of August, 50 percent of the students in the school had at least one schedule conflict. The principal, counselors, and teachers were completely unprepared for this situation. In the process of correcting these students' schedules,
the counselors intentionally moved some courses to different class periods.
This was done to resolve schedule conflicts for a majority of the students in
the class but would inevitably create new schedule conflicts for a few of the
other students. It took six weeks for all of the schedule conflicts to be
resolved, and by the end of this time, 80 percent of the students' schedules had
been changed at least once.

The first two days of school in 1999–2000 were half-days. During these days some students met with counselors for schedule changes. Most students were simply told to go to whatever class their schedule indicated, regardless of whether it was their correct class, or to go to a study hall. The three school counselors then worked through the weekend to make schedule changes. They were able to adjust almost all of the English conflicts. Shortly after they began working on mathematics conflicts, a power outage that lasted for six hours destroyed some of the work that they had previously done and made further work impossible.

By the following Monday, the counselors were still faced with hundreds of students who needed schedule changes. The head counselor asked two friends who were retired counselors from other schools to volunteer their time to help them adjust schedules. Because the counselors' offices were small and could not accommodate the students, the counselors met with them in the gymnasium. The counselors made changes on a first come, first served basis, working with students who had no class during a period. However, so many students needed changes every period that a student might wait for an entire class period and not reach a counselor's station. Students who had a class the next period were told to attend their class, meaning that when they returned to the gym during their next free period, they had to take their place at the end of a line to speak to a counselor. Many students spent significant portions of the first two weeks of school waiting in line. Since there were no computers in the gym, schedule changes were made on paper and later entered into the computer, further complicating the process.

By the beginning of the third week of school, sufficient progress had been made in adjusting schedules to permit the counselors to return to their offices where they had access to computers. However, only about fifteen to twenty students at a time could fit in the counselors' waiting area. The remaining students, between one and four dozen each period, waited in the hallways. It was only at this point that the principal became involved. She was unwilling to have students roaming the halls during class time. When she saw students in the halls, she told them to go to whatever class was on their schedule—even if it was the wrong class—or to study hall, and to try again next period to meet with a counselor.

By the beginning of the fourth week of classes, the number of students with schedule conflicts was small enough for the students to fit in the waiting area of the counselors' office space, restoring order to the hallways. Schedule changes continued each period for the fourth, fifth, and sixth weeks of school. It was only by the end of the sixth week that all of the schedule conflicts resulting from the master schedule problem were resolved and the school could return to normal functioning. Of the 853 students in the school, 684 (80.2 percent) changed their class schedules at least once during the first six weeks of school. The distribution of schedule changes across weeks for 1999–2000 appears in Table 1.

Table 1. Number and Percentage of Students Changing Class Schedules by Week
for First Six Weeks of Semester I, 1999–2000 (N = 853)

	Week	N	%
	1	549	64.4%
	2	319	37.4%
	3	206	24.2%
	4	86	10.1%
	5	59	6.9%
1st "week" = 2 half-days	6	44	5.2%

OBTRUSIVE AND UNOBTRUSIVE CONSEQUENCES OF A BREAKDOWN IN SCHEDULING

One would expect that a massive disruption of instruction such as that caused by the scheduling breakdown would have a significant negative impact on student learning. Past research (Wiley 1976; Heyns 1978; Barr and Dreeben 1983) shows that growth in achievement is positively related to the quantity and quality of instruction. When students are absent from classes due to illness, truancy, or other reasons, they miss instruction and lose ground academically. The longer they are out of class, the greater the negative effect on achievement.

To measure the impact of the 1999–2000 scheduling problem on student learning, two OLS regression models were estimated—one for English and one for mathematics. Students' end-of-semester grades in each subject were regressed on the number of classes students missed in that subject due to scheduling problems, controlling for prior achievement, absenteeism, and background variables (see Kubitschek et al. [2001] for a description of these analyses). The results are presented in Table 2.

Surprisingly, the analysis shows that missed instruction due to schedule changes had no effect on achievement in either subject. No matter how many classes students missed due to scheduling problems, their grades were no lower than those of students who missed no classes.

This result is all the more surprising given the large number of schedule changes made during the 1999–2000 school year compared to the number made in a more typical year. In 2000–01, for instance, only 21 percent of the students had schedule changes at the beginning of the school year, and about 85 percent of these changes involved elective rather than required courses. Most of the remaining 15 percent of the requests were due to the need to reschedule a few classes to redistribute enrollment. All of the necessary changes were made by the beginning of the third week of classes. The far greater number of schedule changes that occurred in the 1999–2000 school year, and the disruption that these changes caused, made it seem likely that an achievement effect should be observed.

However, the absence of a negative effect of the 1999–2000 scheduling

Table 2. Regression of Student Grades in English and Mathematics on Class Periods without Instruction and Other Student Variables

	English N = 693		Mathematics N = 624	
	b	s.e.	b	s.e.
Female = 1	0.23	0.06***	0.31	0.08***
African American = 1	-0.09	0.07	-0.19	0.10
Free Lunch = 1	-0.16	0.07*	0.13	0.10
Age (years, centered by grade)	0.02	0.06	-0.08	0.08
Sophomore	-0.49	0.21*	-0.78	0.28**
Junior	0.13	0.22	-0.34	0.30
Senior	0.08	0.23	-1.00	0.37**
Total Test Composite/10	0.00	0.02	0.01	0.03
Test Composite*Sophomore	0.06	0.03	0.10	0.04*
Test Composite*Junior	-0.02	0.03	0.03	0.04
Test Composite*Senior	-0.00	0.03	0.13	0.05*
Missing Test Composite = 1	-0.14	0.10	-0.00	0.13
Periods Absent	-0.12	0.01***	-0.13	0.01***
Periods Without Instruction	-0.01	0.03	0.03	0.03
Constant	0.19	0.17	0.09	0.21
R square	0.24		0.21	

* = $p < .05$
** = $p < .01$
*** = $p < .001$

problems on student achievement does not necessarily imply that the schedule breakdown had no effect on student learning. Using student grades to measure achievement under atypical circumstances such as these has serious limitations. First, a negative effect of schedule changes on grades would not be seen if teachers had assigned grades for relative growth in achievement, as they typically do when they fit student grades to a normal distribution. Only a measure of progress or change in achievement over time would have revealed the impact of less instruction on student learning. Second, some teachers reported that in response to the scheduling problem, they slowed their rate of instruction to accommodate the students who joined the class after the semester had begun. This strategy effectively reduced the amount of material that students covered during the semester. Since all students were affected in the same way, the impact of this strategy would not be seen in student grades. Third, some teachers indicated that they took the scheduling problem into account when assigning grades because they were unwilling to penalize students for a school-based error. These factors make it unlikely that a reduction in instruction or student learning would be detected by relying on subject grades.

Several other indicators suggest that student learning did suffer due to the 1999–2000 scheduling crisis. Teachers reported more than the usual number of students cutting classes that year; apparently, some students grew accustomed to not being in class and—realizing that the problems confronting the school made them less visible—were more willing than usual to be truant. The large number of students roaming in and out of the gymnasium and hallways in the first weeks of school made leaving school quite easy. When the situation reached a critical point, the principal installed a security guard in the hallways to prevent students from leaving school.

Professional relations among teachers and counselors were strained because of the scheduling difficulties. Teachers could not understand how the scheduling problem could have happened in the first place, or why it took so long to correct. The principal and guidance office offered no satisfactory explanation for the problem. Counselors were annoyed that the teachers did not help by requiring students with incorrect schedules to go to the counselors for schedule adjustments. Negative feelings between teachers and counselors persisted through the school year and may have affected the ability of the two groups to work together to assist students

Many teachers, parents, and students were angry about the loss of instructional time and complained to the school and district office. They were concerned not only that the students would receive lower grades, but also that they would be disadvantaged in taking the statewide standardized achievement test and the PSAT and SAT exams that fall. The district office chose not to intervene since the worst of the crisis was over by the time the parents complained.

In general, the disruption caused by the scheduling breakdown reverberated throughout the school and continued for the duration of the year. Students were restless and inattentive and some became highly critical of the school, especially during the first semester. Teachers were frustrated by the interruptions to their classes and the amount of instruction that the students missed. Counselors were distressed that the time they had to spend on schedule changes prevented them from providing other student services, particularly college counseling for juniors and seniors. Perhaps troubled by the problems that beset the school, the principal announced in January that she would resign at the end of the school year. Administrators, faculty, staff, and students all agreed that the year was a chaotic and dysfunctional one. Consequently, while the statistical analysis showed no effect of the scheduling problems on student grades, the reaction of the school community provided strong evidence that the scheduling crisis had an adverse impact on student learning for the entire school year.

At the same time, despite the negative impact of the scheduling break-down, the school continued to function in a remarkably normal manner. The damage was far less severe than it would have been if the school's structure and organization resembled the complex interactive and tightly coupled technological systems that Perrow described. The simple interactive system that characterized the school and the loose coupling of its units protected it from total collapse. Since each unit in the school performed a designated function in the educational process, scheduling was the sole responsibility of the guidance department. The task of fixing the master schedule and reassigning students to classes was left to the counselors. The counselors themselves decided to ask recently retired high school counselors to assist with the task. The counseling department had the authority to bring in these volunteers without having to obtain special permission from the principal or district office.

Given that the counselors were charged with fixing the scheduling problem, the teachers were free to carry on their designated assignments in the school. They stayed in their classrooms and provided at least minimal instruction to the students in their classes. In classes that had few disruptions, teachers were able to make close to normal progress covering the curriculum. Even in the classes that suffered the most disruptions, the students presumably learned more than they would have if their classes had been canceled. Moreover, the ability of the teachers to carry on their instructional tasks provided a sense of security for the students. In addition, the fact that the teachers were able to continue teaching avoided the public embarrassment of closing the school and the media attention that would have created.

Similarly, the loosely coupled organization of the school allowed the principal to maintain her daily routine, almost as if the scheduling debacle had not occurred. She never became involved in correcting the master schedule or reassigning students to classes. When students skipped classes due to scheduling difficulties, she treated the issue as a disciplinary infraction. She imposed penalties on truant students with no apparent consideration of the impact of the scheduling difficulties on student attitudes and behavior. Nor did she discuss truancy cases with the counselors or teachers in the context of the scheduling crisis. The principal's interactions with the district office and with the community continued as usual, as if no problems were occurring in the school. Even when the scheduling crisis became obvious to parents and the community at large, the principal simply assured these groups that the guidance department had everything under control.

Most students attended classes as usual, even during the worst of the scheduling disruptions and even when they had to drop classes and add different ones later. Cocurricular and extracurricular activities were held as usual. School service functions were carried out, with the cafeteria serving breakfast and lunch on time and the janitorial staff caring for the building as usual. In short, the simple interactive structure and loosely coupled organization of the school enabled faculty, staff, and students to conduct their daily activities in a way that bore a fairly close resemblance to normal times.

CONCLUSIONS

A school may be characterized as a simple linear system with loosely coupled units. Early theoretical work by Bidwell (1965) and Barr and Dreeben (1983) depicts the school as a system of fairly simple linear interactions, task differentiation, and loosely linked, autonomous units. In contrast, Perrow (1984) describes a high-risk technological system as a complex interactive system with tightly connected units. The structural differences between these two kinds of systems have implications for how the systems respond to crisis. When a unit in a complex, tightly connected technological system malfunctions, the whole system is likely to collapse with possibly catastrophic consequences. When a unit in a simpler, loosely connected school fails, built-in redundancies and buffers enable the school to continue functioning—albeit with reduced productivity.

In the school analyzed in this study, an error in the preparation of the master schedule of classes resulted in students beginning the school year with class schedules fraught with errors and inconsistencies. The guidance counselors, who created the original master plan, took responsibility for solving the problems in the schedule. During a period of weeks, they adjusted the master schedule and reassigned students as necessary, leaving the teachers free to continue teaching their classes. While many students lost instructional time, they were able to resume classes as usual once their schedules were adjusted.

The response of this school to the scheduling crisis illustrates how a school's organization affects its reaction to a crisis. The unit autonomy and task differentiation of the school made it easier to isolate and fix the scheduling error because responsibility for the master schedule was relegated to a single unit, the guidance department. The relaxed time frame in which the school conducted its work lessened the danger of total collapse by providing flexibility with the content of the curriculum and the rate of instruction. The loose connections among units in the school—particularly among teachers, counselors, and the administration—enabled schoolwork to continue even when one unit was incapacitated. To a great extent these characteristics protected the school from total breakdown that would have necessitated its closure.

While the simple linear interactive structure and loose coupling of a school provide the advantage of reducing damage when an error or accident occurs, these school features also incur certain costs. Schools are seldom as efficient as high-risk technological systems. Teachers and students spend a considerable amount of time engaged in tasks not related to instruction or learning. Teachers may not be proficient in their jobs and instructional quality may vary. These characteristics reduce the productivity of a school.

Moreover, although a school is unlikely to have a catastrophic accident in Perrow's sense, breakdowns that appear limited to parts of a school may actually have a negative impact on the whole school. In the present study, the breakdown in the scheduling process led to loss of teacher instruction and student learning, truancy, loss of professional status by counselors, animosity between counselors and teachers, general disorder in the school, parental dissatisfaction, and student complaints. Some of these problems persisted throughout the school year. Hence while the simple interactions and loosely connected structure of a school minimize the likelihood of its closing as the result of a crisis, subsystem malfunctioning can have a significant negative effect on the primary functions of the school—student cognitive and social development.

A clear understanding by school personnel of how organizational characteristics of a school affect its functioning can reduce a school's vulnerability to a crisis and minimize the danger of systemic breakdown. The simple linear organizational structure and loosely coupled organization of a school lessen the detrimental impact to the school of human or random error and provide protection against widespread consequences of local unit problems. Unfortunately, these same features of a school also reduce school efficiency and productivity. The challenge to educators is to utilize the advantages derived from structural simplicity and loosely connected units while constantly aiming to increase student learning.

Acknowledgments

The author gratefully acknowledges support for this research from the Spencer Foundation and the Institute for Educational Initiatives at the University of Notre Dame. I am also grateful to Warren Kubitschek for project management and statistical advice and to Stephanie Arnett, Karen Boyd, Gail Mulligan, and Laurie Nelson for research assistance. Finally, I thank the school personnel who provided the data for the analysis.

REFERENCES

Barr, Rebecca and Robert Dreeben. 1983. *How Schools Work*. Chicago: University of Chicago Press.
Bidwell, Charles E. 1965. "The School as a Formal Organization." Pp. 972–1022 in *Handbook of Organizations*, edited by James G. March. Chicago: Rand McNally.
DeLany, Brian. 1991. "Allocation, Choice, and Stratification within High Schools: How the Sorting Machine Copes." *American Journal of Education* 99:181–207.
Heyns, Barbara. 1978. *Summer Learning and the Effects of Schooling*. New York: Academic Press.
Kubitschek, Warren, Maureen T. Hallinan, Stephanie M. Arnett, and Kim S. Galipeau. 2001. "Departmental Differences in Schedule Changes and the Effects of Lost Instructional Time on Achievement." Paper presented at the annual meeting of the American Sociological Association, Anaheim, CA.
Meyer, John W. 1977. "The Effects of Education as an Institution." *American Journal of Sociology* 83:55–77.
Meyer, John W. and Brian Rowan. 1977. "Institutionalized Organizations: Formal Structure as Myth and Ceremony." *American Journal of Sociology* 83:340–63.
Meyer, John W. and Brian Rowan. 1978. "The Structure of Educational Organizations." Pp. 78–109 in *Environments and Organizations*, edited by Marshall Meyer and W. Richard Scott. San Francisco: Jossey-Bass.
Pallas, Aaron M., Gary Natriello, and Carolyn Riehl. 1993. *Tweaking the Sorting Machine: The*

Dynamics of Students' Schedule Changes in High School. Unpublished manuscript, College of Education, Michigan State University.

Perrow, Charles. 1984. *Normal Accidents: Living with High-Risk Technologies.* New York: Basic Books.

Powell, Arthur G., Eleanor Farrar, and David K. Cohen. 1985. *The Shopping Mall High School: Winners and Losers in the Educational Marketplace.* Boston: Houghton Mifflin.

Riehl, Carolyn, Aaron M. Pallas, and Gary Natriello. 1999. "Rites and Wrong: Institutional Explanations for the Student Course-Scheduling Process in Urban High Schools." *American Journal of Education* 107:116–54.

Weick, Karl. 1976. "Educational Organizations as Loosely Coupled Systems." *Administrative Science Quarterly* 21:1–19.

Wiley, David E. 1976. "Another Hour, Another Day: Quantity of Schooling as a Potent Path for Policy." Pp. 225–65 in *Schooling and Achievement in American Society,* edited by William H. Sewell, Robert M. Hauser, and David L. Featherman. New York: Academic Press.

7

Tracking, Instruction, and Unequal Literacy in Secondary School English

Adam Gamoran
Sean Kelly

The publication of Barr and Dreeben's *How Schools Work* in 1983 transformed research on school achievement from the analysis of production functions to the study of the production of achievement at the site of the production process. Instead of limiting attention to school inputs and outputs, the authors looked inside schools to focus on the structural and technological conditions through which learning emerges. With this new vision, Barr and Dreeben presented a sociological analysis of schooling effects. In a sense the analysis of how school structure and activities produce cognitive learning paralleled Dreeben's ([1968] 2002) earlier statement that "what is learned in school" consists of norms that pave the way for the transition from the family to adult society. In both works readers glimpsed the relations among school organization, classroom tasks, and student socialization. Besides the focus on cognitive development, however, what distinguished the later work from the earlier one was the detailed empirical analysis that demonstrated the power of the conceptual model.

The study of the production process pioneered by Barr and Dreeben helps us understand both levels and distributions of achievement within and among schools. Despite concerns about levels of achievement in American society, unequal distributions no doubt constitute a more serious social problem (Berliner and Biddle 1995). Unequal literacy, for example, is an increasingly important determinant of inequality in labor market success (Murnane, Willett, and Levy 1995; Raudenbush and Kasim 1998). Even among persons with the same levels of schooling, literacy skills vary widely (Carbonaro 2000).

Adam Gamoran and Sean Kelly • Department of Sociology, University of Wisconsin-Madison, Madison, Wisconsin 53706.

Stability and Change in American Education: Structure, Process, and Outcomes edited by Maureen T. Hallinan, Adam Gamoran, Warren Kubitschek, and Tom Loveless. Eliot Werner Publications, Clinton Corners, New York, 2003.

Unequal literacy among young people is closely tied to social and economic disadvantages. In the 1999 *National Assessment of Educational Progress* (NAEP), the reading achievement of 17-year-old high school students whose parents had failed to complete high school fell more than 30 points below those whose parents had some postsecondary schooling, a gap of more than one standard deviation (Campbell, Hombo, and Mazzeo 2000). Similar differences were evident among younger children in the fourth and eighth grades. Moreover, these differences have persisted at roughly the same levels for the past thirty years. Substantial gaps also exist among students from different racial and ethnic backgrounds but these have tended to narrow over time. For instance, differences among African American and white 17-year-olds declined from about 1.1 standard deviations in the 1970s to about .7 standard deviations at present (Hedges and Nowell 1999). The NAEP writing results show differences and trends similar to those in reading (Greenwald et al. 1999).

Sources of unequal literacy performance range among family, community, and school contexts. In this chapter we examine school and classroom bases of inequality in writing performance, using new observations of instruction in a diverse sample of middle and high schools.

SCHOOL AND CLASSROOM BASES OF UNEQUAL LITERACY PERFORMANCE

Which aspects of schools and schooling may contribute to unequal literacy? Research in sociology of education has distinguished between *structure*, the way schools are organized and the way people are distributed within and among them, and *technology*, the materials and activities used to accomplish the work of schools—that is, teaching and learning (Barr and Dreeben 1983). Structures set conditions in which technology occurs, but to understand how results are generated (for example, to see how literacy develops in young people), it is essential to witness the technology at work.

Both structural and technological conditions contribute to inequality in literacy performance. Barr and Dreeben's (1983) seminal contribution was to show that technology (that is, classroom instruction) was a major mechanism for the impact of structure, the way students were organized among and within classrooms. In first grade reading, for example, the arrangement of students into schools, classrooms, and reading groups created differentiated learning contexts, but it was instructional variation—differences in the coverage of new words and phonics concepts in the reading series—that accounted for the effects of the structural arrangements on student learning (Barr and Dreeben 1983; Dreeben and Gamoran 1986; Gamoran 1986; Gamoran and Dreeben 1986).

School Effects and Literacy Performance

Although it seems intuitively unlikely, researchers have convincingly demonstrated that differences from one school to the next contribute relatively little to overall variation in achievement (e.g., Coleman et al. 1966). Even the variation that is specifically associated with race, ethnicity, and social class inequality is not closely tied to school-to-school differences. Typically, between 10 and 25 percent of the variance in cognitive performance lies among schools and the rest lies within (e.g., Coleman et al. 1966; Gamoran 1987; Entwisle, Alexander, and Olson 1997). When comparing among schools, bivariate differences such as city versus suburb and public versus private often appear substantial (Donahue et al. 1999; Greenwald et al. 1999), but these differences mainly reflect the different population compositions of the various schools (Gamoran 1987, 1996). Once individual differences within schools are taken into account, very little variation in cognitive performance is attributable to contextual features of student composition, locale, or sector. Recent reports of school quality effects in the economics literature (e.g., Card and Krueger 1996) largely reflect aggregate differences among schools and do not recognize that most of the variation in achievement is internal to schools. At best school resources and other contextual conditions are modestly related to student performance (Greenwald, Hedges, and Laine 1996). Although literacy is distributed unequally among schools, schools on average contribute relatively little to the overall variation because neither the structure nor the technology of schools varies greatly from one school to the next.

Classrooms as Contexts for Inequality

In contrast to modest school effects on variation in literacy, differences at the classroom level are more salient (Murnane 1975; Barr and Dreeben 1983; Rowan and Miracle 1983; Dar and Resh 1986; Gamoran et al. 1995). Classroom differences illustrate how school structure is associated with inequality and how technology mediates the impact of structure. A key structural device in secondary schools is the assignment of students to different tracks and ability groups. Tracking, or dividing students by perceived performance into different classes or groups, is an important axis of differentiation around which instruction differs by classroom (Sørensen 1970). Since the 1970s researchers have recognized that within-school variation in achievement is structured in part by the organization of tracking within schools (e.g., Heyns 1974). Although it is difficult to separate the effects of tracking from selectivity, analyses that attempt to account for selection bias still seem to indicate that tracking plays a causal role in stratifying student achievement (e.g., Gamoran and Mare 1989; Gamoran et al. 1995). Tracking tends to magnify inequality of achievement without doing much to affect the overall level of achievement in a school. That is because students in high groups tend to perform better than their counterparts in other groups, while students in low groups tend to perform worse. At one time American secondary schools were divided into formal program tracks—such as college preparatory, general, and vocational—but now tracking mainly occurs within each subject as students are divided into honors or advanced, regular, and remedial or basic classes

(Lucas 1999). Despite changes in the way it is implemented, tracking remains a powerful source of achievement inequality.

Classes at different track levels constitute varied contexts for learning, in large part because they differ in the quality of instructional materials and activities, the technological elements of schooling (Oakes, Gamoran, and Page 1992). To understand how classroom instruction contributes to literacy, and how variation in instruction may mediate inequalities in literacy, we need a solid conception of instruction and student performance. Barr and Dreeben (1983) developed such a conception at the elementary level, focusing on the pace and coverage of instructional content. At the secondary school level, new empirical analyses can build on recent theoretical progress.

Classroom Instruction and Literacy Performance

Researchers on secondary school English such as Nystrand (1997), Langer (1995), and Applebee (1996) have identified aspects of classrooms that contribute to students' ability to engage with academic content and enhance their abilities to read and write well. According to Nystrand and Gamoran (1991a), much instruction is characterized by *procedural engagement*, in which students go through the motions of compliance without much depth of understanding or commitment. However, some teachers stimulate *substantive engagement*, in which students are actively involved in pursuing academic issues by asking questions and posing problems that students can relate to their own knowledge and experience. In classes characterized by substantive engagement, recitation becomes more like conversation: teachers and students speak with one another because they are truly interested in what the other has to say, not merely to check whether students have absorbed the requisite material (Nystrand and Gamoran 1991b).

Classroom instruction is typically dominated by lecture, recitation, and seatwork (Nystrand 1997). Recitation follows a well-established pattern of what Mehan (1979) refers to as IRE: teachers pose a question (Initiation), students provide an answer (Response), and teachers accept or reject what the students have said (Evaluation). In substantively engaging classrooms, teachers move beyond the IRE pattern. First, instead of asking questions simply to discover whether students know the answer, teachers ask questions because they really want to know what students think. These are called "authentic questions" (Nystrand 1997). Second, teachers build on what students have said in posing subsequent questions, a technique known as uptake (Nystrand 1997). Third, students themselves may ask substantive questions. When they do, they signify their own engagement and they potentially move the content of the lesson in a direction that interests them. Finally, student-teacher exchanges sometimes transcend the IRE pattern to constitute discussion—that is, a free exchange of information among students and between the teacher and students without prompting by teacher questions (Nystrand 1997). Nystrand uses the term "dialogic" (as opposed to "monologic") to characterize classes that are rich in authentic questions and uptake, substantive questions from students, and discussion (see Nystrand et al., in press). An empirical study of eighth and ninth grade English and social studies classrooms indicated that student performance in writing and literature was higher when instruction was more dialogic (Nystrand 1997).

Langer's (1995) notion of *envisionment-building* English classrooms is similar in that it emphasizes thought-provoking instruction that places students' explorations of disciplinary content at the center of discussion, using questions to help students to work through ideas and employing multiple perspectives to address issues. Applebee (1996) further shows how successful English teachers create a sense of coherence and continuity in their curricula. One way to build coherence is to draw connections among different reading, writing, and speaking activities in the classroom.

Tracking, Instruction, and Social Inequality

To what extent should we expect differences in track levels and classroom instruction to mediate race, ethnic, and social class differences in literacy development among secondary school students? We do not expect tracking or instruction to account for differences between schools because most of the variation in these conditions occurs within schools. Racial and social class characteristics of schools are largely unrelated to the use of tracking (Gamoran 1987), and while there may be some aggregate connections between instruction and school composition, they are small compared to the more substantial variation within schools (Gamoran and Carbonaro, 2002–03). By contrast, we expect class-level variation in literacy to be more closely tied to tracking and instruction. Classes are likely to exhibit covariation in their student compositions, track levels, and instructional patterns since disadvantaged students tend to be overrepresented in lower tracks and low-track classes tend to exhibit less dialogic instruction (Gamoran et al. 1995; Nystrand et al., in press). Thus elements of instruction that promote literacy may be most evident among advantaged students and least evident among the disadvantaged, and for that reason may contribute to inequality (Gamoran et al. 1995). Classrooms can also vary in instructional quality independently of tracking, but such variation is unlikely to account for social background inequalities because enrollment patterns within tracks, within schools, are not generally associated with social background.

Instructional effects may also mediate social background effects within classes at the level of individual students. Students differ in their responses to instruction and these differences may be associated with social background. Student responses to instruction (such as turning in homework and responding to teacher questions) reflect what students bring with them to the classroom; they also reflect how students perceive and experience their encounters with teachers and their peers. If we conceive of instruction not as what teachers do to students, but as what teachers and students do together (Nystrand 1997), then student responses are an important component of instructional quality and may contribute to inequalities in achievement both among and within classes.

Sociological research on classrooms and their instructional conditions has had mixed success in documenting instructional effects on learning. Studies with extensive data on instruction draw on limited samples (e.g., Barr and Dreeben 1983; Rowan and Miracle 1983; Gamoran et al. 1997; Nystrand 1997; Mayer 1999). Studies of national surveys provide more representative samples but their evidence on instruction tends to be weaker (see Gamoran 2001). Moreover, national surveys almost never adopt a sampling design that is well suited for studying classroom effects: either they ignore classes altogether, include only one or two classes per school, or sample only a small number of students per class. Our project compromises among competing sampling strategies by studying a relatively small number of schools selected to vary in their contexts and compositions. We focused on schools with sufficient classes per school and students per class to allow a close analysis of how literacy performance is distributed among schools, classes, and students, and how students' experiences of instruction may be linked to unequal literacy.

DATA AND METHODS

Our data were drawn from a larger project designed to replicate earlier findings of Nystrand (1997), Applebee (1996), and Langer (1995) on the relationship between dialogic instruction and student literacy performance, but with a more diverse sample of schools and students than had been employed in the past. Five states were selected for variation in their approaches to high-stakes assessment: California, Florida, New York, Texas, and Wisconsin. Within each state two city and two suburban districts agreed to participate, and within each district one middle school and one high school were selected, for a total of twenty schools: five urban high schools, five urban middle schools, five suburban high schools, and five suburban middle schools. Before the first round of data collection was completed, the Texas urban middle school withdrew from the study, reducing the total to 19 schools. Within each school four classes were selected to represent the array of tracks in the school; generally this included one honors class, one remedial class, and two regular classes. Half of the middle schools did not use tracking. Grade levels were seventh or eighth in the middle schools and tenth or eleventh in the high schools, although one twelfth grade class was included. In one school only two classes agreed to participate, and two other schools contributed only three classes. Three additional classes were dropped from the study due to low rates of student participation, and five classes were excluded from the current analysis because student participation rates in the fall data collection were too low. Thus our sample for analysis consists of 64 classes in 19 schools, with respective participation rates of 95 percent and 84 percent at the school and class levels.

A total of 1,412 students attended the 64 classes for the entire school year and 1,111 agreed to participate in our study, a response rate of 79 percent.

Most of the nonrespondents simply failed to turn in consent forms; very few actively refused. Missing data on fall or spring tests reduced the sample for analysis to 974 students, or 88 percent of the study participants and 69 percent of all students who were in the class for the whole school year.

Variables

Each class was observed four times, twice in the fall and twice in the spring, and the data were averaged across observations. Observers used a computer-based coding scheme to assess classroom activities, focusing especially on allocations of time to particular activities and the types of questions that students and teachers asked (Nystrand 1999). They also made a series of holistic judgments at the end of the class session. In addition, teachers and students completed questionnaires in the spring and student writing was assessed in the fall and spring.

The dependent variable consists of student responses to two writing prompts, one asking them to write about a character they admired from a book or story and one about an important experience. Each response was scored by two raters according to its level of abstraction (scale of 0–5) and the coherence and elaboration of its argument (scale of 1–4). The two raters' scores were averaged; interrater reliability was .7, similar to other writing assessments (Nystrand 1997). The combined ratings on the two scales were summed, resulting in a scale of one to nine. Table 1 provides means and standard deviations for all variables. The spring writing assessment shows a mean of 3.94 and a standard deviation of 1.04.

A similar writing assessment was given in the fall using only one prompt, which asked students about a character from a movie or book. The mean on this assessment was slightly lower (3.66), and the standard deviation slightly higher (1.09). However, the spring-fall writing difference probably should not be regarded as a gain score because the prompts were not identical. Instead, we think of the spring score as reflecting student writing performance and the fall as a control for initial differences in writing skills.

Other background variables were taken from student questionnaires. Gender, race, and ethnicity are indicated by dummy variables. Just over one-half of the respondents were girls; 38 percent were non-Hispanic whites, 32 percent were Hispanic, 18 percent were African American, and 6 percent were Asian American. Six percent reported other ethnicities but these categories are too small for separate analyses. As a proxy for social class, we assessed the availability of home resources such as a daily newspaper, dishwasher, two or more cars, more than fifty books, VCR, computer, and so on. Student responses ranged from one to eleven (the scale maximum) with a mean of 8.68 items.

We took one indicator of instruction from student questionnaires. Students were asked how often they completed their writing assignments for class. We converted their answers, ranging from "never" to "all of the time," to percentages. The mean of 88.43 for completion of writing indicates that stu-

Table 1. Means and Standard Deviations of Variables

	Mean	S. D.	Source
School (n = 19)			
High school (vs. middle)	.53	.51	State data
Urban (vs. suburban)	.47	.51	State data
% Free lunch	.33	.26	State data
% African American	.26	.26	State data
% Hispanic	.28	.27	State data
% Asian American	.06	.11	State data
% Tracked	.79	.42	School & teacher report
Class (n = 64)			
SES	.07	1.63	Teacher questionnaire
% African American	.19	.21	Aggregate student data
% Hispanic	.31	.26	Aggregate student data
% Asian American	.05	.09	Aggregate student data
High track	.20	.41	School & teacher report
Regular track	.41	.50	School & teacher report
Low track	.16	.37	School & teacher report
Proportion of questions by students	.18	.14	Observational data
Proportion of authentic teacher ques.	.19	.13	Observational data
Proportion of questions with uptake	.31	.12	Observational data
Discussion time in minutes per hour	1.70	3.02	Observational data
Coherence scale	7.81	3.86	Teacher questionnaire
Envisionment-building scale	-.04	.78	Observational data
Student (n = 974)			
Spring writing score	3.94	1.04	Spring tests
Fall writing score	3.66	1.19	Fall tests
Home resources	8.68	2.02	Student questionnaire
African American	.18	.38	Student questionnaire
Hispanic	.32	.47	Student questionnaire
Asian American	.06	.24	Student questionnaire
Female (vs. male)	.53	.50	Student questionnaire
Completion of writing assignments	88.43	18.00	Student questionnaire

dents averaged between "most of the time" and "all of the time" in response to this question. A similar indicator for reading assignments was also available, but it proved redundant in multivariate analyses so we have omitted it.

Of the many activities that characterize instruction, the most important for dialogic instruction is the time spent in discussion, defined to reflect free and open exchanges between teachers and students that transcends the usual IRE pattern. The classes we observed averaged 1.7 minutes of discussion per one hour of class time (see Table 1). This may seem like a small amount but it is actually greater than was observed in a previous study using the same definition of discussion (Nystrand 1997).

Three further indicators of dialogic instruction were based on questions asked in class. We measure the proportion of questions that were asked by students rather than the teacher. We also measure the proportion of authentic questions asked by the teacher—that is, questions that do not have a prespecified answer. Finally, we measure the proportion of questions with uptake that incorporate part of what the previous speaker had said.

Indicators of class composition were taken from both student and teacher reports. The class racial and ethnic composition (percent African American, Hispanic, and Asian American) were aggregated from student reports. The social class composition is indicated by a standardized variable reflecting the teacher's estimate of the proportion of students in five social class strata: high, middle upper, middle, lower middle, and lower family income.

Teachers explained the structure of classes so we could identify track levels. We used two class-level dummy variables to indicate honors and remedial classes (respectively) with regular classes as the reference category.

School-level indicators were taken from state and district published records, generally found on the Internet. These included the percentage of students identified as African American, Hispanic, and Asian American, and the percentage receiving free or reduced-price lunches. In addition, dummy variables indicated a high school (as opposed to a middle school) and an urban (as opposed to suburban) location.

Four of the 19 schools did not use tracking to differentiate their English classes. Consequently, we included a dummy variable to indicate tracked schools with untracked schools as the reference category. In our analyses the school-level coefficient for "Tracked" thus refers to students in tracked schools compared to students in untracked schools. The class-level coefficients for honors and remedial classes, termed "High" and "Low" in our tables, reflect differences between students in those classes and otherwise similar students in regular classes in tracked schools.

Methods

We used multilevel models of 974 students within 64 classes in 19 schools to decompose variance in spring writing performance into the student, class, and school levels. Multivariate, multilevel models were then used to attribute this variation to race, ethnicity, and social class, and to uncover school and class sources of inequality in writing performance.

RESULTS

We first decomposed the variance in writing performance into school, class, and student components. This decomposition indicates the levels of inequality that exist and where the inequalities lie. We will subsequently attempt to account for these inequalities on the basis of school and classroom conditions of structure and technology.

An unconditional multilevel model (i.e., a model with no predictors) revealed that 10 percent of the variance was between schools, 29 percent was between classes within schools, and 61 percent was within classes. This is lower than most national estimates for between-school variation, and probably reflects the decision to sample selected classes in their entirety rather than drawing a random sample of students from each school. When we include school level (i.e., high school or middle school), between-school variance shrinks further, constituting only about 4 percent of the variance compared with about 31 percent between classes and 65 percent within classes. All subsequent models adjust for high school versus middle school.

Social Dimensions of Inequality

Next we examined racial and ethnic inequalities at the student, class, and school levels. Recall that the student and class indicators are drawn from student questionnaires, while school data are from public records. The first column of Table 2 shows no signs of inequality at the school level, but classes with higher proportions of African American students scored lower on the writing assessment and Hispanic students scored lower than non-Hispanic whites within classes. About 23 percent (.231) of the class-level variance in achievement is associated with the racial and ethnic composition of classes.

Are these inequalities attributable to social class differences? This seemed likely in light of associations between race/ethnicity and social class in the wider society, but in our results only part of the racial and ethnic differences are associated with social background. Table 2 shows that the coefficient for class percent African American drops from -1.458 in the first model to -1.16 in the second when the teacher's estimate of the social class composition of the class is taken into account. The coefficient for Hispanic students declines slightly from -.133 to -.117. The class and student indicators of social class are statistically significant, but the coefficient at the school level (percent free lunch) is not. This model also controls for gender at the student level and urban versus suburban at the school level (results not shown). This model accounts for close to half of the variance at the class level (.482) and nearly all the variance at the school level (.995).

Class-level differences in achievement along dimensions of race and social class may also reflect the achievement levels of students when they entered the classes in the fall. To address this possibility, we add fall achievement as a control variable at the student level (not shown). Now the coefficients reflect differences in student writing performance in the spring, net of preexisting differences that were evident in the fall. This model explains almost three-quarters of the variance in achievement at the class level. The further decline in the coefficient for percent African American (to -.604, not significant) shows that the relatively low levels of literacy performance in classes with high proportions of African American students were already in place at the beginning of the school year. Racial differences at the class level appear less salient for achievement growth than for initial sta-

Table 2. Distribution of Student Writing Achievement at the School, Class, and Student Levels

| | Race, Ethnic, and SES Differences | | | Track Effects |
| | (1) | (2) | (3) | (4) |
	Baseline	SES	Fall Achiev.	Tracking
School level				
% African American	.700 (.481)	.828 (.473)	.364 (.373)	-.176 (.392)
% Hispanic	.092 (.438)	.288 (.433)	.157 (.341)	-.015 (.404)
% Asian American	.289 (.653)	.157 (.582)	.087 (.455)	.322 (.507)
% Free lunch		1.083 (.767)	.980 (.604)	.586 (.644)
Tracked				-.087 (.169)
Class level				
% African American	-1.458 (.564)***	-1.160 (.489)**	-.604 (.394)	-.211 (.356)
% Hispanic	-.685 (.442)	-.367 (.423)	-.246 (.338)	-.060 (.318)
% Asian American	-.287 (.926)	-.257 (.821)	-.081 (.654)	.098 (.628)
SES		.235 (.064)***	.172 (.050)***	.108 (.050)**
High Track				.423 (.117)***
Low Track				-.337 (.136)***
Student level				
African American	-.119 (.087)	-.116 (.085)	-.089 (.081)	-.087 (.081)
Hispanic	-.133 (.074)*	-.117 (.072)	-.123 (.069)*	-.121 (.069)*
Asian American	-.086 (.117)	-.077 (.114)	-.017 (.109)	-.015 (.109)
Home Resources		.031 (.016)**	.031 (.015)**	.028 (.015)*
Variance Explained[a]				
School level	.906	.995	.995	.429[b]
Class level	.231	.482	.720	.852
Student level	.008	.063	.148	.152

* $p < .10$
** $p < .05$
*** $p < .01$

Coefficients are unstandardized, standard errors are in parentheses.

[a] Variance explained relative to unconditional model, adjusted for school level.

[b] The basis for school-level explained variance changes when tracks are introduced to the model, because schools with no tracks have no variation in tracking. From this point variance explained at the school level refers to variance among tracked schools.

tus. The coefficient for social class also declines from .235 to .172 and the model explains nearly three-quarters of the variance in achievement at the class level (.720). Yet social class remains a significant predictor of achievement at the class level, as do home resources and Hispanic background at the student level. Why is this the case? Which aspects of school structure and technology may contribute to inequalities among and within classes? To address this question, we examine tracking and instruction as predictors of writing performance and possible mediators of social inequality at the class and student levels.

Structural and Technological Sources of Social Inequality

The fourth column of Table 2 (Model 4) shows the distribution of writing performance by social background after taking the organization of tracking into account. The role of social class at the classroom level is further diminished as the coefficient drops to .108, less than one-half its size when it was first introduced in Model 2. Part of the reason that classes with higher average social class produce higher achievement is that they tend to be in higher tracks where achievement growth is steeper.

Social background, prior achievement, and tracking do not account for all of the achievement inequalities we have uncovered; our conceptual framework suggests that instructional differences may also play a role. Instructional conditions are important—first, because they may help us understand variation in writing performance; and second, because they may mediate the effects we have noted thus far, particularly the effects of tracking.

Before introducing instructional variables, we trimmed the model to allow a more stable estimate of instructional effects. Model 5 (Table 3) presents this trimmed model, with race and ethnicity omitted at the school level and Asian American and percent Asian American omitted at the student and class levels, respectively. Models 6–7 display social background coefficients under two different instructional models, which will be described shortly. Comparing columns 6–7 to Model 5, the only notable change is that the individual-level coefficient for home resources diminishes from .029 in Model 5 to .021 in Model 7—a decline of about 28 percent following the introduction of instruction to our model. Overall instructional conditions do little to mediate inequality beyond the effects of tracking. To the extent that classroom events account for social background inequalities, tracking is the main organizing condition.

Effects of Tracking and Instruction on Writing Performance

What are the effects of tracking and instruction on writing performance? Although instruction plays a modest role in mediating background effects beyond the role of tracking, it may be more important as a mechanism through which tracking effects are conveyed. Table 3 presents results for the analysis of the relationship between instruction and achievement. These models include the variables in Models 1–4 as controls, although some of the nonsignificant variables were removed to improve the stability of estimation. The first column of Table 3 (Model 5) shows that, as expected, students in high tracks exhibit better writing performance and students in low tracks exhibit worse performance than students in regular classes who are similar in observed social background, gender, fall achievement, and other school and classroom characteristics. By adding the coefficients to the estimate for tracked versus untracked schools, one may also use these figures to compare students in high and low tracks to similar students in untracked schools. These computations indicate that high-track students scored .394 - .073 =

.321 points higher and low-track students scored -.342 - .073 = -.415 points lower than their untracked counterparts. Posthoc tests indicate that these differences are statistically significant.

Table 3. Effects of Tracking and Instruction on Writing Achievement

	(5) Trimmed Track Effects	(6) Instructional Effects	(7) Discussion X Track Interactions
School level			
% Free lunch	.569 (.553)	.197 (.579)	.449 (.546)
Tracked	-.073 (.152)	-.160 (.145)	-.165 (.129)
Class level			
% African American	-.318 (.260)	-.377 (.256)	-.459 (.244)*
% Hispanic	-.048 (.283)	.140 (.286)	.024 (.278)
SES	.111 (.050)**	.101 (.048)**	.141(.048)***
High Track	.394 (.112)***	.349 (.114)***	.152 (.141)
Low Track	-.342 (.134)***	-.403 (.138)***	-.275 (.150)*
Student Questions		.248 (.378)	.133 (.362)
Authentic Questions		.929 (.533)*	1.429 (.559)**
Uptake		-.302 (.424)	-.273 (.394)
Discussion Time		-.006 (.020)	-.040 (.029)
High Track			.065 (.036)*
Low Track			-.253 (.128)*
Student level			
African American	-.084 (.080)	-.074 (.083)	-.085 (.079)
Hispanic	-.119 (.067)*	-.102 (.069)	-.111 (.066)*
Home Resources	.029 (.015)*	.023 (.015)	.021 (.015)
Writing Completion		.005 (.001)***	.005 (.001)***
Variance Explained[a]			
School level	.570	.771	.966
Class level	.843	.846	.857
Student level	.153	.163	.163

* $p < .10$
** $p < .05$
*** $p < .01$

Coefficients are unstandardized; standard errors are in parentheses.

[a] Variance explained relative to unconditional model, adjusted for school level.

The second column of Table 3 (Model 6) displays the effects of instruction. At the student level, those who more often complete their writing assignments improve their writing more over the course of the year. At the class level, students whose teachers pose a higher proportion of authentic questions also exhibit better writing performance in the spring. Percent of student questions, the use of uptake, and discussion are not significantly related to achievement in this model. These instructional measures have little impact on the coefficients for tracking. (Although coherence and envisionment building are correlated with achievement, they did not contribute independently beyond the other variables in the model and we omitted them after preliminary analyses.) Compared to Model 5, the coefficient for high track is slightly smaller while the coefficient for low track is slightly larger.

Why does instruction not appear to mediate the effects of tracking in Model 6? Two reasons seem most likely. First, the instructional conditions we observed may not vary between tracks. In earlier work we found that authentic questions and uptake occurred with similar frequency across tracks, although the content of the questions tended to differ (Nystrand 1997). Table 4 shows a similar result for these data: authentic questions, uptake, and student questions did not vary consistently by track level, so that they cannot mediate the effects of tracking. Discussion time varied directly with track level since high tracks spent the most time in discussion and low tracks the least. However, the models thus far reveal no effect of discussion on achievement.

Table 4. Instructional Differences across Tracks

	Discussion (minutes)	% Authentic questions	% Questions with uptake	% Student questions
Track level				
Low (n=10)	.70 (1.14)	21.91 (13.94)	31.37 (12.17)	16.89 (17.93)
Regular (n=26)	1.44 (3.10)	19.30 (14.74)	31.48 (12.87)	16.08 (10.24)
High (n=13)	3.30 (4.01)	21.26 (9.00)	29.32 (10.31)	23.20 (17.40)
Mixed (n=15)	1.42 (2.47)	14.05 (9.59)	31.31 (11.84)	15.49 (12.76)

Figures are means with standard deviations in parentheses.

A second concern about our models is that they may misspecify the relationship between instruction and achievement if instruction has different effects in different tracks. In earlier research we found substantial differences between track levels in the ways that dialogic instruction affected achievement (Nystrand 1997). In high tracks authentic questions and discussion had positive effects on achievement, but in low tracks the effects were zero or even negative. This occurred because authentic questions and discussion in high tracks concerned literature, but in low tracks they concerned other—often marginally academic—issues. Consequently, in these data we tested authentic questions, uptake, and discussion for interactions with tracking.

Only discussion yielded significant interactions, and these results are displayed in the final column of Table 3. Here we see that the main effect for discussion, which reflects both regular and untracked classes, is slightly negative and not statistically significant. A multilevel interaction term for discussion in tracked versus untracked schools was not statistically significant, so we excluded it to simplify the model. The interaction term for high-track classes is positive and significant, indicating that discussion adds significantly more to achievement in high tracks than in regular classes. Finally, the coefficient for discussion in low-track classes is negative and statistically significant. Apparently, discussion in low tracks is actually an impediment to achievement, presumably because what students are discussing is not academic content (Nystrand 1997).

Once the interaction between discussion and tracking is taken into account, we find that variation in discussion does help account for the effects of tracking. When no time at all is spent on discussion, the coefficients in the last column of Table 3 (Model 7) indicate that—all else constant—the high-track advantage drops to a nonsignificant .152 points and the low-track deficit is reduced to -.275 points compared to students in regular track classes. These gaps increase as more discussion occurs. For example, if every class spent two minutes on discussion, the advantage of high tracks would be $((-.04 + .065) * 2) + .152 = .202$ points, while students in low-track classes would be behind by $((-.04 -.253) * 2) - .275 = -.861$ points. Thus instructional effects operate both independently of and in conjunction with track effects to produce variation in achievement.

The final model accounts for very large proportions of variance at the school level (.966) and class level (.857) but much less variance (.163) at the student level. This pattern reflects two conditions. First, because very little variance lies between schools, it does not take much to account for it. Variance explained at the class level is much more meaningful for understanding student achievement: over 30 percent of the overall variance exists at that level, compared to less than 5 percent of the variance at the school level once the difference between high schools and middle schools is taken out of the equation. Second, in our data collection strategy, classes are the main sampling unit and the most powerful predictors (tracking and instruction) are measured at the class level. As a result we have much greater success accounting for variance at the school and class levels than at the student level.

DISCUSSION AND CONCLUSIONS

This paper offers a replication and extension of previous research on the sources of achievement inequality. The broad conception of dialogic instruction as portrayed by Nystrand (1997), Applebee (1996), and Langer (1995) is supported with new data that generally replicates Nystrand's (1997) earlier empirical findings. In particular, classes with more authentic questions boost achievement, as does discussion time in honors classes only. It is particularly important that we have found similar results in a national data set instead of a regional one, and with a much larger selection of students from minority groups and economically disadvantaged backgrounds. Not all of Nystrand's findings were supported, however. Coherence among instructional activities and questions with uptake made unique contributions to writing performance in previous work, but not in this study.

This paper also replicates findings about tracking, showing once again that this practice is the chief device for sorting students by classes and differentiating instruction to different groups of students. Moreover, class-level differences in achievement due to social class were partially attributable to tracking, and instructional variation accounted in part for track differences in achievement. Observed differences in achievement among classes with differing racial and ethnic compositions were primarily due to preexisting achievement differences among students entering the classes. Instruction was assessed mainly at the class level, so the study was not well designed to account for within-class differences in literacy performance. In the future observations that are more sensitive to differences within classes, in how different students are treated and how they respond, may help account for within-in-class variation in achievement.

Our analysis locates the sources of unequal writing achievement performance in structures within schools and in classroom technology. We have shown once again that, contrary to the rationale favoring ability grouping, instruction that occurs in high- and low-track classrooms tends to exacerbate the inequalities produced by separating students into different learning environments. More generally, we suggest that the dialogic instruction that occurs in some English classrooms could benefit all students if practiced more widely. The apparent negative effects of discussion in low-track classes—which replicate earlier findings—further indicate that what matters is not only how teachers and students interact, but the curriculum content around which their interaction occurs.

Nearly twenty years after the publication of *How Schools Work*, and over thirty years after *On What Is Learned in School*, researchers still have much to learn about the production of achievement. We know to look for it within classrooms; we have demonstrated the structural role of tracking and the technological role of instruction; but we still need better measures of instruction and achievement to capture the production process more precisely.

Acknowledgments

Research for this paper was supported by the Center on English Learning and Achievement (CELA) at the Wisconsin Center for Education Research, University of Wisconsin-Madison, with funds from the Office of Educational Research and Improvement, U.S. Department of Education (Grant No. R305-A60005). The data were drawn from a larger project directed by Arthur Applebee, Judith Langer, Martin Nystrand, and Adam Gamoran. The authors are grateful for the contributions of their CELA colleagues to this research.

The findings and conclusions in this paper are those of the authors and do not necessarily represent the views of the supporting agencies.

REFERENCES

Applebee, Arthur. 1996. *Curriculum as Conversation: Transforming Traditions of Teaching and Learning.* Chicago: University of Chicago Press.

Barr, Rebecca and Robert Dreeben. 1983. *How Schools Work.* Chicago: University of Chicago Press.

Berliner, David C. and Bruce J. Biddle. 1995. *The Manufactured Crisis: Myths, Fraud, and the Attack on America's Public Schools.* Reading, MA: Addison-Wesley.

Campbell, Jay R., Catherine M. Hombo, and John Mazzeo. 2000. *NAEP 1999 Trends in Academic Progress: Three Decades of Student Performance.* Washington, DC: U.S. Department of Education.

Carbonaro, William J. 2000. *Degrees of Difference: Explaining Variation in the Returns to Literacy Skills and Earnings across Occupations, over Time, and across Nations.* Ph.D. dissertation, Department of Sociology, University of Wisconsin-Madison.

Card, David and Alan B. Krueger. 1996. "Labor Market Effects of School Quality: Theory and Evidence." Pp. 97–140 in *Does Money Matter? The Effect of School Resources on Student Achievement and Adult Success,* edited by Gary Burtless. Washington, DC: Brookings Institution Press

Coleman, James S., Ernest Q. Campbell, Carol J. Hobson, James M. McPartland, Alexander M. Mood, Frederic D. Weinfield, and Robert L. York. 1966. *Equality of Educational Opportunity.* Washington, DC: U.S. Government Printing Office.

Dar, Yehezkel and Nura Resh. 1986. *Classroom Composition and Pupil Achievement: A Study of the Effect of Ability-Based Classes.* New York: Gordon and Breach.

Donahue, Patricia L., Kristin E. Voelkl, Jay R. Campbell, and John Mazzeo. 1999. *The NAEP 1998 Reading Report Card for the Nation and the States.* Washington, DC: U.S. Department of Education.

Dreeben, Robert. [1968] 2002. *On What Is Learned in School.* Clinton Corners, NY: Percheron Press/Eliot Werner Publications.

Dreeben, Robert and Adam Gamoran. 1986. "Race, Instruction, and Learning." *American Sociological Review* 51:660–69.

Entwisle, Doris R., Karl L. Alexander, and Linda Steffel Olson. 1997. *Children, Schools, and Inequality.* Boulder, CO: Westview.

Gamoran, Adam. 1986. "Instructional and Institutional Effects of Ability Grouping." *Sociology of Education* 59:185–98.

Gamoran, Adam. 1987. "The Stratification of High School Learning Opportunities." *Sociology of Education* 60:135–55.

Gamoran, Adam. 1996. "Student Achievement in Public Magnet, Public Comprehensive, and Private City High Schools." *Educational Evaluation and Policy Analysis* 18:1–18.

Gamoran, Adam. 2001. "Beyond Curriculum Wars: Content and Understanding in Mathematics." Pp. 134–62 in *The Great Curriculum Debate: How Should We Teach Reading and Math?* edited by Tom Loveless. Washington, DC: Brookings Institution Press.

Gamoran, Adam and William J. Carbonaro. 2002–03. "High School English: A National Portrait." *High School Journal* 86:1–13.

Gamoran, Adam and Robert Dreeben. 1986. "Coupling and Control in Educational Organizations." *Administrative Science Quarterly* 31:612–32.

Gamoran, Adam and Robert D. Mare. 1989. "Secondary School Tracking and Educational Inequality: Compensation, Reinforcement, or Neutrality?" *American Journal of Sociology* 94:1146–83.

Gamoran, Adam, Martin Nystrand, Mark Berends, and Paul C. LePore. 1995. "An Organizational Analysis of the Effects of Ability Grouping." *American Educational Research Journal* 32:687–715.

Gamoran, Adam, Andrew Porter, John Smithson, and Paula A. White. 1997. "Upgrading High School Mathematics Instruction: Improving Learning Opportunities for Low-Income, Low-Achieving Youth." *Educational Evaluation and Policy Analysis* 19:325–38.

Greenwald, Elissa A., Hilary R. Persky, Jay R. Campbell, and John Mazzeo. 1999. *The NAEP 1998 Writing Report Card for the Nation and the States.* Washington, DC: U.S. Department of Education.

Greenwald, Robert D., Larry V. Hedges, and Richard D. Laine. 1996. "The Effects of School Resources on Student Achievement." *Review of Educational Research* 66:361–96.

Hedges, Larry V. and Amy Nowell. 1999. "Changes in the Black-White Gap in Test Scores." *Sociology of Education* 72:111–35.

Heyns, Barbara. 1974. "Social Selection and Stratification within Schools." *American Journal of Sociology* 79:1434–51.

Langer, Judith. 1995. *Envisioning Literature: Literary Understanding and Literature Instruction.* New York: Teachers College Press.

Lucas, Samuel. R. 1999. *Tracking Inequality: Stratification and Mobility in American High Schools.* New York: Teachers College Press.

Mayer, Daniel P. 1999. "Measuring Instructional Practice: Can Policymakers Trust Instructional Data?" *Educational Evaluation and Policy Analysis* 21:29–46.

Mehan, Hugh. 1979. *Learning Lessons: Social Organization in the Classroom.* Cambridge, MA: Harvard University Press.

Murnane, Richard J. 1975. *The Impact of School Resources on the Learning of Inner-City Children.* Cambridge, MA: Ballinger.

Murnane Richard J., John B. Willett, and Frank Levy. 1995. "The Growing Importance of Cognitive Skills in Wage Determination." *Review of Economics and Statistics* 77:251-66.

Nystrand, Martin. 1997. *Opening Dialogue: Understanding the Dynamics of Language and Learning in the English Classroom.* New York: Teachers College Press.

Nystrand, Martin. 1999. *Class 3.0.* Madison, WI: Wisconsin Center for Education Research.

Nystrand, Martin and Adam Gamoran. 1991a. "Instructional Discourse, Student Engagement, and Literature Achievement." *Research in the Teaching of English* 25:261–90.

Nystrand, Martin and Adam Gamoran. 1991b. "Student Engagement: When Recitation Becomes Conversation." Pp. 257–76 in *Contemporary Research on Teaching* edited by Herbert A. Walberg and Hersh C. Waxman. Berkeley, CA: McCutchan.

Nystrand, Martin, Lawrence Wu, Adam Gamoran, Daniel A. Long, and Susie Zeiser. In press. "Questions in Time: Investigating the Structure and Dynamics of Unfolding Classroom Discourse." *Discourse Processes.*

Oakes, Jeannie, Adam Gamoran, and Reba Page. 1992. "Curriculum Differentiation: Opportunities, Outcomes, and Meanings." Pp. 570–608 in *Handbook of Research on Curriculum,* edited by Philip W. Jackson. New York: Macmillan.

Raudenbush, Stephen W. and Rafa M. Kasim. 1998. "Cognitive Skill and Economic Inequality: Findings from the National Adult Literacy Survey." *Harvard Educational Review* 68:33–79.

Rowan, Brian and Andrew W. Miracle, Jr. 1983. "Systems of Ability Grouping and the Stratification of Achievement in Elementary Schools." *Sociology of Education* 56:133–44.

Sørensen, Aage B. 1970. "Organizational Differentiation of Students and Educational Opportunity." *Sociology of Education* 43:355–76.

8

When Tensions Mount: Conceptualizing Classroom Situations and the Conditions of Student-Teacher Conflict

Daniel A. McFarland

An enduring concern of Robert Dreeben's work is the conditions of classroom instruction (Dreeben [1968] 2002; Barr and Dreeben 1983; Dreeben and Barr 1988). Whether it is the conditions influencing classroom goodwill (Bidwell, Chapter 3, this volume) or the compositional effects on instructional methods, Dreeben repeatedly brings readers' attention to how the social organization of schools relates to instruction and learning. In a similar spirit, this chapter analyzes the conditions of classroom instruction and learning but approaches the problem from a different angle. Rather than examining the conditions of equilibrium and efficiency, it examines the conditions of classroom conflict. Classroom conflicts are galvanizing events that unravel the classroom order. When students argue with their teacher, rebel from authority, or resist instruction, they challenge classroom goodwill and bring instruction to a halt (Bidwell 1965; Dreeben [1968] 2002). However, conflicts—or any breach for that matter—are also windows into the underlying assumptions and methods that actors use to create a sense of normalcy and order (Garfinkel 1967; Wieder 1974). Hence while the focus here is on commonly occurring states of disequilibrium and disorder, the spirit is much the same as Dreeben's attempt to understand the social (dis)organization of schooling and how it relates to instruction.

In order to understand the conditions of classroom conflict and disorder, I present a conceptualization of classroom settings that makes the multiplicity of classroom doings a starting point of exposition. Classrooms are regarded as crowded settings wherein multiple loci of interaction or situated streams of activity take place (Jackson 1968). Actors within classrooms can promote, participate in, and attend to these multiple ongoing streams of activity

Daniel A. McFarland • School of Education, Stanford University, Stanford, California 94305.

Stability and Change in American Education: Structure, Process, and Outcomes edited by Maureen T. Hallinan, Adam Gamoran, Warren Kubitschek, and Tom Loveless. Eliot Werner Publications, Clinton Corners, New York, 2003.

(Goffman [1974] 1986). However, not all streams of activity are related to academic work. Much of what students say and do is wholly unrelated to class tasks or school affairs, and such doing and saying often arises between students while they sit in classrooms and teacher-directed tasks take place.

Two common types of classroom activity are the focus of this paper: academic and sociable affairs. I argue that these doings are understood and interpreted by participants as distinct frameworks of interaction. These interpretive modes of (and for) action have different organizational logics whose definition is anchored in particular activities, relational patterns, form and content of communication, and status systems (Friedland and Alford 1991; Padgett 2001). More often than not, academic and sociable doings have very distinct anchors that result in opposing principles of interpretation and prescribed actions. As a result many classrooms entail competing, incompatible affairs that create latent interpersonal tensions between teacher and students and manifest in classroom conflicts.

This conceptualization of classrooms builds on research currently presented in the education literature. Most researchers describe classroom settings as having discrete segments of academic and sociable activity in which all of the participants in the classroom uniformly engage (Bossert 1979; Doyle 1986; Stodolsky 1988). The general view of classroom situations is that they arise sequentially and with clear switches. The implication is that all of the individuals in a classroom are in the same framework at the same time.

Some researchers complicate this view by suggesting that academic and sociable affairs arise in distinct arenas of the classroom, such as front-stage and back-stage arenas of discourse (or public and private: see Alton-Lee, Nuthall, and Patrick 1993). Some even describe classrooms as having multiple scripts (Gutierrez, Rymes, and Larson 1995) or states of interaction (McLaren 1986) where students act in a manner reflective of sociable or academic interpretations of affairs. While these works recognize the multiplicity of situations, they still depict collective action as uniformly flowing into one framework of interaction after another and do not describe how situations co-occur and interpenetrate.

Every classroom has multiple streams of activity that simultaneously occur and draw the attention and active involvement of participants. In many classrooms it is common for the stream of academic activity to dominate and become the primary mode by which ongoing events are interpreted. Thus during a classroom lesson like recitation, many events will be interpreted with regard to the primary track of activity that retains student involvement in recitation and pushes the task toward its completion. All sorts of subordinate tracks of activity and side-events still arise during the task, but they are usually of secondary concern to most participants and the meaning of such actions are often encased by the primary framework of the academic task (Goffman [1974] 1986). Hence a student's side comment to a peer or a teacher's bracketed joke arise as a secondary stream of activity whose meaning is framed by the main story line of recitation.

However, equally common in classroom settings is the co-occurrence of multiple primary frameworks of interaction that lack hierarchical or nested interrelation. That is, sociable and academic affairs can persist in different arenas of the classroom uninterrupted and uncorrupted by the other's existence, and without either stream's meaning being subordinated to the other. The argument of this chapter is that uniform engagement in a single collective endeavor is an uncommon occurrence in classrooms. However, even the view that classrooms have distinct arenas of interaction and interpretive frameworks is too limiting since it fails to recognize the common process by which these interpretive frames and forms of interaction co-occur and interpenetrate without clear brackets defining their boundaries.

The multiplicity of interpenetrating and competing doings is an accurate, useful conceptualization of classroom settings that helps explain how and why teachers and students behave within them. It is a useful conceptualization because it helps us understand why "cultural dopes" (Garfinkel 1967) or univocal performers of social roles are uncommon, and it helps us understand why a great deal of ambiguity, misunderstanding, and contention arise in the everyday affairs of classrooms.

Since classrooms are crowded settings, multiple arenas of discourse and activity can arise within them. As such, doings and their loci of interaction can spread, recede, dissipate, merge, and compete for adherents. Actors often move across such loci and some even perform in a multivocal fashion to multiple audiences at once (McFarland 1999). Because there are multiple groups and loci of interaction in the classroom, it is frequently the case that situations fail to have clear boundaries. Teacher-prescribed tasks can become confusing as more sociable modes of interpretation and play routines are pirated in, thereby creating mixed situations where it is hard to grasp what is happening. Likewise, tensions can mount when sociable affairs spread and their salience eclipses that of the tasks a teacher prescribes. In short, whenever teacher-prescribed tasks fail to be the primary stream of activity for the majority of classroom participants, problems tend to arise.

In what follows I conceptualize classroom settings as composed of multiple doings and describe how conflict emerges from the relationship between competing academic and sociable endeavors. In the first section, I describe academic and sociable frameworks of interaction and their organizational anchors. Following that I relate how certain frameworks come to dominate settings by the adaptations that subordinate tracks of activity make possible. In the third section, I describe how multiple primary frameworks can co-occur without any holding clear sway over the classroom as a whole. The fourth section describes how multiple primary frameworks can collide and compete for adherents, creating a great deal of discontent within the setting. In the final section, I describe how coalition formation is one means by which political actors develop classroom consensus and focus audience participation in a more uniform fashion.

FRAMES AND CLASSROOM SITUATIONS

As stated in the introduction, two common types of classroom activity are the concern of this paper: academic and sociable affairs. I argue that these doings are understood and interpreted by participants as distinct frameworks of interaction. By *frame* I mean principles of organization that govern the subjective meaning that actors assign to social events (Goffman [1974] 1986). Events, actions, performances, and selves do not always speak for themselves but rather depend on framing for their meaning (Branaman 1997; Steinberg 1999). We can understand the same event, action, or performance as playful or insulting depending on which interpretive frame is applied. Hence we could interpret the actions of two children rolling around on the floor shouting at each other as either fighting or play.

Frames can be applied at multiple levels of analysis. At the microlevel of talk-activities, Tannen and Wallat (1987) write of multiple frames of interaction occurring in a medical interview. There a doctor juggles multiple doings and shifts frames as she moves from one talk-activity to the next: she consults the mother, entertains the child-as-patient, and reports medical diagnoses to a camcorder recording the examination (the consultation occurred at a teaching hospital). Classrooms teachers also juggle multiple doings and frames. As they conduct the routine of recitation, they inform and elicit questions from students one moment and then shift to negative sanctions of off-task students the next. In both cases the actor's effort is on sustaining a larger primary framework or main story line: the check-up or the lesson. All the different talk-activities, registers of talk, and so forth are part of the larger effort to sustain a role-frame of doctor-patient or teacher-student roles.

This chapter is more concerned with the collective promotion and maintenance of certain role-frames than the individual enactment of particular frames of talk-activities that Tannen and Wallat (1987) describe (see also McFarland 1999: Chapter 10). Hence what I call academic or sociable affairs really consist of a set of activities that are enacted to establish particular roles as legitimate identities of the classroom setting. In certain respects what I refer to as an academic or sociable frame of interaction is akin to what Benford and Snow (2000) call a master frame in social movements. The academic frame encapsulates various roles (teacher-student) and the talk-activities particular to them, while the sociable frame encapsulates various roles (friends-enemies) and the talk-activities particular to them (akin to McLaren's [1986] street and student states). The primary doing in each case—whether it is doctoring, educating, or socializing—is accompanied by subordinate tracks of activity that reinforce the primary endeavor of the role-frame. Of central concern in this article is the extent to which participants promote one role-frame over another and the extent to which such promotion results in making audience members constituents and adherents to that framework.

Task Situations and Academic Frames

In well-behaved, highly engaged classes, there arise multiple streams of activity that are primarily interpreted from an academic frame. As such, the academic frame makes sense of various behaviors during tasks so that participants think "we are doing schoolwork." The academic frame's meaning or logic is anchored in certain organizational structures such as teacher-student roles, classroom tasks, the labor relations that they entail, their topics, the status rewards that they afford, and the forms of talk that teacher-prescribed tasks entail.

Academic affairs are distinct from other doings first and foremost because they concern academic topics such as math, science, English, and so on. These topics are often quite distinct from students' lived experiences at home and in their neighborhoods. However, teachers vary in the extent to which they relate course materials to students' lives, thereby decreasing or increasing the social distance between adolescent and subject matter (Cummins 1989; Haroutunian-Gordon 1991). In addition to relevance, course topics differ in cognitive complexity. Teachers vary in the type of knowledge that they seek from students, ranging from fact recall to opinions to problem solving to critical assessments to synopsis and metatheoretical thinking (Mehan 1979; Stodolsky 1988; McFarland 1999). The greater the cognitive demand, the greater the student involvement required. It is of little surprise that scholars find students become more committed to academic work when it entails relevant topics of greater cognitive demand (Stodolsky 1988; Boaler 1997).

The academic frame is also characterized by the formal properties of teacher-prescribed tasks and their patterns of interaction. Classroom activities generate work relations that distinguish teachers and students in interaction. Teachers utilize all sorts of activities through which subject matter is learned: lectures, recitations, discussions, seatwork, group work, student presentations, laboratory work, films, conferences, and so on (Doyle 1986; Stodolsky 1988). Most of these activities organize the learning process in one of three ways: teacher centered, student centered, and student isolated. Teacher-centered activities structure learning so that ideas and skills are transmitted from teachers and incorporated by students (Cummins 1989). Student-centered activities structure task interactions in a more reciprocal or developmental fashion, placing students more at the heart of discourse (Metz 1978). Student-isolated activities force youths to engage the materials by themselves. This third type of activity pertains most often to seatwork but also refers to individual projects and exams. Because seatwork can be either an incorporatist (e.g., crosswords and worksheets) or a developmental (e.g., essay questions and critical thinking) strategy, it is difficult to categorize. Regardless, most classes use activities that organize instruction in either teacher-centered or student-centered ways, favoring one style over the other (Hallinan 1976).

Each style of instruction defines student access to arenas of public discourse (Goffman 1981; Doyle 1986). Transmission classes make access to public discourse the most unequal, so that competition for access and teacher praise is great. Such competition is lessened in developmental classes because student access to public discourse is more open. However, since the teacher is less central, praise is also lessened. Therefore, depending on the task structure, the reward structure and status-logic of task interactions may shift (Michaels 1977; Bossert 1979).

In all of these different task structures, teachers *generally* find ways to position themselves in asymmetrical relationships with their students. Teachers retain their power position because they hold a monopoly on forms of diffuse speech (such as performative, declarative, and informative speech) that are directed at the class as a whole. Typically, a teacher will use these forms of speech while standing in front of a class. Moreover, he or she will utilize an impersonal, authoritative tone. Each of these indirect forms of speech calls on students to be quiet and listen. Any student response would seem awkward and improper (McLaren 1986: Chapter 3). Teachers also have a monopoly on evaluative forms of speech. That is, teachers correct, encourage, praise, sanction, blame, and challenge students far more than students do so in return (Dreeben [1968] 2002; Jackson 1968; Bidwell and Friedkin 1988). Hence teachers may or may not be central to the instructional format of tasks, but they will often retain their monopoly on indirect and evaluative forms of public speech.

Student labor and its evaluation create asymmetric relationships between teachers and students (Hurn 1985) and affect the relationship that adolescents have with one another as students. Students produce work that is evaluated by teachers, creating a unidirectional workflow. Teachers evaluate the quantity and quality of student work and then rank pupils when allocating grades. Students typically value these grades and compete for higher rankings. However, one student's success comes at another's loss because the rankings often shift in a zero-sum manner (Coleman 1961; Michaels 1977). A good example of this is class rankings within grade-cohorts: when the number two student moves up a notch, the number one student moves down.

In sum, organizational anchors reveal several logics or organizing principles that characterize the academic frame: academic topics, incorporative versus developmental activity structures (Metz 1978; Cummins 1989), asymmetry in teacher-talk and workflow (McLaren 1986), and competition among students for status-rankings (Coleman 1961). Of course these logics will vary by classroom, but all share a family resemblance making teacher-student roles recognizable and expected in every classroom setting—a master-frame for all task situations.

Sociable Situations and Sociable Frames

Even the studies of classrooms that describe uniformly engaged audiences note that not all class time is spent completing work and engaging in tasks. A class period may consist of several lessons, each with different segments. Before each class begins, between segments, and after the lesson is completed, there are moments of transition or breaks in the instructional process when the teacher does not prescribe patterns of interaction (Stodolsky 1988). Here, outside the task frame, youth are left to define the situation for themselves.

In undefined segments of class time, public social discourse rises in prominence and becomes the primary current of activity. Other subordinate tracks are then interpreted from a sociable frame and serve to retain adolescent involvement in social affairs. Adolescents will take advantage of free time by turning to their friends and gossiping about the weekend. In the process different cliques will be formed and maintained. In such instances the main story line becomes one of overt gossiping supported by secondary tracks of clarification, side gossip, and elaboration. All secondary tracks support and reinforce the continuation of the main story line of overt gossip.

Meanings in the sociable frame have an organizational logic distinct from the academic frame because they are anchored by sociable topics and activities, as well as by friendships and more playful interactions. When in the sociable frame, youth communicate about certain topics that have little to do with most academic subjects such as dating, parties, sports, television, movies, music, sex, drinking, personal relations, upcoming events, and so forth (Sieber 1979; Mehan 1980; Edelsky 1981; Streeck 1984; James and Drakich 1993; Alton-Lee, Nuthall, and Patrick. 1993; Gutierrez, Rymes, and Larson 1995). Youth have a wide range of social experiences to which they look forward and on which they reflect. This shared set of social experiences generally has referents outside of class, but they are so important that students repeatedly draw on such folkways whenever possible in class (Coleman 1961; McLaren 1986; Fine 1987; Eder 1995).

The sociable frame is also characterized by the formal properties of adolescents' social activities and patterns of interaction (Corsaro and Eder 1990). Sociable activities arise as forms of gossip, collaborative storytelling, sharing, ritual teasing, and play to name but a few (Goodwin 1980; Maynard 1985; Eder 1986; Corsaro and Rizzo 1988; Eder and Enke 1991; Eder 1995). These talk-activities almost always involve egalitarian turn taking and collaboration between participants. Hence social discourse is more evenly distributed and group oriented than task discourse (Metz 1978; Doyle 1986). In addition, sociable talk is fast paced and tends to overlap the discourse of separate speakers, further lessening interpersonal distinctions. Sociable talk arises in the classroom between friends and it develops enclaves of supportive relationships that protect the individual from ridicule when taking the public stage. As a result, an interaction order emerges in the classroom where collaborative efforts are spent preserving interactions that enable ritual selves to be safely performed (Goffman 1983; Rawls 1987; Giordano 1995).

Friendship networks not only reinforce this interaction order; they are also the basis of informal status distinctions between adolescents in the class. The friendship network consists of preexistent, keyed, and emergent types of friends (Goffman [1974] 1986; McFarland 1999). Preexistent friendship relations are those that persist outside of class and predate membership in the course, such as hangout friends. Keyed ties are friendships that form in class on the basis of some other shared affiliation (Simmel 1971). In previous research, for example, I observed class friendships that formed on the basis of shared participation in athletics, theater, or merely race and gender (McFarland 1999). It is not uncommon to see groups of thespians or African American females who view one another as class friends, but who do not get together on weekends. Emergent friendships have neither a keyed nor a pre-existent basis. They emerge in the setting through collaborative participation in sociable activities or simply by way of frequent interaction (Festinger, Schachter, and Back [1950] 1967). As a whole, then, classroom friendship networks entail affective ties that have a pastiche of social origins (Cusick 1973).

In the classroom informal status is given to those who observe group norms and maintain the processes of interaction. These popular individuals and cliques tend to be "regular guys and gals" who are the least threatening to others in the class (Roethlisberger and Dickson 1939; Homans [1950] 1992; Merten 1998). They are adolescents who maintain the interaction order such that ritual presentations of self are safely performed (Goffman 1983; Rawls 1987). This is somewhat counterintuitive since one might expect members of the leading crowd to be the most popular in the classroom (Coleman 1961). Instead, leading crowd members tend to be moderately popular individuals and cliques that are snobbish in their friendship choices. They lack real dominance in many classrooms because sets of students view members of the leading crowd much like a negative reference group (de Waals 1982). In several classrooms I observed athletes and theater students refer to one another with disdain. In such contexts third-party cliques became the most vocal in classroom affairs since they brokered these polarized cliques and enjoyed a degree of esteem (as the least disliked in class: see Kinney 1993; McFarland 1999).

In sum, the academic and sociable frames within many high school classrooms have organizational anchors with distinct form and content. It is often the case that academic and sociable affairs entail very different types of topics, roles, activities, and forms of discourse. Academic affairs in the classroom frequently entail abstract academic topics, teacher-student roles, teacher-centered tasks, more controlled turns at talk, monopolistic use of certain forms of talk, and a status system based on individual competition and rank. In contrast, sociable affairs in the classroom frequently entail topics of a personal or entertaining nature, collaborative activities and egalitarian relationships, overlapping fast-paced turns at talk, and status rewards based on service to the group and conformity to group norms. Consequently, the organizational logic of sociable affairs often exists in juxtaposition to academic work (Gutierrez, Rymes, and Larson 1995).

DOMINANT FRAMES AND SUBORDINATE TRACKS OF ACTIVITY

Task and sociable situations may consist of contradictory organizational logics but nevertheless persist in the majority of classroom settings. Every classroom by definition has an academic situation; otherwise it is no longer a classroom, but something altogether different. Many descriptions of classroom situations describe well-behaved, highly engaged classrooms where one observes the class collectively switch between sociable and academic frames of interaction. Such a uniformly focused class is possible, but it is only one of the possible situational outcomes given the multiplicity of interaction loci and interaction frames that are often present in the classroom setting. In addition, uniformly focused settings almost invariably entail subordinate tracks of activity that sustain a general focus on the main story line and are therefore not truly uniform.

Early work in discourse analysis nicely portrays what uniform, sequential situations look like when they arise in classrooms (Mehan 1979; Cazden 1988). Mehan's (1979) work describes the typical lesson of a classroom as having three parts or phases: an opening, instructional, and closing phase. During the opening and closing minutes of a class period, activity segments of free time, maintenance, or transitions are common and students find that behavioral expectations are rather loosely defined (Stodolsky 1988). During such opening phases, the sociable frame guides interpretations and behavior such that loud, fast-paced, energetic speech acts are common. During these opening moments, one often observes a teacher and students engaging in excited social banter about their weekends and personal lives. After awhile the teacher begins to make announcements and give directives that drown out sociable affairs and draw student attention to academic work. Shortly thereafter public academic talk becomes the primary, dominant track of activity in the classroom. The reverse switch is also observed in the final minutes of class. As tasks are completed and the passing period approaches, students' academic focus wanes as peers again socialize and relate to one another on a more personal basis. Thus we see a switch from the sociable frame's to the academic frame's dominance in the opening phases of most class lessons, and then a switch back to the sociable frame's dominance in the class period's closing minutes (Jackson 1968). In this manner a sequential enactment of activities and roles occurs where adults and adolescents switch routines and identities (akin to changing games and hats) from play routines and egalitarian friendship roles to task routines and asymmetrical relationships of teacher-student roles, and then back again. Unfortunately, in most classroom settings it is the academic frame and tasks that must be actively constructed through a great deal of effort, and it is the sociable frame toward which actors invariably drift when such efforts pause or cease to persist.

During the instructional phase of class periods, public task discourse is generally considered the primary track of activity to which actors attend and adhere (Mehan 1979, 1980). However, few scholars remark on how the main story line of instruction is often accompanied by multiple subordinate tracks of activity that retain student involvement (Goffman [1974] 1986). For instance, high school teachers often lecture to students, informing them about new facts and skills. Students listen but sometimes miss certain points or find others difficult to follow. In an effort to keep up, pupils privately turn to neighbors and ask for clarification or elaboration (Goffman 1981). These instances of private task discourse are adjustments that students make to stay involved in the task. At other points in a lecture, students grow bored and privately turn to neighbors to make a funny face or crack a joke. After the brief repose, these same students fall back into the lecture somewhat refreshed. Here private sociable activity is a secondary track that serves as a release valve and outlet for student sentiments that are publicly discouraged from being voiced during lectures. Privately sociable students temporarily put the task on hold but bracket and conceal their playful behavior. In so doing, they subordinate sociable affairs to the main storyline of the academic lesson (see Goffman's [1974] 1986 discussion of "keying").

Hence a primary stream of activity like teacher-led recitation is maintained by waves of private talk that enable students to adapt to the rigid behavioral demands of the task. Pupils engage in private secondary tracks of activity in order to clarify the task or let off steam. In this manner both student and teacher identities are maintained through the lesson. However, academic work will not always be the dominant activity in a classroom. In the example above, private sociable activity is considered a secondary track to instruction because it sustains student involvement in instruction. But private social discourse can also be a secondary track to public social discourse in other segments of class time. For example, in the opening and closing segments of a class period, private sociable activity has the purpose of sustaining the primary social doing of gossip, play, or collaborative storytelling. In both situations private discourse sustains the primary framework, whether it is related to academic work or sociable affairs. Such a conceptualization enables one to view the classroom as having multiple interweaving strands of secondary discourse that surround and reinforce the primary stream of participant activity. Nevertheless, matters become more complicated when we acknowledge that in some settings there may be multiple, independent streams of activity and that each has its own subordinate tracks of private discourse.

MULTIPLE PRIMARY FRAMES

Many classrooms lack a single interpretive framework that dominates *all* participants' definition of the situation. In these classrooms there are multiple loci of interaction that compete for adherents and lack hierarchical or nested interrelation. A multiplicity of competing situations is a common occurrence in many small group settings. Loci of academic and sociable interaction can become distinct primary frameworks of interaction that entail their own story line, subordinate tracks of activity, and organizational logics. This conceptualization of primary and secondary interpretive frameworks enables us to describe classroom contexts where "what is going on" remains unclear or divided. It also allows us to introduce a political dimension to framing and classroom situations in which definitional work is contested in certain arenas and accepted in others. In many respects this conceptualization improves on

Goffman's description of primary frames by making sensible situations a problematic outcome that political agents joust to establish (as he and others would wish: see Goffman 1981; Manning 1992).

In general, it is the presence of public sociable affairs that creates multiple primary frames in classroom settings. Public sociable affairs tend to arise in classes where adolescents have many friends or are given ample opportunity to interact with one another during and between tasks. Such opportunities arise in student-centered task formats and during long transitions between academic tasks. When friendship roles and relations enter classrooms or emerge within them, youth are obliged to show loyalty and liking to their friends in order to maintain the role relation (Blau [1964] 1996). Moreover, since friends have shared histories as well as similar interests and backgrounds, they will have much to talk about that is unrelated to the class task. Hence by virtue of being friends, there is an inclination to interact on a basis quite distinct from that called for by academic work. Adolescents also socialize when they are given the opportunity to interact, especially during segments in which they are left to define the situation for themselves (e.g., free time) or have greater autonomy over their action (e.g., group work). In addition, like most any person, adolescents wish to interact on a meaningful basis that enables them to present their social selves (Waller 1932; Mead 1934; Goffman 1959). When tasks pertain to abstract topics, youth may activate the sociable frame and reference meanings in their social world outside of class.

Friendship networks and social opportunities interact to have independent and compounding effects on the sociability of students in a class. Hence densely interconnected friendship relations increase sociable behavior, while a sparse friendship network will be less sociable. When the teacher imposes centralized instruction, sociable behavior is dampened because students lack frequent opportunities to interact, but students will be inclined to interact when teachers open access to discourse (McFarland 2001). Therefore students are generally inclined to socialize when they have many friends and many chances to interact. Dense friendship networks and student-centered tasks are therefore associated with high rates and wide distributions of interactions. In contrast, teacher-centered formats hinder sociable interaction and narrow the distribution of interactions as fewer speakers have the opportunity to take the floor. During teacher-centered formats, sequential public turns are the norm and deviations are easily observed. Hence the persistence of sociable affairs is often prevented as teachers administer negative sanctions to these disturbances that threaten the successful performance of a centralized task structure. Consequently, informal relationships and the formal organization of instruction are two key structural anchors that can constrain and enable the presence of multiple primary frameworks.

Which conditions explain how academic and sociable frameworks of interaction interrelate? In some classrooms the coexistence of academic and sociable situations are compatible and do not create problems, while in others these situations compete for adherents and undermine the existence of the other (Willis 1977; Sieber 1979; Mehan 1980; Alton-Lee, Nuthall, and Patrick 1993; Gutierrez, Rymes, and Larson 1995). Which characteristics of classroom settings determine whether multiple situations exist in aligned or oppositional states? *Congruence* between academic and sociable affairs generally arises because students have intrinsic and extrinsic motivations to learn and comply with behavioral expectations of tasks. As stated above, the general inclination or drift in student attention is toward play and sociable affairs. In other words, the variance in adolescents' sociable inclinations is less than the variance in their academic interest. Hence it is assumed that when students are interested in the subject matter, care about grades, and want to attend college, they will be more likely to comply with efforts to make academic affairs the primary interpretive framework. Even though they may drift into socializing during various phases of class lessons, the teacher will find it easier to draw such students back on task.

In some classes academic and social situations *merge* together. By this I mean that meanings of either frame interpenetrate. Such situational mergers occur when students are highly motivated but have tasks organized in student-centered formats such as group work or discussion. Student-centered formats serve to bring classmates into relation with one another rather than with just the teacher. However, by forming work relations between students, the teacher also opens up channels of discourse that may be transformed and imbued with content unrelated to the task (Simmel 1971). That is, interacting students not only talk more about their tasks, they talk more about social affairs. Since teachers often accept a degree of social behavior, a merger of situations is allowed.

Mergers are also facilitated when the content of tasks is relevant to adolescents' social relationships and personal lives. In fieldwork I observed a clear situational merger in a creative writing class. There the teacher conducted lessons where presenters expressed their sentiments and the audience adhered to a norm of giving only positive feedback. In such a context, the teacher deftly merged parts of multiple roles: that of facilitator, boss, confidant, and friend. Similarly, when students orated their papers to classmates, they performed across interpretive frameworks and merged organizational logics. Student orators invoked parts of multiple identities in a pastiche manner, playing the parts of student, male or female, peer, and friend.

Unfortunately, successful mergers such as the one described above are difficult to achieve. In many classrooms the merging of academic and sociable frameworks requires a great deal of compromise (Powell, Farrar, and Cohen 1985). As students bring more sociable meanings to bear on tasks, the activity can get out of hand and be transformed into a game relevant to dating relationships and football rather than the lesson that the teacher had in mind. Moreover, mergers can confuse the students about the appropriate rules of conduct. What is going on may be unclear and endless debate can arise when such lack of clarity is present.

Teachers have tipping points at which they feel that the inclusion of sociable affairs begins to disrupt the completion of tasks (Bidwell and Friedkin 1988). At some point teachers utilize framing strategies to "flood out" problematic behaviors (that is, a directed effort to break down or disrupt certain situations) and "flood in" appropriate ones (Goffman [1974] 1986). If students are highly motivated, the teacher has more leverage over students and is more likely to successfully tweak or realign students back on task, primarily through bridging ties and amplifying beliefs and values that participants already hold (Snow et al. 1986).

WHEN TENSIONS MOUNT: SITUATIONAL MICROPOLITICS

Oppositional states usually arise between academic and sociable affairs in a classroom when students are not interested in the course subject and have little concern for grades (Dreeben and Barr 1988). This lack of academic resolve is partly a result of background and partly a result of the topic's lack of relevance to adolescents' lives (Cummins 1989; Haroutunian-Gordon 1991). In low-resolve settings, youth tend to focus more on sociable affairs and oppose efforts to redirect them on-task. Teachers frequently contain such oppositional tendencies by using teacher-centered task structures and rigid behavioral controls. In such circumstances the social world of adolescents diverges from the academic world but is suppressed or hindered from outward expression. Sociable situations still persist in private and students resent efforts to mobilize them back onto schoolwork.

When unmotivated students enter student-centered tasks, they may take the opportunity to socialize and openly rebel from academic work. In these classrooms tasks are transformed into games or jokes or simply supplanted by sociable affairs (McFarland 1999: Chapter 16; McFarland 2001). Under such circumstances the conflict is in the open and a combative, rebellious atmosphere persists despite teachers' efforts to contain and suppress such behavior. Taking such a conceptualization to its logical outcome, one would hypothesize that classrooms composed of students with low academic resolve, dense friendship networks, and greater sociable opportunities will have the greatest rate and distribution of classroom conflict between students' sociable frames and teachers' task frames.

The potentially combative relationship between academic and sociable affairs is best illustrated through the example (taken from previous research) of an actual classroom and the multiple tracks of activity that take place during a single class period (see McFarland 1999). My observation of one particular class period in an Algebra 2 class demonstrates how sociable and task situations can coexist in a combative manner. It illustrates how students and teacher adapt to one another's behavior, and how social and academic situations persist in spite of each party's attempt to rid the classroom of the other interaction framework. In describing this class period, I will not relate all of the discourse that transpires nor the full retinue of data collected on the set-

ting because my interest here is merely conceptual illustration. Note that
while I use names throughout the account for ease of reference, they are pseudonyms to protect the confidentiality of the subjects.

Algebra 2 class has all the organizational conditions discussed above that
could lead it to become a combative environment. It is composed of students
who are neither very interested in math nor very concerned about grades. The
students are well connected as friends and the class is taught in primarily student-centered formats. The teacher, Mr. Ellis, is a middle-aged African
American male with a degree in mathematics and progressive teaching goals.
On the class day in question, students enter the class and sit in their separate
friendship cliques at three different locations within the room. Because students were able to choose their own seats, their work groups aligned nearly
perfectly with their friendship selections. At the front is a clique of five African
American females in their sophomore year of high school. At the back of the
room is a clique of five white sophomores, two of whom are females and three
of whom are males. These students are the most motivated and attentive but
only mildly moreso than their classmates. On the right side of the room is a
third clique of two junior African American males and two white females, one
of whom is a sophomore and the other of whom is a junior. Both the mixed-
race and African American student cliques have little or no interest in algebra,
but they share a keen interest in their friends.

As students sit in their groups, they excitedly banter about their weekends, parties, boys, girls, and the like, while a few hurriedly copy the homework assignment due at the beginning of the class. As the bell rings, the
teacher takes roll quietly at his desk and exchanges a few sociable remarks
with the black females at the front of the room. After a few minutes, he rises
and begins to lecture, demonstrating how to do various math problems from
an overhead projector. A few of the white students listen, but most of the other
students continue to socialize. The white students at the back of the class are
relatively quiet, but they privately socialize and copy homework problems
from their neighbor as they intermittently listen to what the teacher says.
Every now and then, an African American male student in the mixed-race
clique will complain, "I don't understand what you're saying," or the less serious, "Why don't we ever do field trips like other classes?" Soon the volubility
of social discourse is so high that the teacher struggles to hear his voice over
his students. At this point the teacher turns to the most vocal clique, the
African American females, and makes a few reprimanding remarks. "Clarisse,
why did you bring your biology book in here, and why aren't you listening!?"
Clarisse replies with a joke to which all her friends respond with laughter,
"Ahh, Mr. Ellis I don't listen in there either!" After chastising another member
of the clique, Mr. Ellis turns back to the overhead, but few listen and the
socializing gets even louder. Mr. Ellis begins to make even more dramatic
efforts to acquire control by openly shouting at students, "Sit down!," "Get
your calculator out!," and "I am not going to keep this up!"

About fifteen minutes into the class, the teacher is pacing back and forth at the front of the room and shouting at the top of his lungs, "CAN I HAVE YOUR ATTENTION??!! CAN I HAVE YOUR ATTENTION!!??" It finally gets quieter as students in the mixed-race clique laugh back in low voices that mimic his, "YYEESSS!!!" The classroom is somewhat quieter now and Mr. Ellis asks, "Who did the homework?" Students reply with jokes of their own. One boy from the mixed-race clique shouts, "I was absent!" to which a couple of his friends shout, "Dude, you never do it!" and the teacher laughs in disbelief. Another winks at his friends saying, "I was in real bad shape Friday and got busy this weekend!" (implying he was hung over and partying). Others throw forth their humorous excuses and the teacher once more explodes, "IF YOU ARE NOT LISTENING, SHUT YOUR MOUTH!!" The class grows somewhat quiet again and Mr. Ellis starts to walk around the room with his grade book, noting which students did their homework. As he passes each desk, he tells the student how awful his or her grade currently is. Meanwhile the students go back to socializing and even start announcing their grades to the rest of the class. It becomes a game to see who has the lowest score, and one of the African American males at the side of the room believes he has won, so he stands with his fists triumphantly raised in the air as his classmates laugh and cheer him on. After recording students' completed homework, the teacher publicly chastises the class for its grades and then proceeds to do more problems at the overhead.

The white student clique reacts to the teacher's anger by quieting and paying more attention. The students in the African American and mixed-race cliques react by temporarily relegating their sociable activity to private backstage arenas. This only serves to further distance the sociable situations of the problematic students from the teacher. Hence while the students adjust to the teacher's demands, only the white clique is persuaded to make academic work its primary focus. In contrast, the mixed-race and African American cliques adjust to the teacher's demands but keep the social frame as their primary focus. Their private sociable activity persists as a separate story line that adjusts to its environment. About halfway through the class period, the teacher stops lecturing at the overhead and assigns homework to be started during class. As Mr. Ellis sits down, the students openly socialize once more so that the sociable frame jumps back into public view, where it persists for the rest of the class period. The white clique males and the mixed-race clique males interact more frequently during this phase of the lesson, and this draws the white clique back into sociable affairs.

In sum, the majority of students in Algebra 2 this day only attend to task-related talk as a secondary track of activity. This is especially true for the African American female clique and the mixed-race clique since they make little effort to even conceal their disdain for class tasks. Even when sociable affairs become private, they remain the primary focus for the students who merely tolerate the teacher's lecturing in the background. An occasional joke or complaint voiced at or by the teacher becomes fuel for further sociable conversations among students in their groups. Apart from the white clique, the

Algebra 2 students never really leave their friendship relations and sociable frame behind. The teacher, on the other hand, remains an agent of the academic frame. He succeeds in persuading the white clique to switch its situational focus, but only intermittently. In short, the teacher tries to sustain participation and focus on academic affairs, while the African American female and mixed-race cliques sustain their own sociable situations and interpretive frameworks in juxtaposition to his efforts; and off to the side, a less vocal clique of white students enters and exits the variety of academic and sociable situations throughout the class period.

The example of Algebra 2 class illustrates how two types of primary frameworks can exist in contention and compete with one another for adherents. Throughout the class period, sociable affairs had greater sway over the majority of students. The academic routines led by the teacher only acquired the intermittent commitment of the white student clique during a lecture, and only then because it was amplified by the teacher's negative sanctions and threats. In order to perform a successful lecture, the teacher needed students to make the academic routines and interpretive modes the focus of their attention. However, the relevance of the lecture and its academic rules were undermined by the presence of personal friends and the fact that the students were disinterested in the content of the lesson. When the teacher changed the activity to one of seatwork, students openly disregarded their work and socialized loudly with one another, thereby establishing the sociable frame's uniform dominance in the setting.

DOMINANT INDIVIDUALS, CLIQUES, AND COALITIONS

In many classrooms subsets of students take the lead in play and work situations (Metz 1978; Cohen and Lotan 1997). As such, actor involvement in the construction and elaboration of interaction frames is uneven. Certain cliques and individuals dominate discourse and therefore have greater influence on the definition of classroom situations. These dominant individuals are typically popular among classmates and above-average students (McFarland 2001). If they are not members of the formally dominant clique, then they are at least members of a tightly bound clique (high closure). Students with social support more successfully perform on public terrain than those who are isolates and social pariahs. Student and teacher audiences are highly judgmental and socially reinforced students are the most resilient actors in these moments of sanction and ridicule (Giordano 1995; Merten 1998; McFarland 1999).

Dominant individuals and cliques greatly influence the definition of classroom situations (Cohen and Lotan 1997). As resilient actors they manipulate frameworks in an effort to obtain greater control over interaction. How academic and sociable situations coexist depends in part on how dominant actors form political regimes within classrooms. Regimes can form in classes between a clique and a teacher or among cliques of students. In the former case, we find an allied regime that reigns with the teacher and tasks, while in the latter case we find a warring regime that combats the teacher and tasks. These regimes and alliances lead certain sets of individuals to dominate both academic and sociable affairs, thereby acting as junctures across the multiple primary frames, and the coexistence of multiple situations is allowed as long as the regime or alliance retains its dominance.

In general, dominant students will act in the direction of their social support since they risk losing their status within the group when they behave in ways that counter their audience's proclivities or norms (Sherif 1948; Homans [1950] 1992; de Waals 1982; Fine 1987). Hence in classes with motivated students, the dominant cliques and individuals tend to form alliances with teachers. Such a political coalition between student cliques and the teacher is allowed by the teacher because dominant students facilitate instructional processes by participating in tasks (see Diani [1996] on inclusion). Moreover, this regime is often seen as desirable by the teacher because co-optation of the dominant clique removes resources from the sociable frame, lessening competition with academic endeavors for student adherents. However, this alliance frequently has a price since even the most motivated dominant students will make social digressions, jokes, and occasionally challenge the teacher despite their heightened leadership and involvement in tasks. Hence teacher alliances with dominant students draw in social elements to tasks, but afford such performance privileges only to the more vocal students (Gordon 1957).

Some teachers prefer to ally with the most successful students rather than the most interactive or dominant students (Cusick 1973). This strategy has a mixed effect on the classroom. The teacher bridges to engaged students in an effort to keep the instructional process moving at a good pace and retain control that dominant students sometimes abuse. However, by doing this, the teacher can polarize the social structure of adolescents into specialized cliques. The students aligned with the teacher become active in tasks and the previously dominant students begin to specialize in sociable affairs. This can lead to two separate classroom situations that persist at opposite ends of the room and in contention with one another.

In classrooms where the students are unmotivated, the dominant clique or coalition of students can become a warring regime against the teacher and tasks in an effort to acquire concessions and privileges. Warring regimes adopt certain behavioral tacks or framing strategies in an effort to acquire control of the classroom situation. As described in the case of Algebra 2, the teacher used negative sanctions and indirect forms of speech to breach sociable affairs and flood students out of the public stage. Such a strategy sought to deconstruct the competing frame of interaction not only by making adherence to it more costly through negative sanctions (such as warnings) but by constraining participation, thereby preventing such endeavors from continuing (through loss of resources and commitment).

Dominant individuals and cliques in Algebra 2 used similar strategies to combat academic interpretations of events. Students used complaints and challenges to breach academic affairs. Such complaining and public confessions of confusion serve to slow down the task, draw attention to problems endemic to the endeavor, and basically demobilize student involvement in tasks (Hansen 1989). Students also used jokes to distance the evaluations that the academic frame placed on them through low grades and negative teacher sanctions. Constant joking and ridicule of academic affairs served to devalue its identity-attributions and make sociable activities of play and gossip appear to be more meaningful and rewarding streams of activity in which to participate (McLaren 1986; Woods 1983).

Therefore dominant individuals (teachers or students), cliques, and coalitions use various interaction strategies to deconstruct the competing frame and amplify their own. They do so to redirect audiences and establish a dominant interpretive framework in the classroom. Powerful individuals and cliques find that their efforts to establish a dominant mode of interaction are facilitated by forming coalitions or alliances with others. For instance, in the example of the Algebra 2 class, the friendship structure consisted of three cliques (the African American female clique, the white clique, and the mixed-race clique). During the first semester, these cliques were somewhat loosely interconnected, with the mixed-race clique acting as a unifying bridge between the clique of African American females and the clique of white students. In fact, the African American females and the mixed-race clique of students even mobilized as a coalition against the teacher in many disputes, becoming the locus of conflict in the class. The African American female clique in particular liked to aggravate and disrupt the teacher, and the mixed-race clique reinforced such efforts. Since the class was generally unmotivated, the rebellious coalition even acquired the occasional social support from the clique of white students, making it nearly an uprising at times. Throughout the year the coalition of rebellious students successfully subordinated task interpretations to those of the sociable framework, transforming the classroom situation (see Diani [1996] and Snow et al. [1986] on realignment).

However, political alignments and alliances are seldom static. In today's schools student populations change as pupils move in and out of the classroom and school during the year and even semester. As such, political alliances that establish routines of interaction can readily change the definition of the classroom situation. The greatest change in political alignments arises when a teacher or student leaves the class. Teachers seldom leave classrooms in mid-semester, but in certain instances (e.g., pregnancy, dismissal, or voluntary leave) a teacher will exit the setting, leaving a long-term substitute or new teacher to enter. Even when a teacher falls ill for a day and a substitute shows, there is a noticeable change in student behavior. Hence merely removing or replacing one particularly dominant individual can have drastic effects on political alignments.

When students leave a class, the changes to the classroom friendship network can be more subtle. In my observations the greatest changes in high school classroom networks occur at the start of a new semester. In many year-long classes, a few students alter their course schedule in mid-year, thus leaving a class and entering another class as a new student. The loss or addition of certain individuals creates a shift in the entire social structure, leading certain cliques and coalitions of students to fall apart and others to rise. This in turn alters which individual or clique has more social support and ability to influence public discourse.

Such a shift actually occurred in the example of Algebra 2 class. There the coalition of rebellious students imploded in the second semester when a new African American female, Anice, was introduced to the class and decided to sit with the mixed-race clique. The clique of African American females had previously included all of the African American females in the class. They interpreted Anice's group selection as an act of snobbery and began to insult and gossip about her. This offended the mixed-race clique, who then hardened their clique boundary and dissolved their alliance with the African American female group. Toward the end of the year, the clique of African American females began to socialize more with the teacher, while the mixed-race group socialized with the third clique of white students. As a result of these new political alignments, the classroom situation was slightly reframed. Sociable affairs remained dominant, but they now took place in distinct locales of the class. The African American females took on a playful, flirtatious, but no less disrespectful tone with the teacher; the mixed-race group became more recalcitrant and challenging; and the white students became class clowns (see McFarland 1999: Chapter 16; McFarland 2001).

Not all shifts in the classroom situation have structural leads. Actors can manipulate or tweak frames in an effort to alter student participation. An adept actor can manipulate frames to his or her advantage. Individuals are more successful at such manipulations in situations where they deftly use framing tactics aimed at select individuals with the greatest social clout in the setting (Goffman [1967] 1982). Framing strategies that affect dominant students have the greatest impact on the classroom situation as a whole. However, actors can also succeed without changing the classroom situation. They can simply maneuver through risky social situations without attracting any negative evaluations from either interpretive frame (see McFarland 1999: Chapter 10).

CONCLUSION

This article characterizes classrooms as small group settings wherein multiple streams of activity occur and are interpreted from at least two frameworks of interaction: academic and sociable doings. These situations often arise simultaneously in a classroom and compete for student adherents. The extent to which multiple situations and frameworks of interpretation oppose or align with one another depends on the organizational characteristics of each situation or set of affairs. This work argues that a wedge is placed between task and sociable doings when academic work is not aligned with students' lived experiences and interests, or when students see little value in the content of the curriculum (Dreeben [1968] 2002; Bidwell and Friedkin 1988; Haroutunian-Gordon 1991). Such disillusionment leads adolescents to gravitate away from academic work to sociable affairs and to define the latter in opposition to tasks (Fine 1987; Ogbu 1987). Teachers can contain sociable affairs through teacher-centered routines but the resistance to academic work will remain latent and subversive. When tasks are student centered, latent resistance can manifest in open revolt. Moreover, when dense networks of friends are present in a disillusioned class, they may compete with the teacher's control even in transmittal formats. Nonetheless, the opposite also tends to be true: open instruction for interested, engaged students enables the diffusion and reinforcement of positive academic values and authentic dialogue (Nystrand 1997). Hence the relevance of materials as well as the formal and informal organization of relationships within the classroom greatly defines the manner in which academic and social worlds relate to one another (McFarland 2001). With multiple loci of interaction in classrooms, it becomes evident that teachers are not the only audience to whom students adjust when performing in class. Students outnumber the teacher and the pastiche of interpersonal friendships and alliances can reflect several dominant audience foci. Apart from the teacher, popular students have been found to alter classmate perceptions and behaviors (Cohen and Lotan 1997)—as have friendship cliques of well-connected pupils (Cusick 1973; Bossert 1979; Plank 2000). What has not been fully explored is how and when dominant individuals and groups, whether teachers or students, sway classrooms to adopt one interaction framework rather than another.

Dominant actors and cliques are the political agents of classrooms, and they constantly lay claim to definitions of the classroom situation by promoting particular interpretations and doings. The teacher is invariably an agent of academic affairs and may constantly try to focus students' attention on work and mobilize them to complete prescribed tasks (Jackson 1968; Hammersley 1974, 1976; Snow et al. 1986). Students, on the other hand, can be agents of alternative interpretations of academic affairs and even agents of more playful sociable doings that have nothing to do with prescribed tasks (McFarland 1999). Students frequently comply with the teacher's demands, but such compliance often entails some adaptation of rules and procedures and the outcome of tasks diverges slightly from the script's expected outcome (Hansen 1989). Divergence is even more pronounced when students collude on the sidelines to develop and present counterclaims to the teacher's definition of the classroom situation (Alton-Lee, Nuthall, and Patrick 1993).

Combative political maneuvers are more complex. Resistant pupils adopt behaviors that on the one hand demobilize their peers' adherence to academic work, and on the other draw favorable attention to other collective endeavors and interpretive modes that educators generally find incompatible with the goals of schooling (McLaren 1986). Combative teachers adopt similar behaviors in return and breach adolescents' side conversations and sociable affairs and then redirect student attention by redeveloping interest in academic work (McFarland 1999). As such, the classroom setting is one where commitment to a single endeavor and interpretation is seldom fully won but must be constantly worked out and negotiated (Dreeben [1968] 2002; Powell, Farrar, and Cohen 1985; McNeil 1986).

But interaction strategies are not all that dominant actors need to perform in order to establish their definition of the classroom situation. Also relevant in this world are coalitions or alliances. Since multiple audience foci and situational loyalties can exist in classrooms, teachers frequently reach out and ally with more dominant sets of students by incorporating their interests or giving them privileges of discourse. Such alliances help the teacher focus attention on tasks and mobilize participation toward completing them. In this manner teachers co-opt other loci of activity removing resources (that is, participants) from competing collective endeavors. However, student groups can also ally and present the teacher with a large, unified coalition. Due to their numbers and propensity to act collectively, coalitions of student cliques can draw enough participation away from tasks that academic work never gets done. In other words, student coalitions are capable of commencing and fulfilling classroom rebellions.

This conceptualization views classrooms as small group settings composed of multiple simultaneous frameworks with mechanisms that wedge interpretive frameworks apart, resulting in divergent moral obligations that these misaligned frameworks of interaction can impose on students. Much of social experience is complex and ambiguous (Merton 1976) and a number of contradictory interpretations can be made of the same action. By making the multiplicity of situations a starting point for classroom conceptualizations, we see the logic of behaviors that frequently occur within classrooms. Moreover, we see the natural state of high school classrooms as one where tensions can easily mount. Classrooms are settings wherein order and task behavior are never established as permanent features, but are perpetual questions that teachers and students politically confront and negotiate in the everyday life of school.

Acknowledgments

This research was funded by the National Science Foundation, the Spencer Foundation, and the Institute for Educational Initiatives at the University of Notre Dame. I would like to extend special thanks to Warren Kubitschek for his thoughtful comments that helped give shape to this chapter. I am also greatly indebted to Robert Dreeben, Charles Bidwell, John Padgett, and the late Roger Gould for their helpful comments on earlier drafts of this manuscript.

REFERENCES

Alton-Lee, Adrienne, Graham Nuthall, and John Patrick. 1993. "Reframing Classroom Research: A Lesson from the Private World of Children." *Harvard Educational Review* 63:50–84.

Barr, Rebecca and Robert Dreeben. 1983. *How Schools Work*. Chicago: University of Chicago Press.

Benford, Robert and David A. Snow. 2000. "Framing Processes and Social Movements: An Overview and Assessment." *Annual Review of Sociology* 26:611–39.

Bidwell, Charles E. 1965. "The School as a Formal Organization." Pp. 972–1022 in *Handbook of Organizations*, edited by James G. March. Chicago: Rand McNally.

Bidwell, Charles E. and Noah E. Friedkin. 1988. "The Sociology of Education." Pp. 449–71 in *Handbook of Sociology*, edited by Neil J. Smelser. Beverly Hills, CA: Sage.

Blau, Peter M. [1964] 1996. *Exchange and Power in Social Life*. New Brunswick, NJ: Transaction.

Boaler, Jo. 1997. *Experiencing School Mathematics: Teaching Styles, Sex and Setting*. Buckingham, UK: Open University Press.

Bossert, Stephen T. 1979. *Tasks and Social Relationships in Classrooms: A Study of Instructional Organization and Its Consequences*. Cambridge, UK: Cambridge University Press.

Branaman, Ann. 1997. "Introduction." Pp. xlv–lxxxii in *The Goffman Reader*, edited by Charles Lemert and Ann Branaman. Malden, MA: Blackwell.

Cazden, Courtney B. 1988. *Classroom Discourse: The Language of Teaching and Learning*. Portsmouth, NH: Heinemann.

Cohen, Elizabeth and Rachel Lotan, eds. 1997. *Working for Equity in Heterogeneous Classrooms: Sociological Theory in Practice*. New York: Teachers College Press.

Coleman, James S. 1961. *The Adolescent Society: The Social Life of the Teenager and Its Impact on Education*. New York: Free Press.

Corsaro, William A. and Donna Eder. 1990. "Children's Peer Cultures." *Annual Review of Sociology* 16:197–220.

Corsaro, William A. and Thomas A. Rizzo. 1988. "Discussionne and Friendship: Socialization Processes in the Peer Culture of Italian Nursery School Children." *American Sociological Review* 53:879-94.

Cummins, Jim. 1989. "Empowering Minority Students: A Framework for Intervention." *Harvard Educational Review* 50:18–34.

Cusick, Phillip. 1973. *Inside High School: The Student's World*. New York: Holt, Rinehart and Winston.

de Waals, Frans. 1982. *Chimpanzee Politics: Power and Sex among Apes*. New York: Harper & Row.

Diani, Mario. 1996. "Linking Mobilization Frames and Political Opportunities in Italy." *American Sociological Review* 61:1053–69.

Doyle, Walter. 1986. "Classroom Organization and Management." Pp. 392–431 in *Handbook of Research on Teaching*, 3rd ed., edited by Merlin Wittrock. New York: Macmillan.

Dreeben, Robert. [1968] 2002. *On What Is Learned in School*. Clinton Corners, NY: Percheron Press/Eliot Werner Publications.

Dreeben, Robert and Rebecca Barr. 1988. "Classroom Composition and the Design of Instruction." *Sociology of Education* 61:129–42.

Edelsky, Carole. 1981. "Who's Got the Floor?" *Language in Society* 10:383–421.

Eder, Donna. 1986. "The Cycle of Popularity: Interpersonal Relations among Female Adolescents." *Sociology of Education* 58:154–66.

Eder, Donna. 1995. *School Talk: Gender and Adolescent Culture*. New Brunswick, NJ: Rutgers University Press.

Eder, Donna and Janet Lynne Enke. 1991. "The Structure of Gossip: Opportunities and Constraints on Collective Expression among Adolescents." *American Sociological Review* 56:495–508.

Festinger, Leon, Stanley Schachter, and Kurt Back. [1950] 1967. *Social Pressures in Informal Groups: A Study of Human Factors in Housing*. Stanford, CA: Stanford University Press.

Fine, Gary Allen. 1987. *With the Boys: Little League Baseball and Preadolescent Culture*. Chicago: University of Chicago Press.

Friedland, Roger and Robert Alford. 1991. "Bringing Society Back in: Symbols, Practices, and Institutional Contradictions." Pp. 232–66 in *The New Institutionalism in Organizational Analysis*, edited by Walter W. Powell and Paul J. DiMaggio. Chicago: University of Chicago Press.

Garfinkel, Harold. 1967. *Studies in Ethnomethodology*. Cambridge, UK: Polity Press.

Giordano, Peggy. 1995. "The Wider Circle of Friends in Adolescence." *American Journal of Sociology* 101:661–97.

Goffman, Erving. 1959. *The Presentation of Self in Everyday Life*. New York: Doubleday.

Goffman, Erving. [1967] 1982. *Interaction Ritual: Essays on Face-to-Face Behavior*. New York: Pantheon.

Goffman, Erving. [1974] 1986. *Frame Analysis: An Essay on the Organization of Experience*. Boston: Northeastern University Press.

Goffman, Erving. 1981. *Forms of Talk*. Philadelphia: University of Pennsylvania Press.

Goffman, Erving. 1983. "The Interaction Order: American Sociological Association, 1982 Presidential Address." *American Sociological Review* 48:1–17.

Goodwin, Marjorie. 1980. "He-Said-She-Said: Formal Cultural Procedures for the Construction of a Gossip Dispute Activity." *American Ethnologist* 674–94.

Gordon, Calvin Wayne. 1957. *The Social System of the High School: A Study in the Sociology of Adolescence*. Glencoe, IL: Free Press.

Gutierrez, Kris, Betsy Rymes, and Joanne Larson. 1995. "Script, Counterscript, and Underlife in the Classroom: James Brown versus *Brown v. Board of Education*." *Harvard Educational Review* 65:445–70.

Hallinan, Maureen T. 1976. "Friendship Patterns in Open and Traditional Classrooms." *Sociology of Education* 49:254–65.

Hammersley, Martyn. 1974. "The Organization of Pupil Participation." *Sociological Review* 22:355–68.

Hammersley, Martyn. 1976. "The Mobilisation of Pupil Attention." Pp. 104–15 in *The Process of Schooling: A Sociological Reader*, edited by Martyn Hammersley and Peter Woods. London: Routledge & Kegan Paul.

Hansen, Donald A. 1989. "Lesson Evading and Lesson Dissembling: Ego Strategies in the Classroom." *American Journal of Education* 97:184–208.

Haroutunian-Gordon, Sophie. 1991. *Turning the Soul: Teaching through Conversation in the High School*. Chicago: University of Chicago Press.

Homans, George. [1950] 1992. *The Human Group*. New Brunswick, NJ: Transaction.

Hurn, Christopher. 1985. "Changes in Authority Relationships in Schools: 1960–1980." Pp. 31–57 in *Research in Sociology of Education and Socialization*, vol. 5, edited by Alan C. Kerckhoff. Greenwich, CT: JAI Press.

Jackson, Philip W. 1968. *Life in Classrooms*. New York: Holt, Rinehart and Winston.

James, Deborah and Janice Drakich. 1993. "Understanding Gender Differences in Amount of Talk: A Critical Review of Research." Pp. 281–312 in *Gender and Conversational Interaction*, edited by Deborah Tannen. New York: Oxford University Press.

Kinney, David. 1993. "From Nerds to Normals: The Recovery of Identity among Adolescents from Middle School to High School." *Sociology of Education* 66:21–40.

Manning, Phillip. 1992. *Erving Goffman and Modern Sociology*. Stanford, CA: Stanford University Press.

Maynard, Douglas. 1985. "On the Function of Social Conflict among Children." *American Sociological Review* 50:207–23.

McFarland, Daniel A. 1999. *Organized Behavior in Social Systems: A Study of Student Engagement and Resistance in High Schools*. Ph.D. dissertation, Department of Sociology, University of Chicago.

McFarland, Daniel A. 2001. "Student Resistance: How the Formal and Informal Organization of Classrooms Facilitates Student Defiance." *American Journal of Sociology* 107:612–78.

McLaren, Peter. 1986. *Schooling as a Ritual Performance: Toward a Political Economy of Educational Symbols and Gestures*. London: Routledge & Kegan Paul.

McNeil, Linda M. 1986. *Contradictions of Control: School Structure and School Knowledge*. New York: Routledge & Kegan Paul.

Mead, George Herbert. 1934. *Mind, Self, and Society: From the Standpoint of a Social Behaviorist*. Chicago: University of Chicago Press.

Mehan, Hugh. 1979. *Learning Lessons: Social Organization in the Classroom*. Cambridge, MA: Harvard University Press.

Mehan, Hugh. 1980. "The Competent Student." *Anthropology and Education* 11:131–52.

Merten, Don E. 1998. "The Meaning of Meanness: Popularity, Competition, and Conflict among Junior High School Girls." *Sociology of Education* 70:175–91.

Merton, Robert K. 1976. *Sociological Ambivalence and Other Essays*. New York: Free Press.

Metz, Mary Haywood. 1978. *Classrooms and Corridors: The Crisis of Authority in Desegregated Schools*. Berkeley: University of California Press.

Michaels, James W. 1977. "Classroom Reward Structures and Academic Performance." *Review of Educational Research* 47:87–98.

Nystrand, Martin. 1997. *Opening Dialogue: Understanding the Dynamics of Language and Learning in the English Classroom*. New York: Teachers College Press.

Ogbu, John. 1987. "Variability in Minority School Performance: A Problem in Search of an Explanation." *Anthropology and Education Quarterly* 18:312–34.

Padgett, John F. 2001. "Organizational Genesis, Identity, and Control: The Transformation of Banking in Renaissance Florence." Pp. 211–57 in *Networks and Markets*, edited by James Rauch and Alessandra Casella. New York: Russell Sage Foundation.

Plank, Stephen. 2000. *Finding One's Place: Teaching Styles and Peer Relations in Diverse Classrooms*. New York: Teachers College Press.

Powell, Arthur G., Eleanor Farrar, and David K. Cohen. 1985. *The Shopping Mall High School: Winners and Losers in the Educational Marketplace*. Boston: Houghton Mifflin

Rawls, Anne W. 1987. "Interaction Order Sui Generis: Goffman's Contribution to Social Theory." *Sociological Theory* 5:136–49.

Roethlisberger, Fritz J. and William J. Dickson. 1939. *Management and the Worker*. Cambridge, MA: Harvard University Press.

Sherif, Muzafer. 1948. *An Outline of Social Psychology*. New York: Harper & Brothers.

Sieber, R. Timothy. 1979. "Classmates as Workmates: Informal Peer Activity in the Elementary School." *Anthropology and Education* 10:207–35.

Simmel, Georg. 1971. *Georg Simmel: On Individuality and Social Form* (Donald Levine, ed.). Chicago: University of Chicago Press.

Snow, David A., E. Burke Rochford, Jr., Steven K. Worden, and Robert D. Benford. 1986. "Frame Alignment Processes, Micro-Mobilization and Movement Participation." *American Sociological Review* 51:464–81.

Steinberg, Marc W. 1999. "The Talk and Back Talk of Collective Action: A Dialogic Analysis of Repertoires of Discourse among Nineteenth-Century English Cotton Spinners." *American Journal of Sociology* 105:736–80.

Stodolsky, Susan. 1988. *The Subject Matters: Classroom Activity in Math and Social Studies*. Chicago: University of Chicago Press.

Streeck, Jurgen. 1984. "Embodied Contexts, Transcontextuals, and the Timing of Speech Acts." *Journal of Pragmatics* 8:113–37.

Tannen, Deborah and Cynthia Wallat. 1987. "Interaction Frames and Knowledge Schemas in Interaction: Examples from a Medical Examination/Interview." *Social Psychology Quarterly* 50:205–17.

Waller, Willard. 1932. *The Sociology of Teaching*. New York: Wiley.

Wieder, Lawrence. 1974. "Telling the Code." Pp. 144–72 in *Ethnomethodology*, edited by Roy Turner. New York: Penguin.

Willis, Paul. 1977. *Learning to Labor: How Working Class Kids Get Working Class Jobs*. New York: Columbia University Press.

Woods, Peter. 1983. *Sociology and the School: An Interactionist Viewpoint*. London: Routledge & Kegan Paul.

IV

Teaching as an Occupation

9

The Governance of Teaching and Standards-Based Reform from the 1970s to the New Millennium

William A. Firestone

> Perhaps the distinguishing characteristic of school systems is the vague connection between policy formation at both high and middle levels of the hierarchy and its implementation at the level where instruction takes place—the classroom. (Dreeben 1970:48)

Robert Dreeben was one of a handful of sociologists in the 1960s and 1970s examining teaching as an occupation. One of his contributions over thirty years ago in *The Nature of Teaching* (1970) was to point out and analyze the limited governability of teaching from central sources. In charting the aspects of teaching that made it more or less governable, he provided reasons why it is difficult to direct or control teaching from high and middle levels of the hierarchy. Since then education has become much more an object of governmental attention and educational reform has become a full-time political business—if too disjointed to be called a continuous enterprise. A fair body of research on teaching and policy implementation has grown up along with a whole host of reform efforts. In this chapter I will ask if any of this has made teaching any more governable than it was thirty years ago.

To address this question, I will first review Dreeben's analysis of why teaching is difficult to govern. I will then briefly review some of the less sociological critiques of teaching in the United States, which led some to want to govern teaching more tightly. Next I will describe some of the changes in the governance of education since publication of *The Nature of Teaching* with an emphasis on the recent standards movement. Finally, using data from three states where documentation has been especially extensive, I will explore how state testing—a central element of the standards movement—has influenced the governance of teaching.

William A. Firestone • Graduate School of Education, Rutgers University, New Brunswick, New Jersey 08901.

Stability and Change in American Education: Structure, Process, and Outcomes edited by Maureen T. Hallinan, Adam Gamoran, Warren Kubitschek, and Tom Loveless. Eliot Werner Publications, Clinton Corners, New York, 2003.

THE GOVERNANCE OF TEACHING

In saying that it is difficult to govern teaching, Dreeben does not argue so much that teachers are autonomous as vulnerable. He paints a picture of teachers caught between the directives of government and rigidities of bureaucracy on the one hand and the independence and varied needs of children on the other. To begin with teachers must comply with the directives of their employers: "Teachers are salaried employees; they agree, through a written (or unwritten but formal) contract with a school board on what tasks they shall perform in exchange for pay" (Dreeben 1970:46). The employment contract gives administrators rights to direct the work of teachers. Free professionals (e.g., self-employed doctors and lawyers) do not face the same restrictions. Moreover, schools are environments filled with rules and regulations that teachers as well as students are obligated to understand and follow.

On the other hand, the main task of teachers is to gain the cooperation of students to engage in academic work. While teachers are employees, students are conscripts. This means that up to a certain age they are required to attend, but little else is clearly mandatory. Students are not remunerated. They work for grades and they must follow school rules. Yet according to Dreeben, the teacher's job—especially with younger students—is to teach them the meaning of grades and that it is important to follow rules. Thus the formal bureaucratic rules and incentives only work after teachers have successfully educated students to the meanings of these otherwise abstract symbols. Moreover, teachers always work with groups of students with different needs, capacities, and interests. Teachers often find themselves teaching a common curriculum to divergent students. For all of the exhortations to individualize instruction, the challenge is to do so when the teacher must attend to twenty or thirty different students. Thus while the employment contract governs the work of teachers, there is no comparable control over the numerous students on which teachers' work depends (Dreeben 1970).

This dilemma—that teachers must respond to both administrators and students who have conflicting demands and expectations—might be untenable were it not for a number of mitigating factors that Dreeben (1970) points out. Most of these factors are limitations of formal authority rather than means to gain student cooperation. For instance, while schools are formally bureaucratic with a line authority relationship running from a school board to teachers, there is a competing ideology of professionalism. According to this ideology, professionals undergo extended training, develop specialized expertise, and (in some definitions) undertake to protect the welfare of their clients. In return for applying specialized knowledge to protect the welfare of their clients or patients, professionals are granted considerable autonomy from public and hierarchical oversight.

Dreeben (1970) was aware of the many problems with using the professional ideology to increase teacher autonomy. The question of what is a profession can become a sterile, definitional exercise, but most people agree that teaching is not fully professionalized. When professionals work in organizations, the challenge of reconciling the principles of professionalism and formal organization are quite complex and are resolved differently with different occupations, leaving those occupations with different degrees of autonomy. In addition, the professional ideology assumes that professionals police their own members because they have the expertise to do so, but teachers typically work alone with little knowledge of what their peers are doing. When they try to find out, they have the same problems that principals do. Finally, the major teachers' associations are unions that do not subscribe fully to the professional ideology or seek to get others to comply with it. Thus the idea of professionalism can blunt formal authority, but only to a limited extent.

Another factor that eases teachers' vulnerability to both students and administrators is the nature of school rules. Dreeben (1970) points out that most school rules govern pupil behavior rather than core instructional tasks. Thus much of the regulation in some schools focuses on dress codes, wearing hats, and standing in lines. There is less specification about how teachers teach. The partial exception is that many—though not all—schools and districts have traditionally had centrally developed curricula specifying the content to be taught in which grades and often in what sequence. This is especially true in core content areas and those like mathematics that are seen as sequential, so that certain topics must precede others. Still, modes of instruction are usually left to individual teacher preference.

Others have talked about the zoning of authority that gives teachers considerable autonomy in the classroom and administrators greater control over schoolwide issues. Marks and Louis (1997) recently identified four empowerment domains: school operations and management, students' school experiences (including dress codes and the like), teachers' work life, and control over classroom instruction. They argue that teachers generally have limited impact and interest in the first, a great deal of input into the fourth, and variable input into the middle two. Moreover, empowerment with respect to those middle domains contributes the most to improved teaching.

Another reason that instruction is not extensively regulated is that supervision turns out to be problematic. According to Dreeben (1970), supervision is the task of getting teachers to act according to policy in the instructional domain through a mix of policymaking, surveillance, and help. Some would also add that supervision can be reinforced through the distribution of sanctions. Supervision rarely works well because teachers are observed so infrequently and for such short periods of time that it is difficult to know if supervisors have obtained a reliable, valid assessment of how each one teaches. In addition, even though policies are formalized, criteria for good instruction are typically ambiguous and subject to debate in specific instances. Finally, children may change their behavior during formal evaluation sessions to either protect or undermine the teacher, so that sampled teaching may not be typical. For all of these reasons, principals' diagnoses of teaching problems and prescriptions for improvement rarely have independent legitimacy with teachers.

Even if they did have such legitimacy, principals do not control strong sanctions that can be used to influence teachers. They rarely hire or fire. Merit pay is extremely unusual in schools and then may be tied to test scores, not the principal's judgment. Principals can control important but less consequential factors such as the distribution of plum assignments, but this is not often enough to greatly influence teachers (Dreeben 1970).

When taken together the argument that teaching is at least in part a profession, the zoning of authority in schools, and limitations on principal supervision tend to undermine the force of the employment contract. If not giving teachers substantial autonomy, these factors tend to ease the tension between formal demands and student independence. Beyond that dilemma, though, is another source of teacher vulnerability: ambiguity about intended outcomes (Weick 1976). This ambiguity has many sources. For instance, teachers engage in short-term activities (teaching specific lessons) in order to have the long-term outcome of students' knowledge. Because knowledge develops over the long term, it is often difficult to know to whom to attribute results when a child succeeds or fails. In addition, teachers teach more than the academic curriculum. They socialize students to appropriate adult behavior, and the very structuring of the experience of school contributes to that in ways that go beyond the explicit actions of individual teachers—as Dreeben ([1968] 2002) explains in *On What Is Learned in School*. Finally, while there is agreement on which subjects should be taught in school, there is not always agreement on what should be taught within each subject. Nor, in spite of formal curricula, is the coordination of what is taught across grades very effective. The result is often considerable repetition and wasted time (Schmidt, McKnight, and Raizen 1996). These and other sources of ambiguity may contribute to Dreeben's (1970) observation that teachers would often like more—rather than less—guidance from administrators about what they should teach.

CRITIQUES OF TEACHING

To address issues of educational improvement, the organizational and occupational analysis of teaching that Dreeben was so important in developing needs to be linked to understandings of the general nature of teaching and how it influences what students learn. Teaching has been criticized extensively during the twentieth and early twenty-first centuries, perhaps more than it deserves to be (Berliner and Biddle 1995). Moreover, the criticisms have come from so many directions that it is sometimes hard to imagine what teachers could do to appease all their critics.

One common criticism is that teaching is emotionally flat and intellectually unchallenging (Elmore 1996). Cuban (1993) points to the persistence of teacher-centered instruction in American education. In this form of teaching, teachers do most of the work. They spend huge amounts of time telling students facts and giving them circumscribed assignments to carry out. Students have little choice in what they study, limited opportunity for movement, and few chances to work together on projects. This strategy effectively reduces teacher vulnerability to students, but at best it is a more effective strategy for teaching children facts to remember than a way to help them explore ideas, make applications to out-of-school settings, or develop habits of inquiry. In the 1980s several research teams pointed out how in negotiating with students, teachers exchanged limited intellectual demands for order and compliance (Powell, Farrar, and Cohen 1985). This was a related mechanism to cope with vulnerability and administrative emphasis on decorum at the expense of intellectual development.

Criticism of the limited intellectual depth of American education took other forms. Some pointed to the quick coverage of topics, limited depth, and excessive repetition of the same topics at the same low level in the curriculum (Schmidt, McKnight, and Raizen 1996). In mathematics Stigler and Hiebert (1999) suggest that teachers follow an endless process of demonstrating procedures and having children practice them, occasionally broken up by checking homework. The emphasis is on learning to carry out procedures with little consideration of application, the larger mathematical ideas behind these procedures, or the connections among ideas.

Critiques of teaching in the United States are much more extensive than I have described here. Defenders of the American educational system have been less likely to argue that it works well than that some children, notably those with wealthy parents and families with more extensive intellectual capital, do well in the system. The real losers are the children of the poor (Berliner and Biddle 1995). These criticisms and the partial defenses provided an important context for thinking about what form educational policy should take when governments became more active in the educational arena.

THE CHANGING GOVERNMENTAL CONTEXT OF TEACHING

Although *The Nature of Teaching* was written over a decade after the Brown desegregation decision and its enforcement by federal troops in Little Rock and five years after federal civil rights legislation and the first Elementary and Secondary Education Act, Dreeben (1970) was still right in describing education as primarily a local enterprise. In most places a locally elected school board raised funds and hired a superintendent who ran the educational bureaucracy. Teachers and administrators were vulnerable to parents and taxpayers but relatively independent of other levels of government.

While the local governance structure of schools has remained in place, higher levels of government—especially the state—have become increasingly intrusive. The increasing state role is partly a response to the changing funding of education. In the nineteenth century, education was locally funded. However, the state share increased gradually after World War I through the 1980s. Since then the proportions have been fairly consistent, with state and local governments each contributing 42 percent and the balance coming from the federal government (National Center for Educational Statistics 2000).

Increasing state funding has enhanced state governments' interest in education. This interest has been enhanced further by school finance litigation, which has often forced state governments to invest more in education and direct most funding to the poorest districts. As suits became more frequent in the 1990s and the grounds of these suits shifted to the inadequacy of the education received by poor children, the pressure to engage more directly in defining an adequate education and ensuring that it is provided has increased. At the same time, state capacity to make—and sometimes oversee the implementation of—policy increased. State education bureaucracies more than tripled between 1957 and 1986. They added analytic capacity and chief state school officers became more aggressive and policy oriented. State legislatures also grew during the same period. There were simply more people to make state policy (Firestone 1990). As states made more policy, it seems unlikely that they gained influence at the expense of local boards and districts. Instead, it appears that more policy was made overall as districts and schools became important filters, amplifiers, and interpreters of state edicts. The results of all this activity were difficult to predict (Fuhrman and Elmore 1990).

One of the most important expansions of state policy was the movement to adopt standards and assessments. Because it is a rather direct attempt to increase the central direction of teaching while rationalizing the educational process, this movement is especially useful for pursuing Dreeben's analysis of the governance of teaching.

At least two streams feed into the current thinking about state standards. One has been an interest in increasing the accountability of local entities, local educators, and students to the state. Many ideas about accountability come from the business world and are developed in the fields of economics and political science. As thinking about accountability has become more explicit, there has been a shift from accountability for input and capacities (such as funding, buildings, and appropriate certification) to outcomes as measured through student assessments. A standards-based accountability system would, at a minimum, include content standards specifying the knowledge or skills that students are expected to acquire and tests or assessments aligned with those standards. In a weak accountability system, the publication of testing data should provide incentives for local entities and educators to improve. In strong systems student performance standards would be added to define proficient performance and rewards and punishments would be linked to the achievement of proficiency. These rewards and punishments can include student promotion and graduation, individual or collective merit pay for teachers, school takeovers by the state, and removal of staff. They are intended to provide more powerful incentives than those existing in weak accountability systems (Adams and Kirst 1999).

The accountability stream is strong on ensuring responsiveness to state standards but does little to clarify the content of standards. This gap has been filled in some states by professional associations of content experts that include, but are rarely dominated by, teachers. The National Council of

Teachers of Mathematics (NCTM) has led the effort that has achieved greatest visibility. In the association's first efforts to specify standards, its definition of mathematical power as "an individual's abilities to explore, conjecture, and reason logically, as well as the ability to use a variety of mathematical methods effectively to solve non-routine problems" signaled an attack on the intellectual vapidity of American teachers criticized by others (National Council of Teachers of Mathematics 1989:5). Later documents have set out a suggested content and a preferred pedagogy to accompany that content (National Council of Teachers of Mathematics 2000). The latter is notably at odds with the historically dominant American approach to teaching described by Cuban (1993) and others.

The relationship between the accountability and content streams of thinking about state standards is uneasy. The NCTM's most recent documents have been ambivalent about state testing systems that are not designed to provide diagnostic information to teachers (National Council of Teachers of Mathematics 2000). While some states have tried to model their standards on those of the NCTM and related agencies, it is not always clear that the advocates of strong accountability are consistently comfortable with the content associations' definitions of high achievement.

Still, standards and assessments spread rapidly in the last thirty years. While New York State has had its regents' exams for a very long time, many people date the rise of state testing from Florida's adoption of a minimum competency test in the 1970s. By 1982, 36 states tested students (Odden and Dougherty 1982). Now almost every state has at least the minimal elements of a standards-based accountability system. Forty-seven states have some kind of state standards, all fifty test students in at least one grade, and 45 provide report cards on school test scores, thereby providing the key elements of a weak accountability system (Editorial Projects in Education 2001).

While everyone has adopted standards at some level, there is also considerable variation in the standards and assessment policies that states are enacting. For instance, 44 states test students in mathematics but only 23 do so in social studies. States differ in the grades in which students are tested, how often they are tested, and the test formats used. Moreover, there is little agreement among states that they should adopt strong accountability systems. Only twenty states have policies that reward high-performing schools (sometimes these rewards are quite small) and only fourteen administer punishments to low performers. Some states always seem to be in the process of strengthening their accountability system, often postponing the date by which sanctions will really be administered (Editorial Projects in Education 2001).

Moreover, state standards and assessments programs have faced a variety of technical and political problems. For instance, in the early 1990s content experts and cognitive psychologists (among others) advocated moving away from multiple-choice tests to performance assessments requiring multiple responses or portfolios of student work as a way to encourage more intellectually challenging instruction (Resnick and Resnick 1992). A few states experimented with such strategies but they proved problematic. The idea of modeling more intellectually challenging tasks ran afoul of the need for high reliability in accountability systems where rewards and punishments, or even school reputations, were on the line. The new assessments also appeared more expensive and time consuming. Other states had problems in setting cut points for what would constitute proficient performance and changed the numbers of students reported to pass a particular test.

There were also some dramatic changes in assessment systems. At one point content experts pointed to California as a state that exemplified high standards and useful assessments. However, the political climate of the state changed quickly, leading to new standards that rejected the views of the content associations and a more conservative approach to assessment (Kirst and Mazzeo 1996). Arizona adopted and then rescinded a performance-based assessment system in about one year amidst a plethora of problems including implementation difficulties, technical problems with assessments, and bickering among leaders of the state's Republican party (Smith, Heinecke, and Noble 1999). In other states parents and students have protested and boycotted new assessments although advocates of such systems could always point to surveys showing that, for the most part, parents support the idea of testing students (Olson 2000; Public Agenda 2000).

In sum, most states have adopted some elements of standards-based reform but states differ substantially in the elements adopted and the quality of policy enactment. Moreover, the popularity of such policies varies noticeably.

THE STANDARDS MOVEMENT AND CHANGES IN TEACHING

In theory the standards movement should have substantial influence on teaching. One of the classic ways to control work is to measure and reward its outcomes (Mintzberg 1983). The standards movement certainly measures important outcomes and in that regard might intervene into the process of teaching more than many other state or federal policies. There is, in fact, a substantial body of research and criticism on the evils of what is referred to colloquially as "teaching to the test," which suggests that such policies can affect teaching substantially and often negatively (Corbett and Wilson 1991; Smith 1991; McNeil 2000). I now review recent findings from three states (Maryland, Kentucky, and New Jersey) that have introduced new standards and assessments that reflect, to some extent at least, thinking similar to that in the professional associations' standards statements and with varying strength of sanctions linked to those standards (see Table 1). Where possible the focus is on late elementary or middle school mathematics tests. I also summarize findings from a study of four states to provide an overview of the effects of standards policies on teaching.

Table 1. State Policies and Teaching Practice

	Maryland	Kentucky (1992–98)	New Jersey
Assessments	Multipart, constructed response assessments that assess communication and reasoning and let students choose how to solve problem.	Assessment using constructed response items and writing and (for a short time) mathematics portfolios.	Assessments using multiple-choice and open-ended items that require more reasoning and explanation than in the past.
Sanctions	Threat to take over low-performing schools.	Distinguished educators to help and possible state takeover. Cash incentives.	Ambiguous and limited.
Changes in Content	Shift in subjects to tested areas and to more challenging topics within subjects.	More time on writing. Time on subjects higher in tested years. Move to nontraditional topics within subjects.	Shift to topics tested on assessments with lower pass rates. More challenging topics in math. Instability in science.
Changes in Instruction	Extended tasks like those on test but with minimal change in basic instructional approaches.	More open-ended and challenging tasks were presented, but potential was not always realized.	Sensitizes teachers to new instructional approaches with limited actual change.

Maryland

Maryland introduced a new assessment system in 1991 and has persisted with it for a long time. The Maryland State Performance Assessment Program (MSPAP) includes multipart, extended constructed-response items that require students not only to calculate, but also to show and justify their work using pictures, text, and mathematical notation (Firestone, Mayrowetz, and Fairman 1998). The system includes the threat of reconstitution, a form of state takeover for schools failing to show sufficient progress toward a very high pass rate on the quite challenging state tests.

The history of Maryland's program shows the multiple factors that are required for state sanctions to have their impact (Firestone, Mayrowetz, and Fairman 1998). The state's sanctions had limited impact and other factors were at work. For instance, after a few years it became clear that the only

Maryland schools likely to be taken over were a few schools in high-poverty areas in Baltimore and surrounding suburbs. In other schools the probability was low but attention grabbing. As one administrator explained, "Even if the fire isn't on your block, if it's three blocks away, you check your fire insurance" (Firestone, Mayrowetz, and Fairman 1998:108).

Other governance arrangements had an impact. Maryland had county-wide school districts with board members either appointed or elected at large. By contrast, Maine—another state included in the study—had very small districts with members elected from voting districts. Board members were closer to their communities in Maine and the communities showed little interest in state testing unless scores were very low. Maryland board members were more isolated from their communities, and Maryland administrators met regularly in very effective job-alike groups with their opposite numbers in the Maryland State Department of Education who reminded them of state requirements, consulted with them, and generally had considerable impact on local thinking. Moreover, Maryland provided some training opportunities for teachers that brought state ideas directly to some of those in the classroom. Thus effective state-district communication reinforced formal sanctions (Fairman and Firestone 2001).

As predicted in past research, Maryland teachers reported spending more time on tested subjects and less on those not tested. They also changed their curriculum emphasis within subjects but in ways that were more positive than suggested by earlier research on teaching to the test. They deemphasized the more rote aspects of subjects and added more challenging topics. In writing, teachers somewhat decreased their focus on spelling and grammar to focus more on writing for many purposes, analysis of text, and comprehension. In math, number facts were deemphasized to focus more on mathematical communications and applications, areas stressed in the NCTM standards (Koretz et al. 1996).

Almost half the teachers in one survey reported a shift in materials used to those like the state test (Koretz et al. 1996). These were long, multipart activities that often required students to collect and analyze data in relatively realistic situations—for example, survey their peers or measure the height of a water tower using its shadow and that of an object of known length and principles about congruent shapes. These activities provided opportunities for deeper mathematical thinking and making connections between taught topics and the real world. However, when the emphasis was on preparing for tests, teachers tended to teach procedures for the complex tasks, showing students how to organize their work to score high. Moreover, similar changes were taking place in Maine districts not so influenced by state tests but with access to university-based professional development. The instructional changes were often in the form of particular behaviors that were assimilated into ongoing instructional practices. Moreover, they were rarely greater than those that might have been brought about by local professional development programs in districts sensitive to national trends but without strong accountability systems (Firestone, Mayrowetz, and Fairman 1998).

Kentucky

The Kentucky Instructional Results Information System (KIRIS), later changed to the Commonwealth Accountability Testing System, was introduced as one of the most comprehensive state educational reform efforts in America. Resulting from school finance reform litigation that eventually found the whole state educational system unconstitutional, the larger reforms encompassed local governance, finance, assessment, accountability, and teacher education among other areas. The state developed broad standards that were operationalized through the KIRIS. The testing system was changed several times (Poggio 2000). Beginning with off-the-shelf items, it quickly developed as a test relying almost completely on open-ended performance items with scored portfolios of student writing and, for a short time, mathematics assignments. From the beginning, however, the KIRIS was to be part of a strong accountability system with formally designated "distinguished educators" to help low-performing schools, state takeovers in the most extreme cases, and cash incentives for teachers in high-performing schools. By the mid-1990s numerous reliability and other technical measurement issues had arisen. In order to support the state assessment system more reliably, open-ended items and the mathematics portfolio were dropped or deemphasized after 1998.

Kentucky also provides some evidence on mechanisms working in strong accountability systems. In a study of six schools that received cash awards, Kelley and Protsik (1997) found evidence that supported theories about how incentives should influence practice. Teachers in these schools generally understood what was required of them, believed that the tasks were realistic, and saw a connection between their effort and ultimate performance. There was some contradictory evidence, however. Teachers in these schools believed that high student mobility and year-to-year variation in student ability undermined the validity of the state tests as measures of their own performance (an issue that Dreeben raised about supervision) and doubted that they would receive rewards until the checks arrived. They had been more motivated by threats of sanctions. Other research has confirmed that the threat of sanctions was more powerful than the promised rewards. Rewards had limited value both because of doubts that they would be provided and because teachers reported being motivated more by intrinsic incentives, to the point that some found the idea of cash bonuses insulting (Kannapel et al. 2000).

At best, then, the data on rewards from Kentucky are ambiguous. On the other hand, Kentucky has invested more in helping schools meet accountability system goals than have other states—most notably with its Distinguished Educator program and the Kentucky Leadership Academy. A mix of test score data and teacher interviews suggests that the Distinguished Educator program was helpful in changing practice although it sometimes did so by focusing attention on short-term tactics for raising test scores (Kannapel and Coe 2000).

Kentucky teachers adjusted the content taught to the tests. Some of these responses were not as constructive as in Maryland. For instance, by the mid-1990s the quantity of testing had become so extensive that the state was testing reading, writing, and science in fourth grade and mathematics, social studies, and arts and humanities in fifth grade. In one study teachers reported increasing the amount of time that they devoted to subjects in the years that they were tested. They spent 30 percent more time on mathematics in fifth grade than in fourth and 45 percent more time on writing in fourth grade than in fifth (Stecher and Barron 1999). Other researchers confirm in particular the increased emphasis on writing at the expense of some untested areas and suggest that the new focus was a response to both the writing and mathematics portfolios. These researchers suggest that testing in arts and humanities led to increased attention to those subjects in rural high schools (Kannapel et al. 2000).

Within subject areas the focus on topics shifted so that teachers spent less time on traditional topics and more time on newer ones, especially in tested years. Thus fifth grade math teachers devoted more attention to algebraic ideas, statistics and probability, and mathematical communication than their fourth grade colleagues. These led many teachers to worry that they were not attending sufficiently to the basics although this might have been applauded by national content experts (Stecher and Barron 1999; Kannapel et al. 2000). Especially during the period when the math portfolio was required, the KIRIS encouraged teachers to change their materials and strategies. In mathematics they moved to longer, more open-ended tasks that required more extensive reasoning and greater comprehension. Even with the portfolio, however, there was some tension between instructional needs and assessment requirements. Some of the teachers who best understood the requirements of the portfolio system found that "scaffolding" to help students learn to think mathematically came close to providing assistance and guidance that would raise students' scores and would therefore be viewed as inappropriate interference (Borko and Elliott 1999). Teachers who did not fully understand the subject taught or challenging instructional methods often used open-ended tasks as teaching materials. However, they provided such explicit steps for solving open-ended problems or detailed scoring rubrics that the students had little discretion in how to proceed; the cognitive challenge was lost (Kannapel et al. 2000).

New Jersey

New Jersey's fourth grade Elementary School Performance Assessment (ESPA) was introduced in math, science, and language arts in 1999. The tests are intended to be aligned with state standards that reflect national standards, especially in mathematics and science. For instance, the mathematics standards expect students to "develop the ability to pose and solve mathematical problems in mathematics, other disciplines, and everyday experience" and "communicate mathematically through written, oral, symbolic, and visual forms of expression" (New Jersey State Department of Education 1996:4–9). The tests include a mix of multiple-choice items and performance tasks that require relatively short responses but do ask children to describe the steps in their work, interpret charts and graphs, and generally press beyond the traditional mathematics curriculum. The state has set targets for school performance: specific percentages of students should score at proficient level and, where that level is not reached, certain improvement goals should be met. However, neither rewards nor punishments are clearly stated. Moreover, while the state expects teachers to receive one hundred hours of professional development every five years, and there is a broad expectation that this professional development will be aligned with the state standards, regulations identifying which professional development activities count toward the one hundred hours and which ones do not are extremely ambiguous. The state does not directly support any school improvement efforts (Firestone et al. 2001).

Even without incentives, topics covered within subjects have changed since the ESPA was introduced. In mathematics there was a clear movement away from more to less traditional topics in the first two years of test implementation. Teachers spent less time on whole number operations and more on patterns, functions, statistics, and other areas. This change clearly reflected the content of the state tests and state standards. In science, teachers reported increasing the attention to almost all topics in 1999—the first year that tests were administered—and decreasing the attention to almost all topics the following year. A more rigorous comparison of time spent on specific topics identified four with statistically significant decreases between 1999 and 2000. What seems to have happened is that before tests were administered and scores were released, local educators were generally anxious about the science test and focused on it more than they had in the past. When scores were actually released, proficiency rates in science were uniformly higher than in language arts and educators went back to their earlier emphasis on the latter area. This example suggests that teaching content covered on tests can result not only from the items used or from the presence or absence of tests, but also from the comparative difficulty of different subject area tests (Firestone et al. 2001).

The ESPA sensitized teachers to new instructional strategies. In interviews with 58 teachers, 25 said that they tried to get students to explain their thought processes more; 26 used manipulatives more in mathematics and hands-on materials more in science; 23 required more writing in mathematics and science; and 22 emphasized problem solving more. Yet changes in practice were much smaller. Direct observation confirmed extensive use of manipulatives but showed that in most cases manipulatives were not used as intended by their developers to explore mathematical ideas. Instead they became new tools for practicing algorithms in highly structured ways. Teachers still had students practice procedures rather than explore ideas in both subjects, and in mathematics teachers focused on procedural knowledge rather than mathematical ideas or the connections between them (Firestone et al. 2001).

The New Jersey research suggests that as assessments use a greater variety of formats, teaching to the test may become more differentiated. A survey of practices related to test preparation identified some practices (like teaching test mechanics) that seemed to reflect a narrow focus on the assessment, while other activities (like having students use rubrics to score each other's work) were closer to some of the newer ideas dominating the content associations. The latter were more closely correlated with reports of increasingly challenging instructional practices (e.g., having students explain their work or write about mathematics) than the former.

Comparative Research

There is very little research comparing the effects of different states' standards and assessment policies. One exception, by Wilson and Floden (2001), combines both school case studies and surveys in four states. Two of these (Maryland and Kentucky) have been reported on elsewhere in this paper, and two (Michigan and California) have not. Among their observations is the conclusion that standards-based reform not only means different things in different states, but also that it is interpreted differently by different people in the same state and even the same school. Thus in spite of assessments, orienting documents, formal presentations, professional development, and experience with the program, consensus on the changes required by programs is limited. The effect of this ambiguity is that teachers become the real locus of authority in their own classrooms for which practices are adopted and which practices are not.

Another important factor in decision making about instruction is students. When teachers rate the importance of different influences on their practice, they rank the needs of students first—slightly ahead of state and district standards and state assessments. Even allowing for a possible reporting bias, teachers still attend a great deal to whom they are teaching as well as governmental forces.

When looking at instruction, there is evidence of the effects of assessment on instruction but those effects do not overwhelm or greatly modify conventional practice. In fact, the most striking observation is that among teachers, schools, and states, teachers are balancing the old and the new, basics and problem solving, phonics and whole language instruction. A more careful analysis suggests a tilt toward the traditional in both mathematics and language arts. As the authors conclude:

> Teaching remains largely traditional, with some additions. Teachers tinkered, adding selected innovative strategies like writers' workshop or manipulatives, weaving those practices into a recognizable, relatively stable practice. (Wilson and Floden 2001:208)

DREEBEN AND THE STANDARDS MOVEMENT

The standards movement was intended to make education more governable by central authorities. It explicitly sought to define educational outcomes, measure those outcomes, and use the resulting data to influence instruction— either simply by providing authoritative feedback or by linking results to rewards and punishments. Recent studies of teachers' responses to the standards movement suggest some shift away from the fundamental ungovernability of teaching identified by Dreeben, but not much. Extended central control is most apparent with regard to curriculum coverage. What gets taught is at least partially a response to such policy levers as the content of state standards, subjects tested, topics tested within a subject, years in which subjects are tested, item format, and even the passing scores set for particular tests. Responsiveness, however, is not the same thing as improvement. Taking the viewpoint of national subject matter associations, one sees some positives— the deemphasis of topics that experts think have received too much time in favor of others that have received too little. But there are also clear negatives, most notably inconsistencies from grade to grade or year to year that make little educational sense but reflect the exigencies of a large bureaucracy implementing a complex new system.

Instructional approaches are less amenable to, although not immune from, central control. The major pattern seems to be the addition of specific practices that accommodate the test without changes in teachers' basic instructional paradigms, such as MSPAP-like items in Maryland or the addition (but not necessarily appropriate use of) manipulatives in several states. The changes noted have potential in that they could be the first steps on the way to greater reform of practice. However, as they stand they usually represent short-term accommodations. Whether they lead to a fundamental rethinking remains to be seen.

This balance with greater influence on curriculum than instruction appears to be an accentuation of the pattern that Dreeben noted over thirty years ago. He pointed out then that local districts influenced content more than instruction, and that central authorities seem to influence curriculum relatively more than instruction. These findings apply to state interventions today.

What is interesting is the uniformity of effects in spite of the variety of state practices. Both Wilson and Floden's (2001) analysis and mine here note the similarity among states despite differences in formal incentives and a variety of state assessment characteristics, although the number of states included is still low. It may be that states have simply not mobilized enough authority to change the way that teachers achieve their balance between responding to central authority and the needs of children. This might be Dreeben's response, and it makes a good deal of sense in light of the variation in how people interpret the same policy. Accountability-oriented critics would recommend strengthening the incentives in light of this analysis.

It may also be that the problem is not one of authority but knowledge. Another set of critics has suggested that no matter how strong the incentives, teachers simply lack the knowledge to do what the content-association reformers in particular advocate. Part of the argument here is that government spends too much time fiddling with incentives and not enough time analyzing what needs to be learned when new policies are adopted and how that learning can be facilitated (Berman 1986; Cohen and Barnes 1993). Moreover, when one examines the actions and decisions of expert teachers using these approaches, the demands are considerable and quite different from what might have been learned from observing one's own teachers as a child (Shulman 1987; Carpenter et al. 1989). If that is true, then at least part of the response should be to increase learning opportunities for teachers, but that policy response is exceedingly rare and usually inadequate.

What is striking is how few analyses of the implementation of new policies have examined the tension between the demands of policy and the realities of the classroom. Wilson and Floden's (2001) observation about how teachers respond to children's needs first remains unusual. It needs to be verified since it depends on survey data where response bias could enhance the rating given to that factor. More generally, Dreeben's work suggests that it would be extremely useful to investigate how policy implementation reconciles the demands of central authority and students, and then to use a range of methods to ask how this issue is defined and responded to in a variety of settings.

Acknowledgments

The preparation of this paper was supported by two grants from the National Science Foundation: #9804925 and #9980458. The opinions expressed here are those of the author and neither NSF nor Rutgers University.

REFERENCES

Adams, Jacob E. and Michael W. Kirst. 1999. "New Demands and Concepts for Educational Accountability: Striving for Results in an Era of Excellence." Pp. 463–90 in *Handbook of Research on Educational Administration*, 2nd ed., edited by Joseph Murphy and Karen Seashore Louis. San Francisco: Jossey-Bass.

Berliner, David C. and Bruce J. Biddle. 1995. *The Manufactured Crisis: Myths, Fraud, and the Attack on America's Public Schools*. Reading, MA: Addison-Wesley.

Berman, Paul E. 1986. "From Compliance to Learning: Implementing Legally-induced Reform." Pp. 46–62 in *School Days, Rule Days: The Legislation and Regulation of Education*, edited by David Kirp and Donald Jensen. Philadelphia: Falmer Press.

Borko, Hilda and Rebekah Elliott. 1999. "Hands-on Pedagogy versus Hands-off Accountability: Tensions Between Competing Commitments for Exemplary Math Teachers in Kentucky." *Phi Delta Kappan* 80:394–400.

Carpenter, Thomas P., Elizabeth Fennema, Penelope L. Peterson, Chi-Pang Chiang, and Megan Loef. 1989. "Using Knowledge of Children's Mathematics Thinking in Classroom Teaching: An Experimental Study." *American Educational Research Journal* 26:499–531.

Cohen, David K. and C. A. Barnes. 1993. "Pedagogy and Policy." Pp. 207–39 in *Teaching for Understanding: Challenges for Policy and Practice*, edited by David K. Cohen, Milbrey W. McLaughlin, and Joan E. Talbert. San Francisco: Jossey-Bass.

Corbett, H. Dickson and Bruce L. Wilson. 1991. *Testing, Reform, and Rebellion*. Norwood, NJ: Ablex.

Cuban, Larry. 1993. *How Teachers Taught: Constancy and Change in American Classrooms, 1890–1980*, 2nd ed. New York: Teachers College Press.

Dreeben, Robert. [1968] 2002. *On What Is Learned in School*. Clinton Corners, NY: Percheron Press/Eliot Werner Publications.

Dreeben, Robert. 1970. *The Nature of Teaching: Schools and the Work of Teachers*. Glenview, IL: Scott, Foresman.

Editorial Projects in Education. 2001. *Quality Counts 2001: A Better Balance; Standards, Tests, and the Tools to Succeed*. Bethesda, MD: Editorial Projects in Education.

Elmore, Richard F. 1996. "Getting to Scale with Successful Educational Practices." Pp. 294–329 in *Rewards and Reform: Creating Educational Incentives that Work*, edited by Susan H. Fuhrman and Jennifer A. O'Day. San Francisco: Jossey-Bass.

Fairman, Janet and William A. Firestone. 2001. "The District Role in State Assessment Policy: An Exploratory Study." Pp. 124–47 in *From the Capitol to the Classroom: Standards-Based Reform in the States*, edited by Susan H. Fuhrman. Chicago: University of Chicago Press.

Firestone, William A. 1990. "Continuity and Incrementalism after All." Pp. 143–66 in *The Educational Reform Movement of the 1980s: Perspectives and Cases*, edited by Joseph Murphy. Berkeley, CA: McCutchan.

Firestone, William A., David Mayrowetz, and Janet Fairman. 1998. "Performance-based Assessment and Instructional Change: The Effects of Testing in Maine and Maryland." *Educational Evaluation and Policy Analysis*, 20:95–113.

Firestone, William A., Lora Monfils, Gregory Camilli, Roberta Y. Schorr, Jennifer Hicks, and David Mayrowetz. 2001. "The Ambiguity of Test Preparation: A Multi-method Study of One State." Paper presented at the annual meting of the American Educational Research Association, Seattle, WA.

Fuhrman, Susan H. and Richard F. Elmore. 1990. "Understanding Local Control in the Wake of State Educational Reform." *Educational Evaluation and Policy Analysis* 12:82–96.

Kannapel, Patricia J. and Pamelia Coe. 2000. "Improving Schools and School Leaders." Pp. 159–76 in *All Children Can Learn: Lessons from the Kentucky Reform Experience*, edited by Roger S. Pankratz and Joseph M. Petrosko. San Francisco: Jossey-Bass.

Kannapel, Patricia J., Pamelia Coe, Lola Aagaard, B. D. Moore, and Cynthia Reeves. 2000. "Teacher Responses to Rewards and Sanctions: Effects of and Reactions to Kentucky's High-stakes Accountability Program." Pp. 127–48 in *Accountability, Assessment, and Teacher Commitment: Lessons from Kentucky's Reform Efforts*, edited by Betty L. Whitford and Ken Jones. Albany: State University of New York Press.

Kelley, Carolyn J. and Jean Protsik. 1997. "Risk and Reward: Perspectives on Implementation of Kentucky's School-based Performance Award Program." *Educational Administration Quarterly* 33:474–505.

Kirst, Michael and Christopher Mazzeo. 1996. "The Rise, Fall, and Rise of State Assessment in California: 1993–96." *Phi Delta Kappan* 78:319–23.

Koretz, Daniel, Karen Mitchell, Sheila Barron, and Sarah Keith. 1996. *Final Report: Perceived Effects of the Maryland School Performance Assessment Program*. Los Angeles: National Center for Research on Evaluation, Standards, and Student Testing.

Marks, Helen M. and Karen Seashore Louis. 1997. "Does Teacher Empowerment Affect the Classroom? The Implications of Teacher Empowerment for Instructional Practice and Student Academic Performance." *Educational Evaluation and Policy Analysis* 19:245–75.

McNeil, Linda M. 2000. *Contradictions of School Reform: Educational Costs of Standardized Testing*. New York: Routledge & Kegan Paul.

Mintzberg, Henry. 1983. *Structure in Fives: Designing Effective Organizations*. Englewood Cliffs, NJ: Prentice-Hall.

National Center for Educational Statistics. 2000. *Digest of Educational Statistics, 2000.* Washington, DC: U.S. Department of Education.

National Council of Teachers of Mathematics. 1989. *Curriculum and Evaluation Standards for School Mathematics.* Reston, VA: National Council of Teachers of Mathematics.

National Council of Teachers of Mathematics. 2000. *Principles and Standards for School Mathematics.* Reston, VA: National Council of Teachers of Mathematics.

New Jersey State Department of Education. 1996. *Core Curriculum Content Standards.* Trenton: New Jersey State Department of Education.

Odden, Allan and V. Dougherty. 1982. *State Programs of School Improvement: A 50-State Survey.* Denver: Education Commission of the States.

Olson, Lynn. 2000. "Worries of a Standards 'Backlash' Grow." *Education Week,* April 5, pp. 1, 12–13.

Poggio, John P. 2000. "Statewide Performance Assessment and School Accountability." Pp. 73–97 in *All Children Can Learn: Lessons from the Kentucky Reform Experience,* edited by Roger S. Pankratz and Joseph M. Petrosko. San Francisco: Jossey-Bass.

Powell, Arthur G., Eleanor Farrar, and David K. Cohen. 1985. *The Shopping Mall High School: Winners and Losers in the Educational Marketplace.* Boston: Houghton Mifflin.

Public Agenda. 2000. *Survey Finds Little Sign of Backlash against Academic Standards or Standardized Tests.* New York: Public Agenda.

Resnick, Lauren B. and Daniel P. Resnick. 1992. "Assessing the Thinking Curriculum: New Tools for Educational Reform." Pp. 37–75 in *Changing Assessments: Alternative Views of Aptitude, Achievement, and Instruction,* edited by Bernard R. Gifford and Mary Catherine O'Connor. Boston: Kluwer Academic.

Schmidt, William H., Curtis C. McKnight, and Senta A. Raizen. 1996. *A Splintered Vision: An Investigation of U.S. Science and Mathematics Education.* Working paper, Third International Mathematics and Science Study, Michigan State University.

Shulman, Lee. 1987. "Knowledge and Teaching: Foundations of the New Reform." *Harvard Educational Review* 57:1–22.

Smith, Mary L. 1991. "Put to the Test: The Effects of External Testing on Students." *Educational Researcher* 20:8–12.

Smith, Mary L., Walter Heinecke, and Audrey J. Noble. 1999. "Assessment Policy and Political Spectacle." *Teachers College Record* 101:157–91.

Stecher, Brian M. and Sheila I. Barron. 1999. *Quadrennial Milepost Accountability Testing in Kentucky.* Los Angeles: Center for Research on Evaluation, Standards, and Student Testing.

Stigler, James W. and James Hiebert. 1999. *The Teaching Gap: Best Ideas from the World's Teachers for Improving Education in the Classroom.* New York: Free Press.

Weick, Karl E. 1976. "Educational Organizations as Loosely Coupled Systems." *Administrative Science Quarterly* 21: 1–19.

Wilson, Suzanne M. and Robert E. Floden. 2001. "Hedging Bets: Standards-based Reform Classrooms." Pp. 193–216 in *From the Capitol to the Classroom: Standards-Based Reform in the States,* edited by Susan H. Fuhrman. Chicago: University of Chicago Press.

10

The Regulation of Teaching and Learning

Tom Loveless

Americans spent over $2.7 trillion on K-12 public education in the 1990s. Public demand for reform, which burst forth as a potent political force in the 1980s, did not abate. School reformers turned their attention to improving the quality of teachers. This essay analyzes two different regulatory regimes. The first regulates instruction and is associated with long-standing efforts to change how teachers teach. Policies define the characteristics of good instruction and induce teachers to use particular instructional practices in the classroom. The second regime regulates teaching's outcomes and is associated with the school accountability movement. It defines the student learning toward which teachers should direct their instruction (in particular, the learning measured by achievement tests) and offers teachers incentives for attaining the desired results.

This essay compares and contrasts the assumptions of the two approaches and describes their politics and policies. Both approaches have encountered problems. Robert Dreeben's ideas on the state of teaching's technology are introduced to highlight the most serious threat to both regimes. I argue that attempts to regulate teaching are unlikely to have a substantive effect until a well-tested body of knowledge systematically links teaching practices to valued outcomes. The essay concludes with a discussion of the future of regulating teaching, including implications for teaching as a profession.

TWO REGULATORY STRATEGIES: ARGUMENTS AND ASSUMPTIONS

Two reform movements that appear to have little in common, the push to alter classroom instruction and the school accountability movement, are alike in attempting to regulate teaching. That is not how the movements' leaders view their own causes. Leaders of both movements routinely denounce regulation, which they detect in the other movement's reforms. But they insist that their own recommendations would allow teachers more freedom, not less. They are

Tom Loveless • Brown Center on Education Policy, Brookings Institution, Washington, D.C. 20036.

Stability and Change in American Education: Structure, Process, and Outcomes edited by Maureen T. Hallinan, Adam Gamoran, Warren Kubitschek, and Tom Loveless. Eliot Werner Publications, Clinton Corners, New York, 2003.

right about each other but wrong about themselves. Regulations limit the discretion of practitioners, in this case classroom teachers. That is precisely what
both reform movements attempt to do. The instructional reform movement
seeks to limit *how* teachers teach; the school accountability movement seeks
to limit *what* they teach (Hanushek 1994; National Commission on Teaching
and America's Future 1996; Darling-Hammond 1997).

Similar regulatory tools are employed by both regimes. Regulators of
instruction use teacher certification, learning standards, curriculum frameworks, tests, professional development, and bureaucratic oversight to promote
some forms of teaching and discourage others. Regulators of results use learning standards, tests, rewards and sanctions, and bureaucratic oversight to per-
suade teachers to teach some knowledge and skills and not others. The two
regimes are not mutually exclusive. To the contrary, they overlap and coexist
in most states' efforts to improve schooling.

A crucial difference between regulating instruction and regulating student
learning lies in these approaches' assumptions about teaching and learning.
For the first approach, teaching is all important and often indistinguishable
from learning. After all, advocates point out, the quality of one's education
depends almost completely on how one is taught. To provide a good education, the characteristics of good teaching must be known and encouraged. A
core activity of teaching is deciding, for a particular group of children at a particular point in time, what pupils should learn and how they should learn it.
A lesson that leaves children excited about learning and clamoring for more is
surely valuable, even if one cannot specifically describe what has been
learned. It logically follows that the primary control over both curriculum and
instruction should be in the hands of teachers, or some other authority with
intimate knowledge of teaching, rather than district administrators, parents,
the public, taxpayers, or state legislators—all of whom are distant from classrooms.

For the results-oriented approach, learning is not only paramount; it is
analytically distinct from the teaching that produces it. Children go to school
to acquire a body of knowledge that society's political institutions, through
democratic processes, have deemed essential to learn. The style of teaching
that goes into producing such knowledge is of little importance. Outcomes are
paramount. A results orientation holds that good teaching is any teaching that
produces students who know how to read and have mastered mathematics,
history, and science. The fifty to sixty teachers that the average student
encounters from kindergarten through high school graduation will employ a
variety of instructional methods representing a broad spectrum of educational philosophies. The value of an education stems from what is learned, not
how it is learned. If students graduate from high school not knowing what
should be known, it is inconceivable that exposure to a particular type of
teaching can compensate for that ignorance.

Despite their differences, both points of view share the assumption that
teachers make rational choices about how to act in classrooms. Those who

would regulate instruction believe that these choices should be shaped by the teaching profession's definition of an accomplished teacher and the institutions that train and certify teachers. Those who would regulate results believe that teachers are more likely to select productive means of teaching if incentives are offered that make raising student achievement especially attractive. Thus both points of view are optimistic about the power of public policy to influence teachers. Each has spawned a regulatory regime to implement its objectives.

POLICIES REGULATING INSTRUCTION

An effort to regulate instruction typically begins with an elite group of experts. A blue ribbon commission is convened that includes professional educators, experts on teaching, politicians, corporate executives, and representatives of teachers unions and other interest groups. One of the commission's tasks is to define the characteristics of good teaching. After an evidence-gathering phase that includes a review of the relevant research and the taking of testimony at public hearings, the commission issues edicts in an official document. These publications usually include a list of preferred instructional practices but, because such commissions are formed on the belief that conventional schooling needs to be changed, a list of discredited practices may also be offered.

In the short period from 1996 to 2001, an alphabet soup of prestigious panels issued this type of report, among them the National Commission on Teaching and America's Future; the National Board for Professional Teaching Standards (NBPTS); the National Commission on Math and Science Teaching for the 21st Century (known as the Glenn Commission for its chairman, John Glenn); the President's Committee of Advisors on Science and Technology; and the National Reading Panel (NRP). In addition, the National Research Council issued blue ribbon reports summarizing the research on effective teaching practices in mathematics and reading.

Most commissions release reports to great fanfare and are never heard from again, but the NBPTS and NRP have the potential to endure. The NBPTS was established as an ongoing entity by grants from several philanthropic foundations, most notably the Carnegie Corporation, and has received more than $109 million from the federal government. It awards honorary national certificates to selected teachers after an elaborate screening process that costs applicants $2,000 (usually paid for by local districts). Successful candidates receive salary bonuses in 44 states (Blair 2001; Archer 2002).

The National Reading Panel was created by act of Congress. Panel members were appointed by the director of the National Institute of Child Health and Human Development (NICHD), which funded a series of groundbreaking research projects on reading instruction in the 1990s. These studies documented the importance of phonemic awareness and phonics, especially for youngsters who experience difficulty in learning how to read. In a series of metanalyses, the NRP reviewed the NICHD research and other studies meeting high standards of quality, narrowing the analysis to research with experimental and quasi-experimental designs. The panel found that techniques featuring direct instruction, in which teachers systematically teach skills to youngsters, are the most effective methods for teaching reading. This conclusion drew intense criticism from supporters of whole language and other student-centered approaches (Coles 2001; Ehri and Stahl 2001; Garan 2001). In the 1990s the NICHD studies became a favorite of state legislators authoring phonics legislation (Allington 2001). In 2001 the NRP's recommendations were embraced by the Bush administration as providing the scientific basis for a national reading program.

National standards have been another source of instructional regulation. They also feature elite groups. Most of the groups writing standards were organized by professional associations representing educators in such subject areas as math, English, history, and so on (Ravitch 1995). Describing the content of a rigorous curriculum and spelling out "what students should know and be able to do" was advertised as the standards writers' chief task. And indeed, reforming the curriculum received attention. However, the reform of classroom teaching was also a top priority of several of the committees. Standards emerged with extensive, detailed, and prescriptive discussions of pedagogy, most notably the math standards of the National Council of Teachers of Mathematics (NCTM), the science standards of the National Academy of Sciences, and the English-language arts standards jointly authored by the International Reading Association and the National Council of Teachers of English (National Council of Teachers of Mathematics 1989; National Research Council 1994; International Reading Association and National Council of Teachers of English 1996; National Council of Teachers of Mathematics 2000).

Of the standards documents, the NCTM's *Curriculum and Evaluation Standards for School Mathematics* was almost immediately the most influential. In a historical context, this is surprising. The NCTM's instructional reforms embrace tenets of progressive education that, despite nearly a century of passionate advocacy, have failed to be accepted by teachers, parents, or the public (Cuban 1993; Ravitch 2000). In 1980—several years before the campaign for national standards had begun—the NCTM released *An Agenda for Action*, a document endorsing virtually every one of the instructional reforms that would surface again in the 1989 *Standards*. The *Agenda for Action* was ignored. But by draping the banner of national standards around the same set of instructional prescriptions, the NCTM's proposals flourished (Loveless 2001).

What, specifically, would the NCTM change about traditional math teaching? The standards target several facets of instruction, including how teachers should present lessons (child centered, an emphasis on solving real-world problems), utilize technology (extensive student use of calculators starting in kindergarten), employ textbooks and materials (less drill and practice, more frequent use of manipulatives), assess student learning (items with no single right answer on tests), and integrate math with other subjects to forge an interdisciplinary curriculum (students are to keep logs of their math learning and write reports about math). The standards also urge teachers to deemphasize the development of traditional skills, stating, "Clearly, paper-and-pencil activities cannot continue to dominate the curriculum or there will be insufficient time for children to learn other, more important mathematics they need now and in the future" (National Council of Teachers of Mathematics 1989). In addition to winning almost instant recognition as the nation's math standards, the NCTM standards were harnessed to several policy instruments. At the federal level, the NCTM doctrine was reinforced by hundreds of millions of dollars in grants offered by federal agencies, most notably the Office of Educational Research and Improvement and the National Science Foundation (NSF). It is important to note that most of these grants were not offered to study whether the NCTM reforms actually work—that was assumed—but only to facilitate their dissemination and implementation (Hoff 2001; for an exception see Klein et al. [2000]). John Bradley, mathematics program officer for the Education and Human Resources (EHR) division of NSF, told the *Christian Science Monitor* that the EHR spent "about $86 million in the past decade to fund thirteen multiple-grade level math-curriculum projects and build four implementation centers" (Clayton 2000). The NSF spent an additional $427 million dollars on a series of Systemic Initiatives that promoted the NCTM math reform and new science programs in states and local school districts (McKeown, Klein, and Patterson 2000). Other federal programs also provide support. Following the NCTM reform is a criterion for receiving honors from the federal government's Blue Ribbon Schools Program (Loveless 2000; Loveless and DiPerna 2001). The math portion of the National Assessment of Educational Progress (NAEP) is patterned after the NCTM, as is the federal Eisenhower Program that funds professional development in science and math.

The NCTM's influence extends down to states and local school districts. More than forty states model their state math standards on those of the NCTM, which means that they too diverge from content and promote particular teaching strategies in reforming school mathematics (Raimi and Braden 1998). States that have crafted their own criterion-referenced assessments use the NCTM standards as a model. The criteria for issuing state teaching certificates in mathematics invariably cite the NCTM as the reigning authority on good instruction. Local school districts use the NCTM's prescriptions to screen new math teachers for employment, as evaluation instruments for administrators' annual observations of math teachers' lessons, and in granting tenure to math teachers. Across the country districts hold professional development programs that train teachers to implement the NCTM pedagogy.

The NCTM standards are an excellent example of how elite opinion can coalesce around a common agenda—in this case changing the content and teaching of school mathematics—and then promote that agenda through an interlocking network of experts, bureaucrats, and political actors. This political dynamic is not unique and can be found in the development of regulatory policies on smoking, health research and cancer, energy, the environment, and agriculture (Ripley and Franklin 1987; Browne 1995; Fritschler and Hoefler 1996). The result is a regulatory regime with considerable power. Within a decade of the *Standards* release, the NCTM's view of good and bad teaching had been institutionalized in a broad swath of federal, state, and local policies. Converting elite opinion into public policy is no small accomplishment, but the real test for instructional reform is whether teachers change their day-to-day practice. In the case of the NCTM, this is particularly daunting when an organization that represents math teachers argues that most math teaching is deficient. The NCTM wants math teachers to teach differently than they currently do and differently than they have in the past. Change is not cost free. Substantial costs in time, materials, and autonomy are imposed on teachers. Resisters will bear the largest costs. The educational progressivism of the NCTM standards makes them unattractive to a large number of teachers.

The point being made here is irrelevant to the NCTM's educational philosophy. Regulations of any ideological stripe reduce teachers' discretion. As mentioned above, the National Reading Panel staked out a much different philosophical position than the NCTM, recommending that reading teachers use direct instruction to teach phonics. Several states passed legislation influenced by the NRP recommendations, and many progressive-minded teachers oppose the state mandates as restrictive. Teacher discretion has also been reduced (Coles 2001).

In the following sections, I discuss ideology at greater length. First, however, I describe results-based policies that regulate student learning.

POLICIES TARGETING LEARNING

An effort to regulate teaching's results typically begins in a political institution. Education was one of the most important issues in state and local political races in the 1990s. Responding to the public clamor for greater accountability and increased student learning, a state legislature, state board of education, or local school board defines a set of desired outcomes, devises a testing system for measuring student achievement, and offers incentives to schools for achieving goals. The simplest system, found in 45 states, issues school report cards on individual schools. Twenty-seven states feature accountability systems that either rate all schools by their performance or identify low-performing schools. States offer rewards and sanctions (sometimes both) as incentives. Twenty states give awards ranging from a public ceremony recognizing exemplary schools to cash awards granted to teachers and principals (Editorial Projects in Education 2001).

Sanctions vary. Simply publicizing student test scores might shame many low-scoring schools into improving, but fourteen states wield formal sanctions that penalize schools for low performance. In several states schools threatened with sanctions receive mandated assistance from the state for a period of time, culminating in a state takeover if necessary. Since 1988, when the state of New Jersey assumed control of the Jersey City School District, eighteen states have taken full or partial control of forty districts. This figure includes states that have disbanded elected school boards and created new boards under mayoral authority (Lemann 1998; Mezzacappa 2001). Florida is unique in offering vouchers to students in persistently low-performing schools.

Southern states were the earliest to establish monetary incentives for changes in student test scores. In 1984 the first state reward system was established in South Carolina. From 1984 to 1991, individual teachers and principals were singled out for rewards. The system was not based exclusively on student learning. Candidates had to be evaluated by their immediate supervisors. They were required to participate in professional development and could not have missed more than ten days of school during the school year. Educators nominated themselves for consideration. Teachers complained that the system pitted teacher against teacher (Flax 1991; *Education Week* 1993). After seven years the South Carolina legislature revamped the accountability system, instituting sophisticated calculations that used student background characteristics to predict schools' year-to-year gains on a norm-referenced achievement test. Schools that exceeded their Adjusted Gain Index qualified to share a statewide pot of money. The awards ranged from $15,000 to $20,000, but the money had to be spent on the school's educational program (e.g., books, computers, personnel) and could not go directly to teachers. The system received favorable reviews from accountability experts, but many educators complained that the entire system relied on a basic skills test that was incompatible with the state's curriculum standards (Clotfelter and Ladd 1996).

This system remained in effect until the legislature passed the Educational Accountability Act of 1998. A new criterion-referenced assessment (the Palmetto Achievement Challenge Test) was developed and tied to the state's curriculum frameworks. It was first administered in 1999 and school report cards were launched in 2001. The legislature complemented the incentive system with other reforms. Training in teaching styles using the state's standards, literacy coaches in fifty districts, and a training academy for principals were offered. Teachers and principals in highly ranked schools could receive up to $1,000 in salary bonuses. The accountability act also provides for state intervention in low-performing districts, and the state superintendent used this provision to strip the Allendale County School Board of power in June 1999 (Richard 2001, 2002).

Policymakers in South Carolina confronted several thorny questions as the state's results-based system evolved: describing learning goals with enough specificity to signal teachers what they are expected to teach; creating a valid test matching state curriculum standards; deciding whether to focus on gain scores or absolute levels of achievement; figuring out how to provide assistance to schools that fail; and deciding whether to offer rewards to individual teachers or entire school staffs. These questions surfaced again and again as states debated accountability systems in the 1990s.

THE POLITICS AND PITFALLS OF REGULATION

Understanding the politics of the two regulatory regimes begins with appreciating their intellectual origins. Seminal ideas have been generated by scholars inside and outside the field of education representing different disciplinary traditions. Typically (and I am painting with a broad brush here) the most powerful ideas about regulating instruction have come from scholars who study and write about instructional practice, the professionalization of teaching, and teacher training—in other words, from researchers in schools of education. Ideas about holding educators responsible for results (on the other hand) have come from outside education, mainly from the fields of management, economics, and political science. Indeed, in domains other than education, phrases such as "accountability for quality," "emphasizing outcomes," and "regulating for results" are common in public policy discussions (Wilson 1989; Moore 1995; Behn 2001).

This inside-outside pattern shapes the politics of regulation. Instructional regulations are likely to draw political support from educational experts; advocacy groups for professional educators; reform organizations; and officials in federal, state, and local educational bureaucracies. The elite commissions and standards-writing panels that produced the 1990s documents in instructional regulation were dominated by this constituency. Accountability regulations—on the other hand—are usually championed by governors, state legislatures, school boards, and other elected representatives pushing for change from outside the system.

These political tendencies pull most instructional regulation toward the ideology of progressive education and most results-oriented regulation toward the academic skills prized by the public. As surveys of the Public Agenda Foundation have shown, progressive ideas about how teaching should be conducted are extremely popular with scholars at education schools (Farkas, Johnson, and Duffett 1997). Such ideas are not popular with the public, which wants students to master the basics. In the 1990s candidates for public office seized on education as a winning campaign issue. In dozens of states, both Democratic and Republican governors were elected by promising to hold schools accountable for teaching children how to read, write, and compute proficiently.

Populist resistance is a serious threat to instructional regulation. Complaints about the NCTM pedagogy, for example, reached a critical mass in several locales (Loveless 1998). In California a coalition of parent groups and mathematicians mounted a vigorous campaign against the state's 1992 math framework, which faithfully followed the NCTM standards. They cited the NAEP statistics showing California students lagging behind almost every other state in math achievement. Even students from the most privileged socioeconomic circumstances scored abysmally. The state's board of education threw out the NCTM-influenced framework and adopted new state standards in 1997. The most noticeable characteristic of the standards is their strict neutrality on instructional practice, except for taking a firm stance against the use of calculators until the middle grades (California State Board of Education 1999). Nevertheless, critics complain that the standards endorse a "back to basics" approach, emphasizing computation at the expense of conceptual understanding and problem solving. Some predict that students will graduate from California schools without a grasp of mathematical concepts and incapable of solving complex math problems (Trafton, Reys, and Wasman 2001).

Problems for instructional regulation also arise when innovative approaches are implemented in schools. In one of the earliest implementation studies of NCTM-like math reform, David Cohen and Deborah Ball (1990) found that teachers frequently misinterpret recommendations about how to teach. Teachers might use manipulatives during a lesson, for example, but only as a prop to teach the algorithms and procedures that have always been taught—not as a tool for students to solve complex problems or model mathematical concepts. Yet these same teachers believe that they are employing the new instructional strategies that reformers urge them to use. In education such misinterpretations are commonplace because of spotty enforcement by administrators and lack of follow-up to professional inservice. Classroom instruction is rarely monitored.

Other problems of NCTM-inspired regulation are particular to certain grade levels. Elementary teachers lack the mathematical knowledge needed to teach effectively in the manner envisioned by the NCTM reformers (Ma 1999). High school teachers resist reorganizing the math curriculum from the traditional sequence (algebra, geometry, algebra II, calculus) to a series of integrated courses in which algebra, geometry, and calculus are taught together. In the ideal integrated courses, students tackle progressively more sophisticated material each year while exploring the connections among math's domains. Math at all grade levels is plagued by poorly designed materials. After studying textbooks that were written to follow the NCTM guidelines, Richard Askey (2001) identified several with shoddy mathematics.

Regulations targeting results have also experienced pitfalls. Teachers and principals resent policies that hold them accountable for student achievement, pointing out that a student's individual effort, family life, and peers (as well as other factors outside educators' control) strongly affect how much pupils learn. School accountability garners strong backing in public opinion polls, but the support of parents is strongest when student accountability is judged in the abstract. In several states parent groups have joined educators in opposing accountability systems. These protests have been loudest in states where students must demonstrate a minimum level of learning, usually on an exit examination, before they can graduate from high school (e.g., Virginia, Massachusetts, Arizona). Even though protesters seem to represent a minority of parents, they have succeeded in persuading states to delay graduation requirements or lower passing scores on exit examinations (Public Agenda 2000; Kennedy Manzo 2001).

A growing body of scholarship raises concerns about the possible adverse effects of accountability systems. This literature pointedly questions the wisdom of using testing and incentives to improve schooling. Linda McNeil (2000) has written extensively about Texas schools narrowing the curriculum to what is covered on the Texas Assessment of Academic Skills and teachers spending inordinate amounts of classroom time on test-taking skills. Daniel Koretz (1996) has documented the phenomenon of score inflation, how test scores rise irrespective of real learning when high stakes are tied to outcomes. Reasons for score inflation range from the innocent (students and teachers becoming comfortable with a test's format) to the unethical (educators preventing low-performing students from taking examinations). In a few cases, outright cheating has been discovered. Other studies have focused on the impact of accountability systems on low-achieving students, showing that students who are held back because of low test scores learn no more in subsequent years than similar students who are promoted. Moreover, there is evidence that tough standards increase the likelihood of marginal students dropping out of school (Jacob 2001). However, the effect may be offset by including school-level dropout statistics in state accountability systems (Bishop, Mane, and Bishop 2001).

In addition to opposition from parent groups and educational researchers, accountability systems have been plagued by technical problems. Errors in reporting test scores have been embarrassing to officials. Minnesota denied diplomas to 54 high school seniors in June 2000 before discovering during the summer that an error had been made in scoring the state's exit examination (Bowman 2000) and that the students had not really failed. New York City mistakenly ordered 9,000 students to mandatory summer school in 1999 based on faulty test data (Steinberg and Henriques 2001). Maryland postponed release of its 2001 tests scores when some schools registered swings in test scores that were so large as to be unbelievable (Argetsinger 2001). Vermont's early accountability system, which departed from standardized testing and rated portfolios of student work, was found to produce inconsistent evaluations from rater to rater (Koretz et al. 1994). Other states attempted to create criterion-referenced tests keyed to their own learning standards, a costly and time-consuming process. Relying on off-the-shelf standardized tests, even if not a perfect match with a state's curriculum, is far less expensive.

Thomas Kane and Douglas Staiger (2002) identified a persistent and potentially damaging technical flaw in accountability systems. All accountability systems rely on test scores to allocate rewards and penalties. School test scores, like any other measurement, contain naturally occurring error. A certain amount of variation will occur in an individual school's annual scores even if the school's underlying, real level of achievement remains unchanged. Kane and Staiger used California and North Carolina, which reward schools for a single year's improvement in scores, to illustrate the arbitrary nature of incentives ignoring this basic statistical property. Small schools, by virtue of having fewer students, exhibit more volatility in scores than large schools. In comparison to large schools with identical levels of achievement, small schools are more likely to be singled out as either having significantly improved (thereby deserving rewards) or having significantly declined (thereby deserving penalties). The lesson is clear: policymakers must take into account the statistical properties of tests that anchor incentive systems. Otherwise schools will be inadvertently rewarded or penalized based on characteristics irrelevant to performance (Kane, Staiger, and Geppert 2001).

The regulatory regimes that were erected in the 1990s to improve classroom teaching face several obstacles. Whether they direct the style and form of teachers' instruction or mandate the learning outcomes that teachers must pursue, today's education reformers encounter problems experienced by reformers of the past: political opposition from the public, distrust and resistance from teachers, the technical limitations of testing, and an array of shortcomings that do not become evident until policies are enacted. These obstacles cast a cloud over the future of both regulatory regimes. They could be overcome, however, if progress is made on strengthening teaching itself—especially when it comes to teaching's weak technology. Robert Dreeben has analyzed this aspect of the teaching profession from several angles.

DREEBEN ON TEACHING'S WEAK TECHNOLOGY

In *The Nature of Teaching*, Dreeben (1970:206) states that "the central problem of teaching as an occupation is *the state of its technology*" (see also Labaree 1997). This statement is as true today as it was when Dreeben made it in 1970. The state of teaching's technology has not progressed much in the intervening three decades. By technology Dreeben was not referring to today's computers, Internet-based learning, virtual instruction, or anything having to do with wireless devices or Silicon Valley. He meant a coherent set of principles and activities joining the means and ends of teachers' work and an authoritative body of knowledge—backed by science and accessible to practitioners—spelling out the essential tasks of teaching, how to do them, and why they are done.

The two types of regulation discussed in this essay are predicated on the existence of an effective technology. For the first type of policy, which directly regulates instruction, the assumption is explicit. Instructional regulations tell teachers how to teach. Consider teacher certification. Staffing classrooms based on certification systems that train and license teachers assumes that we know the tasks that teachers should be trained to do and how they should do them. Similarly, for veteran teachers certification by a national board assumes that mastery of a particular set of skills constitutes professional knowledge worthy of honor.

Dreeben discussed the quality of technology in four areas of teaching skill: the instructional process, motivating students, classroom control, and managing the social organization of classrooms. His conclusion is sobering.

This list clearly does not exhaust the full range of teaching activities (its technologies), but its components are both familiar and obvious. Though it refers to parts of the teacher's job that are both central to the occupation and the

subject of considerable research in the past, there is not a single area included which has well-known and established modes of proceeding such that
means, outcomes, and appropriate conditions can be related systematically.
That is, teaching is still carried on primarily according to uncodified rules of
thumb and through accumulated individual experience amounting to little
more than lore. At the same time there probably exists enough knowledge
and experience stored in individual heads to provide the basis for sophisticated technologies—were that knowledge and experience ever brought
together, codified, tested for efficacy, and communicated to teachers both in
training programs and on the job. (1970:87–88)

Three decades later Frederick Hess summarized the situation in words echo-
ing those of Dreeben. "In the case of education, there is no established and
research-based canon of essential knowledge" (2001:14).

The technological weakness of teaching undermines instructional prescriptions such as those of the NCTM. When dictating classroom instruction
to veteran teachers, retraining them and persuading them to employ new
approaches is the policy challenge. This is difficult to do if the recommended
strategies are not backed by a convincing body of research. There is research
supporting some of the NCTM's general ideas—for example, if organized cor-
rectly, having students work in small groups can be productive—but even
admirers of the standards acknowledge that the NCTM recommends practices
that have not been subjected to rigorous evaluation (Schoenfeld 1994; Hiebert
1999; Gamoran 2001).

The NCTM standards neither convey a technology nor employ a technological view of teaching. As a consequence they do not describe the conditions
under which the recommended practices function either well or poorly. The
question of calculator use illustrates the shortcoming. The standards assert
that calculators should be used in every grade, beginning in kindergarten.
This is based on studies of varying quality that show a slightly positive effect
on math problem solving—and no effect on students' computation skills—
when calculators are used in conjunction with traditional textbooks and
paper-and-pencil activities (Suydam 1979; Hembree and Dessart 1986; Smith
1996).

Set aside the issue of whether calculators are a good or bad idea and consider teachers' practical questions. How should calculators be used to facilitate
the learning of basic math skills? Can they be used to teach multiplication
facts to students who do not know their times tables? Should calculators be
used to allow students who do not know basic arithmetic to move on to algebra? Should they be used to teach basic skills and algebra simultaneously?
Which contributes more to success in mathematics, elementary students'
knowledge of arithmetic or problem-solving skills? Are there any dangers to
the use of calculators? The NCTM cannot give research-based answers to a
teacher posing these questions because not enough research has been conducted to guide classroom practice at this level of detail.

One might think that accountability systems are immune from being affected by teaching's technological weakness. Regulations that dictate content appear to operate independently from the selection of teaching strategies, but that is not true. By leaving it to teachers to determine how to produce student achievement, results-based policies assume that selecting the means of instruction is a manageable task for teachers once the ends of instruction have been clearly defined. In other words, this type of regulation also depends on the existence of an effective technology. Otherwise the logic of incentives collapses. Incentives are only effective if teachers can rationally select the approaches that reap rewards and avoid sanctions. If teachers choose effective instructional strategies based on hunch or luck, then good instruction should be regarded the same way as winning a lottery or picking the winner of a horse race. That is unacceptable for a rational system of incentives.

The two regulatory regimes discussed in this essay share a common problem, then, and it seriously threatens their potential to effect real improvement in classroom teaching. Without a reliable technology linking teaching's means and ends, the regulation of teaching is largely symbolic. Dreeben's distinction between the means and ends of teaching is crucial to this point. Regulating instruction targets the means of teaching; regulating learning targets the ends. Yet as Dreeben and countless other researchers have noted, the body of knowledge linking the two is exceedingly thin. Once severed from each other, statements of ideal teaching and learning cannot rise above the level of platitude since the relationship between cause and effect has not been established empirically. In the first case, teachers are told that they must teach a particular way but the recommended practices are either self-justifying (e.g., teachers must ask children to solve problems because problem solving is good) or they lead nowhere—certainly not to students learning the basic skills and knowledge that the public demands. In the second case, teachers are told that they must teach students particular content but are not told how the task can be accomplished. Declaring that all students will know the primary causes of the Civil War by the end of eighth grade is a goal, not a technology. How do teachers teach this knowledge and ensure that every student has learned it? The increased regulation brought by these two reform movements makes teaching's weak technological foundation more obvious, but the core problem has been around as long as teaching itself.

Dreeben does not argue (and I am not arguing here) that a science of teaching is impossible—only that a sound, consistent base of essential occupational knowledge has not yet been discovered, organized coherently, and codified in a way that teachers would find useful. Teaching is purposeful. Among the many tasks of elementary school teachers in a typical day, they may organize and reorganize the physical space of the classroom; divide a class of children into groups for instruction and bring them back together as a whole class; and ask questions, explain procedures, pose problems, set aside time for practice, assess learning, and administer discipline. A technological view of teaching sees teachers as carrying out this work in informed ways, choosing courses of action that are appropriate to certain situations and intended to accomplish certain ends.

Barr and Dreeben (1983) studied the teaching of reading in first grade classrooms and documented many of the technological elements of reading instruction. The study is considered a classic by educational scholars for its formulation of how schools produce learning. Education's production function is of special interest to economists. In most regression equations that explain student learning, education's production function is rarely modeled with variables specifying what teachers do when instructing children. If included in the analysis at all, teacher quality is typically modeled by the number of years that teachers have taught, their test scores, the courses that they have taken, or the academic degrees and teaching certificates that they have earned. These are descriptions of teachers' career attainments, not their work in classrooms.

The Dreeben and Barr (1988) study analyzes several components of reading instruction: coverage (how many new words are taught); difficulty of materials (the number and complexity of new words, skills, and concepts introduced in basal materials); time (how much time is devoted to whole class instruction, small group instruction accompanied by seatwork, and supervised reading); and the organization of reading groups by ability (how teachers create groups, assign students to them, and transfer students among groups when appropriate). Although constrained by district and school policies, teachers make decisions regarding these elements of instruction that profoundly shape the quality of reading instruction from classroom to classroom. The study describes low-aptitude groups that did not learn very much because the reading materials were too difficult and instructional time was too short, and high-aptitude groups that did not learn very much because the materials were too easy and scant time was devoted to instruction. Effective reading teachers must find the right balance of time, materials, and student aptitude and must be able to organize and reorganize their classes to maintain that balance. These tasks are technological in nature.

In presenting his ideas and research on teaching, Dreeben (1970) argues against the notion that teaching is largely intuitive or more art than science—a vocation for which common sense, creativity, and a deep caring for children are the primary qualifications. Common sense, creativity, and caring are valuable attributes for any teacher to possess, but they provide insufficient guidance on which instructional approach is best in a classroom situation. For teaching to be seen as an art does not obviate the need for technologies, Dreeben explains. Artists of all types rely on technology. Knowledge of brushes, paints, and canvases and how they are used together both properly and improperly surely does not interfere with a painter's aesthetic endeavors.

I conclude by considering what Dreeben's ideas may mean for the future of teaching as a profession and the continued efforts of reformers to regulate its practice.

CONCLUSION: THE FUTURE REGULATION OF TEACHERS AND TEACHING

I have examined two popular education reform movements of the 1990s and the regulatory regimes that they inspired to improve teaching. Both are handicapped by the absence of a strong, reliable body of knowledge linking instruction to student learning. At different points in his career, Dreeben has hinted that a sound technology of teaching would go a long way toward solving the occupational ills that have hampered teachers for generations: low salaries, constant political interference, the public's lack of confidence in teachers' competence, efforts to bureaucratize and standardize teaching, rigid administrative supervision of teachers' work, and persistently inadequate resources. How could a robust technology remedy all of this? Mainly by convincing outsiders that teachers do valuable work. Professionalism will not come from pleading for it or by renaming teaching's activities to make them sound more sophisticated. Dreeben warns, "The prestige of professionalism accrues to those occupations whose members serve the public and monopolize an esoteric expertise (and gain public respect thereby). Respect derives from competent performance, not from the perquisites and appearances of professionalism" (1970:206).

With this warning in mind, I offer a few observations on what the future holds. They are necessarily speculative. A pessimistic outlook would assume that nothing changes and that the trends reported in this essay simply continue. Regulations muddle along; ideology continues to govern the debates over what is taught and how teachers should teach; good and bad teaching occurs, but almost randomly; policies are passed and implemented that are mostly symbolic; teaching remains a quasi-profession with middling occupational status.

An optimistic scenario can be imagined, ironically, even if current efforts to regulate teachers fail. Such a failure may spur the development of a true science of teaching and ultimately a viable technology. Teachers who follow instructional regulations that fail subsequently demand alternatives. In the twentieth century, the collapse of educational fads laden with instructional dictates—be it life adjustment in the 1940s, the New Math in the 1960s, or whole language in the 1990s—led to heightened demand for approaches that work. Educators want tools that equip them to perform their jobs well. Similar demands come from the public when test scores reveal that large numbers of students are not learning much in school. Pressure mounts to overthrow floundering instructional programs, winnow out ineffective practices, and boost test scores through better teaching (Slavin and Fashola 1998). All of this could lead to technological discoveries that improve teaching and enhance the status of the teaching profession.

These events have transpired before, however, and they simply led to another cycle of fads, failure, and more fads—not to breakthroughs in the science of teaching. Why should this time be any different? Because this time it is already different. Only recently has student learning truly mattered in the sense of being measured, made public, and convincingly linked to valued outcomes. Poor performance in academic subjects was just as widespread forty or fifty years ago, probably moreso, but achievement measures were crude and few people knew about them. Achievement scores were kept to insiders. The economy provided lots of decent-paying jobs for children with poor academic skills, even for high school dropouts, and academic disappointments could be easily swept under the rug. That has changed. Not only have researchers discovered that test scores in youth predict adult earnings, but studies are beginning to link them to other quality-of-life indicators such as health, criminality, teen pregnancy, life expectancy, and so on. The public now pays attention to test scores. Its interest will not be fleeting. Irrespective of state accountability systems that elevate the importance of student achievement in the realm of public policy, higher test scores matter a lot more in the real world than they ever have.

Educational research is changing as well. Social scientists are making great strides in improving program evaluation in all fields of social policy (including education) by conducting carefully crafted experiments that feature random assignment of subjects to experimental and control groups. Although its findings are controversial, the National Reading Panel's (2000) approach of sifting through hundreds of studies and identifying sound research sets a high standard for the future. Even the critics of phonics and direct instruction have had to meet the NRP report on its own terms by talking about reading as a recognizable skill, not as a mysterious, "reformed" activity. The result is a vigorous debate about how to teach reading. These are small steps, to be sure, but as a consequence more is known about how to teach reading than ever before; solid progress has been made toward a technology of teaching in that subject (Coles 2001; Ehri and Stahl 2001; Garan 2001).

Finally, I offer a few observations regarding the future politics of regulation. Such politics are bound to become more intense. Denser regulatory environments produce entrenched interests. Once connected to stable revenue streams, interests fight for survival. Instructional regulations support a booming industry of professional developers since teachers need to be trained in the new techniques and new teaching materials are developed. Financial benefits flow to the expert network that pressed for more regulation in the first place. Accountability systems create demand for commercial enterprises that develop, score, and analyze student tests; textbook and software manufacturers; and producers of learning materials that are supposedly scientifically based. These interests will join the existing ideological warriors to fuel a very competitive politics in the future.

One should also expect turbulence in state regulatory policies. I expect ideological changes in states' policy goals even though regulatory structures remain unaltered. That is one of the interesting aspects of the overthrow of the NCTM mathematics standards in California and Massachusetts. The structures for regulating instruction—curriculum frameworks, tests, and incentives for performance—were not dismantled. They were hollowed out, the NCTM's progressivism was extracted, and the structures were refilled with traditional mathematics content. These regulatory regimes do not seem inherently wedded to particular ideologies. Liberals and conservatives, traditionalists and progressives, can be found supporting both of them although, as discussed above, there are definite tendencies. The point is that regulatory regimes are sensitive to shifts in political climate; the ideological basis of regulation is subject to change.

I save the safest prediction for last. States invariably adopt hybrid reforms when they try to improve public schools. The two regulatory regimes examined in this essay, one devoted to instruction and the other to learning, usually sit side by side in state policy. That will not change. In the public's mind, meaningful school reform will always be linked to spelling out what schools should teach and increasing the capacity of teachers to teach it. Those aspirations are certainly correct, but the ability of public policy to turn such aspirations into accomplishments remains unproven. Evidence that policies can reach into classrooms and improve the core activities of teaching and learning is as elusive as ever. We do not need more proclamations. It is easy to proclaim best practices or the knowledge that students should learn. The challenge is to develop a technology of teaching that will systematically connect these ideals and, by doing so, bring them closer to reality.

Acknowledgments

I am grateful to Paul DiPerna and John Coughlan for research assistance on this chapter.

REFERENCES

Allington, Richard L. 2001. "Does State and Federal Reading Policymaking Matter?" Pp. 268–98 in *The Great Curriculum Debate: How Should We Teach Reading and Math?* edited by Tom Loveless. Washington, DC: Brookings Institution Press.

Archer, Jeff. 2002. "National Board Is Pressed to Prove Certified Teachers Make Difference," *Education Week*, January 30, p. 1.

Argetsinger, Amy. 2001. "State Finds Problems in MSPAP Scoring; Broad Discrepancies Force Outside Review," *Washington Post*, November 7, p. B1.

Askey, Richard. 2001. "Good Intentions Are Not Enough." Pp. 163–83 in *The Great Curriculum Debate: How Should We Teach Reading and Math?* edited by Tom Loveless. Washington, DC: Brookings Institution Press.

Barr, Rebecca and Robert Dreeben. 1983. *How Schools Work*. Chicago: University of Chicago Press.

Behn, Robert D. 2001. *Rethinking Democratic Accountability*. Washington, DC: Brookings Institution Press.

Bishop, John H., Feran Mane, and Michael Bishop. 2001. *Is Standards-Based Reform Working?* Unpublished paper, School of Industrial and Labor Relations, Cornell University.

Blair, Julie. 2001. "New Organization Aims to Develop Tests for Teachers." *Education Week* online, October 17.

Bowman, Darcia Harris. 2000. "Minnesota Extends Testing Contract despite Scoring Mistakes." *Education Week* online, September 6.

Browne, William P. 1995. *Cultivating Congress: Constituents, Issues, and Interests in Agricultural Policymaking*. Lawrence: University Press of Kansas.

California State Board of Education. 1999. *Mathematics Content Standards for California Public Schools: Kindergarten through Grade Twelve*. Sacramento, CA: California State Department of Education.

Clayton, Mark. 2000. "How a New Math Program Rose to the Top." *Christian Science Monitor*, May 23, p. 15.

Clotfelter, Charles T. and Helen F. Ladd. 1996. "Recognizing and Rewarding Success in Public Schools." Pp. 23–64 in *Holding Schools Accountable: Performance-Based Reform in Education*, edited by Helen F. Ladd. Washington, DC: Brookings Institution Press.

Cohen, David K. and Deborah Loewenberg Ball. 1990. "Policy and Practice: An Overview." *Educational Evaluation and Policy Analysis* 12:233–39.

Coles, Gerald. 2001. "Reading Taught to the Tune of the 'Scientific' Hickory Stick." *Phi Delta Kappan* 83:204–12.

Cuban, Larry. 1993. *How Teachers Taught: Constancy and Change in American Classrooms, 1880–1990*, 2nd ed. New York: Teachers College Press.

Darling-Hammond, Linda. 1997. *The Right to Learn: A Blueprint for Creating Schools that Work*. San Francisco: Jossey-Bass.

Dreeben, Robert. 1970. *The Nature of Teaching: Schools and the Work of Teachers*. Glenview, IL: Scott, Foresman.

Dreeben, Robert and Rebecca Barr. 1988. "The Formation and Instruction of Ability Groups." *American Journal of Education* 98:34–64.

Editorial Projects in Education. 2001. *Quality Counts 2001: A Better Balance; Standards, Tests, and the Tools to Succeed*. Bethesda, MD: Editorial Projects in Education.

Education Week. 1993. "States Move from 'Inputs' to 'Outcomes' in Effort to Regulate Schools." *Education Week* online, March 17.

Ehri, Linnea and Steven A. Stahl. 2001. "Beyond the Smoke and Mirrors: Putting Out the Fire." *Phi Delta Kappan* 83:17–20.

Farkas, Steve, Jean Johnson, and Ann Duffett. 1997. *Different Drummers: How Teachers of Teachers View Public Education*. New York: Public Agenda.

Flax, Ellen. 1991. "S.C. Considers Schoolwide Salary-Bonus Program." *Education Week* online, June 5.

Fritschler, A. Lee and James M. Hoefler. 1996. *Smoking and Politics: Policy Making and the Federal Bureaucracy*. Upper Saddle River, NJ: Prentice-Hall.

Gamoran, Adam. 2001. "Beyond Curriculum Wars: Content and Understanding in Mathematics." Pp. 134–62 in *The Great Curriculum Debate: How Should We Teach Reading and Math?* edited by Tom Loveless. Washington, DC: Brookings Institution Press.

Garan, Elaine. 2001, "More Smoking Guns: A Response to Linnea Ehri and Steven Stahl." *Phi Delta Kappan* 83:21–27.

Hanushek, Eric A. 1994. *Making Schools Work: Improving Performance and Controlling Costs*. Washington, DC: Brookings Institution Press.

Hembree, Ray and Donald J. Dessart. 1986. "Effects of Hand-Held Calculators in Pre-College Mathematics Education: A Meta-Analysis." *Journal for Research in Mathematics Education* 17:83–99.

Hess, Frederick M. 2001. *Tear Down This Wall*. Charlottesville, VA: Progressive Policy Institute.

Hiebert, James. 1999. "Relationships between Research and the NCTM Standards." *Journal for Research in Mathematics Education* 30:3–9.

Hoff, David J. 2001. "NSF Plots New Education Strategy." *Education Week*, November 7, pp. 1, 20.

International Reading Association and National Council of Teachers of English. 1996. *Standards for the English Language Arts*. Urbana, IL: International Reading Association and National Council of Teachers of English.

Jacob, Brian A. 2001. "Getting Tough? The Impact of High School Graduation Exams." *Educational Evaluation and Policy Analysis* 23:99–122.

Kane, Thomas J. and Douglas O. Staiger. 2002. "Volatility in School Test Scores: Implications for Test-Based Accountability Systems." Pp. 235–83 in *Brookings Papers on Education Policy 2002*, edited by Diane Ravitch. Washington, DC: Brookings Institution Press.

Kane, Thomas J., Douglas O. Staiger, and Jeffrey Geppert. 2001. *Assessing the Definition of 'Adequate Yearly Progress' in the House and Senate Education Bills.* Working paper, Brown Center on Education Policy, Brookings Institution.

Kennedy Manzo, Kathleen. 2001. "Protests over State Testing Widespread." *Education Week* online, May 16.

Klein, Stephen P., Laura Hamilton, Daniel McCaffrey, Brian Stecher, Abby Robyn, and Delia Burroughs. 2000. *Teaching Practices and Student Achievement: Report of First-Year Findings from the 'Mosaic' Study of Systemic Initiatives in Mathematics and Science.* Santa Monica, CA: Rand Corporation.

Koretz, Daniel. 1996. "Using Student Assessments for Educational Accountability." Pp. 171–96 in *Improving America's Schools: The Role of Incentives,* edited by Eric A. Hanushek and Dale W. Jorgenson. Washington, DC: National Academy Press.

Koretz, Daniel, Brian Stecher, Stephen P. Klein, and Daniel McCaffrey. 1994. "The Vermont Portfolio Assessment Program: Findings and Implications." *Educational Measurement: Issues and Practice* 13:5–16.

Labaree, David F. 1997. *How to Succeed in School without Really Learning.* New Haven, CT: Yale University Press.

Lemann, Nicholas. 1998. "Ready, Read!" *Atlantic Monthly* online, November.

Loveless, Tom. 1998. "The Use and Misuse of Research in Educational Reform." Pp. 279–318 in *Brookings Papers on Education Policy 1998,* edited by Diane Ravitch. Washington, DC: Brookings Institution Press.

Loveless, Tom. 2000. *The Brown Center Report on American Education: How Well Are American Students Learning?* Washington, DC: Brookings Institution Press.

Loveless, Tom. 2001. "A Tale of Two Math Reforms: The Politics of the New Math and the NCTM Standards." Pp. 184–209 in *The Great Curriculum Debate: How Should We Teach Reading and Math?* edited by Tom Loveless. Washington, DC: Brookings Institution Press.

Loveless, Tom and Paul DiPerna. 2001. "In Praise of Mediocrity: Tattered Blue Ribbons at the Department of Education." *Education Matters* 1:30–34.

Ma, Liping. 1999. *Knowing and Teaching Elementary Mathematics: Teachers' Understanding of Fundamental Mathematics in China and the United States.* Mahwah, NJ: Erlbaum.

McKeown, Michael, David Klein, and Chris Patterson. 2000. "The National Science Foundations Systemic Initiatives." Pp. 313–69 in *What's at Stake in the K-12 Standards Wars,* edited by Sandra Stotsky. New York: Peter Lang.

McNeil, Linda M. 2000. *Contradictions of School Reform: Educational Costs of Standardized Testing.* New York: Routledge & Kegan Paul.

Mezzacappa, Dale. 2001. "Lessons from School Takeovers: Big Changes at Districts, Less So in Classrooms." *Philadelphia Inquirer,* November 4, p. A1.

Moore, Mark H. 1995. *Creating Public Value: Strategic Management in Government.* Cambridge, MA: Harvard University Press.

National Commission on Teaching and America's Future. 1996. *What Matters Most: Teaching for America's Future.* New York: National Commission on Teaching and America's Future.

National Council of Teachers of Mathematics. 1989. *Curriculum and Evaluation Standards for School Mathematics.* Reston, VA: National Council of Teachers of Mathematics.

National Council of Teachers of Mathematics. 2000. *Principles and Standards for School Mathematics.* Reston, VA: National Council of Teachers of Mathematics.

National Reading Panel. 2000. *Teaching Children to Read.* Bethesda, MD: National Institute of Child Health and Human Development.

National Research Council. 1994. *National Science Education Standards.* Washington, DC: National Academy Press.

Public Agenda. 2000. *Is There a Backlash against State Standards?* New York: Public Agenda.

Raimi, Ralph A. and Lawrence S. Braden. 1998. *State Mathematics Standards: An Appraisal of Math Standards in 46 States, the District of Columbia, and Japan.* Washington, DC: Thomas B. Fordham Foundation.

Ravitch, Diane. 1995. *National Standards in Education.* Washington, DC: Brookings Institution Press.

Ravitch, Diane. 2000. *Left Back: A Century of Failed School Reforms*. New York: Simon & Schuster.

Richard, Alan. 2001. "Policy Update: South Carolina." Pp. 178–79 in *Quality Counts 2001: A Better Balance; Standards, Tests, and the Tools to Succeed*. Bethesda, MD: Editorial Projects in Education.

Richard, Alan. 2002. "Report Card Days." *Education Week*, January 9, pp. 32–39.

Ripley, Randall B. and Grace A. Franklin. 1987. *Congress, the Bureaucracy, and Public Policy*. Chicago: Dorsey Press.

Schoenfeld, Alan H. 1994. "What Do We Know about Mathematics Curricula?" *Journal of Mathematical Behavior* 13:55–80.

Slavin, Robert E. and Olatokunbo S. Fashola. 1998. *Show Me the Evidence: Proven and Promising Programs for America's Schools*. Thousand Oaks, CA: Corwin Press.

Smith, Brian A. 1996. *A Meta-Analysis of Outcomes from the Use of Calculators in Mathematics Education*. Ph.D. dissertation, College of Education, Texas A & M University.

Steinberg, Jacques and Diana B. Henriques. 2001. "When a Test Fails the Schools, Careers and Reputations Suffer." *New York Times*, May 21, p. A1.

Suydam, M. N. 1979. *The Use of Calculators in Pre-College Education: A State-of-the-Art Review*. Columbus, OH: Calculator Information Center.

Trafton, Paul R., Barbara J. Reys, and Deanna G. Wasman. 2001. "Standards-Based Mathematics Curriculum Materials: A Phase in Search of a Definition." *Phi Delta Kappan* 83:259–63.

Wilson, James Q. 1989. *Bureaucracy: What Government Agencies Do and Why They Do It*. New York: Basic Books.

V

Sociology of Education as a Field of Inquiry

11

Sociology of Education: An Overview of the Field at the Turn of the Twenty-First Century

Barbara Schneider

Having written several significant pieces on the state of sociology of education—including "The Sociology of Education: Its Development in the United States" (1994), which won the Willard Waller prize for outstanding scholarship—Robert Dreeben has marked the intellectual boundaries of the field. That is why, when asked to write about sociology of education as a field of study, I felt an overwhelming sense of responsibility, for clearly Dreeben's analysis exemplifies the finest scholarship on this topic. Relying on historical sources and bringing his keen analytic perspective and creativity to the task of describing the field, Dreeben's chapter traces the provenance of sociology of education both theoretically and methodologically, ending with a critique of his own omissions and challenges for the future. In addressing what vulnerabilities lie in the essay, Dreeben—in his modest way—understates the importance of his identification and analysis of the theoretical streams that characterize both previous work in the field as well as several current studies not discussed in the text.

In this chapter I briefly describe the history of the field of sociology of education from the 1900s through the 1970s. A more in-depth chronology of the field can be found in Dreeben (1994) and Bidwell and Friedkin (1988); recent volumes by Levinson, Cookson, and Sadovnik (2001) and Hallinan (2000) provide a broader view of sociology of education. The focus of this review is on some of the major ideas set forward in these publications, paying particular attention to several themes identified by Dreeben and connecting them with three other conceptual strands: inequality and social justice, global expansion of education, and social networks and their influence on behaviors and social norms. These ideas increasingly characterize much of the work being pursued in the field, and the significance that these topics may have for future scholarly activities is explored.

Barbara Schneider • Department of Sociology, University of Chicago, Chicago, Illinois 60637.

Stability and Change in American Education: Structure, Process, and Outcomes edited by Maureen T. Hallinan, Adam Gamoran, Warren Kubitschek, and Tom Loveless. Eliot Werner Publications, Clinton Corners, New York, 2003.

TRACING THE ROOTS OF SOCIOLOGY OF EDUCATION

A common adage, particularly among sociologists of education, is that every truly great sociologist has written one major work on education or given substantial attention to a key aspect of it, such as the acquisition of knowledge and skills and its influence on social mobility. Certainly among the early sociologists, education appears in the writings of Americans Lester Ward ([1883] 1968) and Albion Small (1897) and in the works of their European counterparts, Karl Marx ([1887] 1971), Emile Durkheim ([1922] 1956, [1925] 1961, [1938] 1977), and Max Weber ([1922] 1947). Although having a distinguished pedigree of intellectual forebears, sociology of education remained in a state of relative incubation until the 1960s when it became one of the major constructs in understanding social stratification as defined and modeled by Duncan and Hodge (1963) and Sewell, Haller, and Straus (1957). Whereas Duncan and Hodge were primarily interested in understanding occupational attainment, Sewell and his colleagues attempted to identify the mechanisms through which occupational attainment operated beginning with the educational experiences of young men in high school. Sewell showed how social inequalities in income and occupational status were found to be the consequences of family and individual characteristics, at the core of which were academic ability, the educational background of one's parents, and the educational expectations that their parents held for them. This interest in social stratification has clearly dominated the field, primarily because of the prolific empirical writings of Sewell, Hauser, and their colleagues and the intergenerational impact they had on their graduate students and subsequently on the latter's students. The importance of Sewell's work to sociology of education is comprehensively discussed in Dreeben's review of the field (1994).

Changing the Social Order

Sociology of education originated from the desire to promote societal reforms through changes in education (Bidwell and Friedkin 1988; Dreeben 1994). In essence, from its inception sociology of education focused on the social applications of sociology—that is, whether education can improve society and by what means. In the early part of the twentieth century, education was broadly conceived by sociologists as the process of integrating or socializing individuals into society, a society that was undergoing enormous changes both in terms of industrial production and population expansion (Weber [1922] 1947; Durkheim [1925] 1961). Sociologists who wrote about education viewed it as one of the primary mechanisms of modernization. These scholars envisioned a holistic role for mass schooling that would stimulate the economy by increasing worker knowledge and productivity and foster a spirit of nationalism among the growing numbers of immigrants inhabiting American cities. Adopting renowned educator John Dewey's conception of education, they viewed education not just as academic achievement but as the mechanism through which individuals learned about citizenship, sportsmanship, group participation, leadership, and social responsibility (Dewey 1900). Social reform would and could only occur if young people had educational opportunities that provided them with activities that were cognitively challenging and socially appropriate. This interdependent relationship between the expansion of education and positive social change formed the theoretical foundation of sociology of education for over a hundred years.

Although sociologists recognized the importance of education for social change, sociology of education was not formalized as a subdiscipline until the late 1920s. In 1927 New York University's School of Education became the official home of the National Society for the Study of Educational Sociology, which produced the *Journal of Educational Sociology: A Magazine of Theory and Practice*. Following New York University's lead, a handful of institutions began to develop subspecializations in sociology of education within their sociology departments. Most universities now either teach a course in sociology of education or have a subspecialization in this area. Schools and colleges of education also offer sociology of education courses and programs, usually as part of foundation studies and sometimes cross-listed in sociology departments (Schneider 1987).

The low status of teacher-training institutions—and the suspect quality of the teachers whom they produced—foreshadowed the problem that schools and colleges of education, even those in elite universities that trained sociologists of education, would later encounter. For example, the training and placement of sociologists of education continues to be a concern of many professors within sociology, which led most recently to a special committee within the American Sociological Association to examine this problem (Pallas 1998). There appear to be at least two major underlying reasons for these problems. First, aligning sociology with education—a field that many do not consider an academic discipline—has placed scholars in sociology of education in the unenviable position of having to discredit the work of educators or trying to legitimize their work to doubting sociologists. Second, the fact that sociologists of education could be trained in schools or colleges of education further eroded the legitimacy of these scholars as true sociologists. Under these circumstances it is not surprising that sociology as a discipline has been somewhat recalcitrant in considering sociology of education as central to its disciplinary core, despite the contributions of such luminaries as Bourdieu, Coleman, Sewell, and Sørensen.

Reviewing the contents of the first issue of the *Journal of Educational Sociology*, one is struck by the inherent tension between the discipline of sociology and the practice of education, a tension that continues to dominate the field. The majority of these initial articles consistently attacked the purposes and practices of education, particularly in elementary and secondary schools. A consistent theme was the inadequacy of schools in fulfilling their role of educating the whole child into "the life of the group, to train him in the use of its institutions, to teach him to cherish and guard its possessions, and to instill in him the desire to promote its welfare" (Counts 1927:12). Teachers and the institutions responsible for their training were often perceived as the source of this inadequacy.

In his paper "Sociological Basis of the Normal School Curriculum," Payne launched a strong criticism of normal schools, arguing that "educational theory and practice has not been concerned at all with the type of knowledge, habits, and attitudes that would affect social behavior" (Payne 1927:5). From his perspective society was in the midst of a social lag. That is, advances in commerce and industry had not infiltrated into classrooms, and consequently social behaviors remained substantially unchanged. The immediate problem of education was to take up the social slack by changing the social order. His prescription for accomplishing this is not too far afield from the measures suggested by recent comprehensive school reformers (see, for example, Stringfield, Ross, and Smith 1996; Slavin and Madden 2000; Fullan 2001). The first of Payne's recommendations was the "development of scientific knowledge" by using the scientific method for study and incorporating advances in science into the classroom. The second was raising the qualifications of teachers and providing them with more comprehensive pretraining so that they could understand the specific "social needs and aspirations of the communities in which they work" (1927:10).

Substantively, the work that developed from these early investigations in sociology of education would, by today's standards, be viewed as somewhat pedestrian and in some instances more practical than sociological in content. A survey of topics covered in sociology of education in the late 1920s included junior high school life, hygiene of the school child, and applied psychology (Ellwood 1927). That is not to say that sociology of education was dormant at this time. Rather, it was conducted by individuals such as Sorokin who tended to see themselves not as sociologists of education, but as sociologists. These were sociologists who viewed education as the nexus of social reform and societal institutions, and it is their ideas that shaped the work of what we today would consider sociology of education.

It is important to view sociology of education in the late 1920s in relation to the study of sociology more generally. This was not a period of methodological sophistication and most articles, even those in journals such as the *American Journal of Sociology*, tended to publish manuscripts that promoted social changes within cities, industries, and occupations (Abbott 1999). The dominant methodology was the case study in the Chicago School style, with occasional surveys where cross-tabulations involving a small number of variables such as sex, age, and occupation tended to be the form of analysis (Raftery 2001). It was not until the late 1930s that analyses of large data sets became more scientifically viable, with the development of practical methods for probability sampling that offered a comprehensive theoretical framework for drawing inferences to populations of fixed and finite size (Groves, Singer, and Lepkowski 2001). It was another twenty years before statisticians were able to develop models and means of analyses for explaining why a phenomenon occurred, as described by regression coefficients and other measures of relationships, and how these measures applied to situations where there were errors of measurement and issues of nonresponse.

In 1963 the field became marginally legitimated when the American Sociological Association assumed responsibility from New York University for the *Journal of Educational Sociology*. Moving oversight from a single educational enterprise to a professional association connected the field more closely with the discipline. At the same time that the journal was being relocated, work in sociology more generally (and sociology of education in particular) was becoming predominately quantitative in its methodological approach. Quantitative work that used large data sets was seen as more scientific and working with more sophisticated mathematical models garnered more status within the field (see Bidwell 1989).

Raftery (2001) contends that sociology has always relied on quantitative methods, commenting that Comte was quite explicit about the importance of grounding work in sociology using empirical data. Early evidence of this is apparent in the work of Durkheim, who relied on such data to form his theory of suicide, originally published in 1897 (1951). Durkheim also used a more qualitative form of data and analysis in *The Elementary Forms of Religious Life*, originally published in 1912, relying on prior material and arranging facts in "strictly ethnographic and geographical order. Each continent and within each continent, each tribe or ethnic group, is studied separately" ([1912] 1995:90). This form of qualitative analysis, which was prominent in the early part of the last century, spawned variations that have become more widely used today, although within sociology heated debates persist over the rigor and value of quantitative and qualitative data and their analytic methods.

In describing sociological work in the first half of the last century, Dreeben (1994) identified three themes that had particular relevance to education and were studied by sociologists: social mobility of education, community influences on education, and the social organization of schools (including the occupational structure of teachers). Though not discrete in content, at a basic level they encompass key questions that have continued to guide the field and are addressed in much of the research and scholarship today.

Social Mobility and Social Stratification

Dreeben (1994) and Bidwell and Friedkin (1988) argue that the importance of education as part of the concept of social mobility was first and elegantly developed by Sorokin ([1927] 1963). It was Sorokin who underscored the importance of institutional structures and the mechanisms that they use to channel individuals into positions of economic and political power. Sorokin describes schools as one of several institutional channels of social mobility— along with the military, government, and religious institutions—in which individuals are funneled and eventually placed based on established criteria. As Dreeben (1994) points out, what distinguished Sorokin's work was his view of education as one (though not the only) context that profoundly influenced the social status of individuals throughout their lives. What is particularly useful about Sorokin's work is the introduction and development of theories explaining why social mobility is constrained by this sorting process based on a set of criteria. The sorting process itself is viewed as having different effects and consequences depending on where and when one gets sorted, placed, or pushed. Sorokin argued that schooling would not provide equal opportunities for everyone primarily because, as institutions, schools had their own internal mechanisms of tests and grades that were designed to differentiate students from one another for purposes of awarding social status to those who succeeded.

Dreeben contends that these early notions of social reform and social mobility were in fact precursors to the concept of social stratification—that is, the process by which individuals are differentiated into various social strata. Although Sorokin's ideas were compelling, the evidential basis for his arguments was less persuasive. It was the theoretical and empirical work of Sewell, who was interested in how much variation in educational and occupational aspirations depended on social status and intelligence, that brought the status attainment model into the forefront of studies in sociology of education. Linking family background characteristics to social psychological factors, academic achievement, and educational expectations, Sewell set out to determine the extent to which these constructs accounted for variations in individual social mobility. The Sewell model (Sewell, Haller, and Straus 1957; Sewell and Hauser 1980) laid the foundation for the Wisconsin Studies, a substantial and important body of empirical work that tested and affirmed the importance of education for achieving occupational success.

The study of status attainment became the prevailing topic in sociology of education from the 1960s through today, as researchers tried to refine the model beyond family socioeconomic characteristics and individual student ability, searching for new variables that could explain educational attainment. Concerned that the Wisconsin framework had individualistic biases with respect to race, gender, and geographical location and that it insufficiently emphasized contextual factors that shape educational expectations, scholars set about reexamining the Sewell model with the original as well as new data sets. Expanding on the models and testing them with other and more diverse populations, investigators began by exploring why some students held higher educational and occupational aspirations than others, paying closer attention to curriculum tracking, school and neighborhood contextual effects, and various methodological issues (Alexander and McDill 1976; Kerckhoff 1976; Rosenbaum 1976). Among these subthemes research on curriculum tracking has overshadowed work in this area, examining how program or course placements in high school affect student achievement, college matriculation, and more recently college persistence. Because this research area has so dominated the field, it is not reviewed here since there are many sources that provide more comprehensive coverage (see, for example, Oakes, Gamoran, and Page 1992).

Using more sophisticated methods and longitudinal data from various national and international data sets, researchers have continued to investigate variations in educational and occupational aspirations among different populations over time (Hauser and Anderson 1991; Morgan 1996) and linked them to outcomes such as college attendance and entry into the labor force (Kerckhoff 1996, Shu and Marini 1998; Kerckhoff, 2001). Economists have also been interested in linking education, in the form of human capital, to later occupational and economic success (Schultz 1961; Becker 1964). One of the major distinctions between sociologists' and economists' perspectives on employability is that to sociologists what is learned and how it is learned—including experiences at home, in school, and in the community—are seen as important as the educational credential itself.

At the time that Sewell and Hauser were developing their model, the majority of American youth ended their formal schooling when they graduated from high school. College attendance was accessible only to youth from middle- and upper-class families (Trow 1973). This trend persisted and, even as late as the 1980s, the majority of high school seniors entered the labor force full time immediately after graduation. Consequently, sociology of education as a field has paid considerable attention to the educational experiences (Willis 1977; Oakes 1985; MacLeod 1987; Brint and Karabel 1989) and the types of full-time jobs taken by young adults who stopped their education after high school (Borman 1991; Rosenbaum and Jones 2000).

On the educational side, students placed in vocational programs in high school were found to be diverted from challenging courses, had lower academic performance, and were less likely to complete high school than those in academic programs (Gamoran and Mare 1989; Natriello, Pallas, and Alexander 1989). This evidence on the effectiveness of vocational education programs did not go unnoticed and was used in redesigning the high school work-related programs of the 1990s (see Secretary's Commission on Achieving Necessary Skills 1992).

The reasons why young people choose different types of employment have been tied not only to family characteristics and individual abilities and interests, but also to the employment opportunities that they have as adolescents in high school (Entwisle, Alexander, and Olson 2000). Researchers have argued that the skills acquired on the job and that the values working imparts—such as punctuality, responsibility, cooperation, and shaping long-term goals (e.g., seeking new employment or returning to school)—constitute important socializing experiences for adult full-time employment (Mortimer et al. 1994; Mortimer and Johnson 1998). However, as more young people have opted to attend college, the long-term employment and social benefits of teenage work seem less salient than in the past, especially if the nature of the work is low skill (Schneider and Stevenson 1999).

By the 1990s things changed and nearly 70 percent of high school seniors matriculated to some type of postsecondary institution soon after high school graduation. This increase in college attendance rates is bringing new meaning to the concept of educational stratification, not only because of the change in the numbers of young people now entering college but also because of their family background characteristics. The fastest growing segment of the population now attending college consists of students whose parents never attended college and have limited financial resources (National Center for Educational Statistics 2001). As the transition from high school to college and adult employment continues to change and becomes increasingly complex, given labor market uncertainties, understanding this process becomes more important to sociologists. Numerous studies are now being conducted on decisions regarding high school courses, work experiences, and college choice (Arum 1998; Schneider and Stevenson 1999; Rosenbaum and Jones 2000; Rosenbaum 2001).

Social mobility today is often viewed within the context of social inequalities; that is, individuals are denied social mobility because of the poor quality of their schools, the conditions of their neighborhoods, and the background characteristics of their parents. Students who leave school before obtaining a high school diploma are not necessarily the victims of having inadequate mental capacity, but may be the recipients of insufficient resources or may be attending schools that push them out (Gambetta 1987; McNeal 1997; Rumberger and Thomas 2000). The test score criterion that Sorokin identified, used for placing and sorting individuals in schools, looms over and haunts young people as they move through or out of the educational system. Recent work on understanding longitudinal differences in test scores among racial and ethnic groups is inextricably tied to concepts of social mobility. If young people are not learning at the same rate as their peers, then the types of learning and social opportunities that their peers have access to will be denied to them (Hedges and Nowell 1999; Hallinan 2001).

The idea of social mobility—that is, how one moves through society attaining economic and occupational status either similar to or different from one's parents—is the backbone of the status attainment literature. In earlier work notions of social mobility were modeled primarily at the individual level, and in much of the work today we find a similar approach, although some models do incorporate characteristics of the individual's peer group or characteristics of the school. But the overriding question is fundamentally about individuals moving through the system. In contrast, Marx ([1887] 1971) and other theorists such as Bowles and Gintis (1976) address social mobility as a societal condition. More macrosocietal conditions socialize individuals into social groups, and movement from one group to another is difficult. Society reproduces social status; all aspects of the social world reify social positions, not just one's parents, teachers, or friends. One of the major reasons that sociologists had problems examining individuals nested within social systems was primarily methodological. Now with more sophisticated methods we are able to address both the individual and social system in the same empirical models (Bryk and Raudenbush 1992; Goldstein 1995), which has provided a clearer picture of how social contexts influence academic achievement and attainment. Research using hierarchical models has examined contextual effects in the school (Lee and Bryk 1989; Lee and Smith 1995; Shouse 1997), family (Pong 1998), community (Blau et al. 2000), and labor market (Grodsky and Pager 2001).

Education and Community Studies

Community influences on education was a second theme identified by Dreeben as central to sociology of education in the first half of the twentieth century. This early line of research is best exemplified in the work of Lynd and Lynd (1929), Hollingshead (1949), and Havighurst and his associates (1962). These studies sought to examine the value structure of the social context together with the social institutions that support and derive their legitimacy from it. By focusing on the community, these investigations attempted to capture the situational factors that influenced the values, attitudes, and educational outcomes of the students who attended schools in the same neighborhood. Relying primarily on field-based methods including surveys, interviews, and observations, these investigators focused on the meanings and understandings (or the values and norms) that characterized a specific community. Through their analyses they showed how these social subjective notions were tied to certain processes, such as how young people interpret their social place in the community, which norms and values are held by the community, and how these norms and values are reflected in social institutions—primarily by the schools.

One study not generally perceived as being representative of community studies was James Coleman's *The Adolescent Society* (1961), an intensive analysis of ten American high schools located in ten diverse communities in the Midwest. Coleman found that the high school was its own social entity, a community unto itself separated from the larger society, and this separateness was reinforced by parents and the structure of the school. Comparing values, norms, and rituals among these ten high schools, Coleman sought to identify those important activities that confer social status on students who participate in them. As might be expected, there were variations among the high schools in the importance given to scholastic achievement, family background, popularity with the opposite sex, and athletics or cheerleading. For Coleman this was a study of how social systems function and how individuals' actions are shaped within these systems. Thus there are two conclusions drawn from this work. The more general finding was that youth in high schools had their own society. But the second finding, more within the community tradition, was that the norms and values shared by an adolescent social system were not consistent among high schools, and this inconsistency was influenced by the parents and teachers in each community.

Forty years later Glen Elder and Rand Conger (2000) returned to this subject, focusing on eight communities in rural Iowa to examine how values and norms shape adolescents' views of their lives. Longitudinal in design, this study captures the lives of adolescents and their parents, siblings, grandparents, and schools using data from surveys, interviews, videotapes of family interactions, and historical public records. Following up on earlier work that demonstrated how economic conditions affect the intellectual and social development of adolescents (Elder 1999), Elder and Conger were interested in how the lives of adolescents were being affected by the great farm crisis of the 1980s. Instead of defining these adolescents as existing within their own separate society, they refer to these young people as living in small worlds of overlapping spheres of family, school, church, and community that are linked through activities with adults and peers who share values, norms, and understandings. Adolescent academic competence, social competence, and self-esteem are strengthened in these closed communities by parent interaction and strong social ties with friends, community members, and religious leaders and congregants.

Several other studies that examine the relationship between norms and values and social mobility are *Home Advantage* (Lareau 2000), *Classrooms and Corridors* (Metz 1978), and *Preparing for Power* (Cookson and Persell 1985). Observing in several classrooms in two schools, Lareau shows how educational advantages are transmitted to children by their parents and teachers in and out of school. Much like Elder and Conger, Lareau carefully and systematically describes how parents attempt to maximize their social and economic resources for their children's educational advantage—in this instance, primarily in school. Using a cultural capital perspective—that is, how resources are transmitted through families (Bourdieu and Passeron 1977; DiMaggio 1982)—Lareau details how parental activities are linked to social class differences, suggesting that social mobility is more easily attained when one's parents adopt more middle-class strategies for interacting with the school and construct strong safety nets when their children fall behind academically.

Metz (1978) also adopts a social class concept to understand how children interact in middle school, demonstrating that parents with greater resources are more likely than those with fewer resources to interfere in school management when their child is at risk. There is a substantial literature in sociology of education that examines the involvement of parents in their children's education. These studies are highlighted here because, much like earlier community studies, they use extensive field methods to reach their conclusions. Additional studies on parent involvement, although not in this methodological tradition, are concerned with the relationship between parent values and actions and achievement (see, for example, Baker and Stevenson 1986; Schneider and Coleman 1993; Epstein and Sanders 2000; Epstein 2001).

Cookson and Persell (1985) also use field methods to describe the lives of adolescents in elite private boarding schools. Much like Coleman in *The Adolescent Society*, they focus on small segregated high school communities, examining what is valued among the students and how those values are formed and reinforced through the actions of teachers and school staff. In contrast to the world of the 1950s, however, the desire for popularity is replaced by the desire to gain entrance into highly competitive colleges and, after completing one's education, attaining positions of leadership and power in American society.

What all of these studies have in common is that the unit of analysis is situational; that is, they are centered on a specific geographical community or a limited set of schools, and the conceptual focus is solidly on the relationships between the activities of the individuals and the norms and values held by them and others in the social systems that they inhabit. A family's decision to have its child play soccer depends in part on who else is participating in this activity and the perceived value that the community and school place on this particular team sport. In each of these studies, social class is expanded to include concepts and ideas that are linked to formal structures and given new and sometimes different meanings. Motivation for action becomes an integral component for understanding differences in behavior, whether it is participating in sports or choosing to attend a private school. Among private boarding school students, for example, attending an elite college socializes them into a leadership role in society, providing the social networks that make this goal a more realistic possibility.

Although not entirely in the field-based methodological genre, two other studies in the 1990s identified several theoretical constructs for describing communities that provided a rich understanding of how community norms, values, and activities influence student learning and social development. In *Public and Private Schools* (Coleman and Hoffer 1987), the focus is not on a single geographical community but rather on a religious community (that is, Catholic schools) and the authors tie social organizational characteristics, values, and norms to the academic performance and school continuation of the individuals who are part of this wider community. Using the national longitudinal database High School and Beyond (HS&B), the authors show that Catholic schools have slightly higher achievement test scores than public schools and substantially higher school completion rates. They attribute the success of these schools to the social norms and sanctions that are transmitted across generations and that arise out of the social structure of a community that both reinforces and perpetuates itself. Characterizing Catholic schools as functional communities, they link shared community norms and values—created through closed intergenerational parent interests—to specific student outcomes.

Catholic Schools and the Common Good by Bryk, Lee, and Holland (1993) presents perhaps the most concrete example of a recent version of a community study that uses a mixed methods approach. Relying on large-scale data sets and field-based cases, they expand Coleman and Hoffer's community concept, finding that the higher academic performance of students in Catholic schools is less dependent on family background and personal circumstances and thus produces a common school effect. Connecting the formal curriculum structure and the norms and values held by the students, parents, and educational staff, they explain variations in academic achievement between Catholic and public high schools. Through their school case studies, they illustrate how the communal organization of the school and the inspirational ideology of the teachers—which supports moral values, trust, and commitment to the students—instill a sense of community that encourages academic performance. Their quantitative analyses of the HS&B data are perhaps more closely linked conceptually with the third Dreeben theme, the social organization of schooling, for it is in this analysis that they empirically model what happens within the school to create the common school effect.

There have been several criticisms of the Coleman and Hoffer and Bryk, Lee, and Holland conceptualizations of functional communities or common school effects as not being refined enough in their conceptions of school communities and consequently overstating the positive effects that these particular organizational properties may have on various student outcomes (see Morgan and Sørensen [1999] and the responses by Hallinan and Kubitschek [1999] and Carbonaro [1999]). Nevertheless, it is important to underscore the value of this work for subsequent theoretical development and empirical testing. How important is generational closure, particularly in our highly mobile school population where most students travel to high schools outside their neighborhoods? Are there other types of schools that do a better job at minimizing family background effects on performance? Do these schools share the same organizational characteristics as Catholic schools? How can a school maintain academic standards and norms and values when the characteristics of the student body and the teachers are constantly changing?

The Social Organization of Schooling

The social mobility studies examine individuals, their ascriptive characteristics, and somewhat simplified measures of the social systems of which they are a part. Community studies identify a social entity such as a town, neighborhood, or religious school as the unit of analysis and examine the values and norms that influence group behaviors and attitudes. Studies that explore the social organization of schooling—the third theme identified by Dreeben—move inside the school, investigating not only the teachers and students but also other relevant actors (including parents, peers, and administrators) to understand the relationships between the social structure and the individuals within it. Few of these types of studies were conducted until the late 1960s when a backlash to conclusions reached in the *Equality of Educational Opportunity* study, often referred to as the Coleman Report (Coleman et al. 1966), sparked a renewed interest in how schools function and the influence that they can exert on the academic behaviors, social skills, and psychological development of their students. Centered primarily on classrooms, this body of work links the formal and informal organizational properties of schools with the educational and social experiences of the students and their teachers.

Unquestionably, the archetype of this conceptual strand is Willard Waller's *The Sociology of Teaching* (1932). In this book Waller focused on the middle grades and high school in a small town to formulate his conceptions of the occupation of teaching. Relying on his own observations and those of his students, Waller provides an analysis of the school as an organization and describes how the social relationships—particularly among teachers, students, and their parents—form a mechanism of social control. The everyday rituals of teachers and their students and the institutionalized ceremonies of schools are used as a backdrop to describe the normative roles of administrators, teachers, parents, and students that continue to characterize many of the social relationships found in schools today (Plank 2000). How teachers attain legitimate authority over the students and their parents and share it with their colleagues remains a central topic in sociology of education, although more recent studies follow the argument shaped by Stinchcombe (1964) and later by Swidler (1979) and delve into the nature of resistance by students and their parents to the teachers' authority (Valenzuela 1999; Dance 2000).

Waller argues that his analyses apply to the lives of urban school teachers, and it would appear from fieldwork conducted by Becker twenty years later (1952, 1953) that the exercise of authority by teachers in cities was even more problematic than in other contexts. Richly descriptive, Becker's work complements Waller's analysis of the absence of a vertical career path for teachers but only touches on the ways in which formal organizational factors influence teacher and student interactions. This missing component was not fully developed until 1965 when Bidwell's seminal "The School as a Formal Organization" presented a comprehensive conceptualization of the organization of schooling and its implications for the socialization of students from elementary through secondary school. Although this focus on the social organization of schools was innovative at the time, the underlying concerns of sociology of education continued to be primarily with the purposes of education, not with how schools were organized. Using concepts from organizational studies such as the division of labor, role-sets, and rationalization, Bidwell articulated a theoretical framework that described how schools function by taking into account the student-teacher relationship, teacher autonomy, and the organizational properties of the school system. Supported by numerous empirical studies that previously had been viewed as thematically unrelated, he conceptually linked the bureaucratic organization of the educational system from the school to the state with the experiences of teachers and students in classrooms.

One of Bidwell's key arguments concerns the nature of the teaching profession and how its effectiveness in socializing students for adulthood has been shaped by a residentially mandated clientele, a weak incentive structure, and an imperfect licensure process. Whereas educational scholars have focused their attention on how teachers should instruct their classes in specific subject areas such as mathematics and reading, more recently sociologists have tended to relate the occupational structure of the profession and the organization of the school and classroom to teacher beliefs, commitments, and collegial and student interactions (Rowan, Raudenbush, and Cheong 1993;

Talbert and McLaughlin 1994). Sociological studies of the professions tend to examine issues of prestige and social structure rather than the actual work that is done and the expertise needed to do it (see Abbott 1988). The sociological studies of teaching clearly deviate from this pattern, turning their attention to the nature of teaching itself. The most relevant examples of this are Dreeben's *Nature of Teaching* (1970), which presents an extensive analysis of the relationships of the teacher with her class and individual students, and Lortie's *Schoolteacher* (1975), which takes a broader approach that is more cursory in its discussion of the actual work of teaching but casts a wider net to explain why teachers enter the profession and how they are socialized into their roles.

The role and professionalization of teachers continues to be an area of strong sociological interest since teachers continue to be held chiefly accountable for failures in student learning, with critics identifying the profession— in its preparation, socialization experiences, and reward structure—as the primary source of the problem (Firestone 1994). Some of the most recent work in this area has been conducted by Bidwell and colleagues (Bidwell and Bryk 1994; Bidwell, Frank, and Quiroz 1997), who have categorized different teacher types, how they function, and how their interactions influence organizational efficiency, including student socialization and learning. Using a field-based approach, Moore-Johnson (1990) has constructed an expansive, detailed view of the teacher's worklife including physical settings and resources, quality of relationships, influence in governance, opportunities for professional development, and salary inequities. Ingersoll (1996), employing large-scale national databases, has shown the consequences to student learning when teacher certification practices are compromised by assigning teachers to classrooms where they have limited knowledge of the subject matter that they are expected to teach.

The study of schools as social organizations involves more than an analysis of the role of the teaching profession. Dreeben (1994) suggests that it was Parsons (1959) who first covered an extraordinary conceptual range of issues pertaining to the social organization of schooling, including the separation of school populations into different learning opportunity structures and the consequences this has for occupational placement and status attainment as well as an individual's participation in society. It may be that Dreeben's humility and perhaps reverence for his teacher are somewhat overplayed and his own contribution understated. Dreeben's analysis of the organizational structure of school systems, schools, and classrooms provides one of the richest conceptualizations of how the educational system is organized and operates, and the consequences these factors have on the achievement of students and the lives of their teachers (Dreeben [1968] 2002, 1970, 1973; Barr and Dreeben 1983). One of the common themes in all of his work is the importance of distinguishing between the formal organizational structure of schools (including membership and authority) and a more sociological approach that views schools on the basis of activities, technology, affiliation, and values (Dreeben 1973).

The concept of curriculum differentiation—that is, how learning opportunities in classrooms are unequally dispersed among students, and what gets learned either formally or informally through this differentiated process—is theoretically and empirically unique to Dreeben. While Parsons's contribution to these issues initially provoked considerable controversy, the lack of empirical evidence did little to advance the field. In contrast, Dreeben's work (1970) and that of his colleague Barr (Barr and Dreeben 1983; Dreeben and Barr 1987) opened a new line of inquiry by examining the internal structure of schools, including the relationship between teachers and students and—perhaps more important—how social and material resources are allocated for instruction.

In the work of Dreeben (1970), Barr and Dreeben (1983), and Hallinan and Sørensen (1983), which focused on classrooms in elementary schools, the intricate and complex decisions of classroom management and instructional practice are revealed as having significant effects on student learning. How the teacher organizes the class for instruction, on what basis students are grouped for instruction (Hallinan and Sørensen 1983; Sørensen and Hallinan 1986), how instruction and content vary among these groups (Dreeben and Gamoran 1986; Gamoran 1987), and what effect being in one group versus another has on achievement and friendship patterns (Hallinan and Williams 1989; Cohen 1997; Carbonaro 1998) all demonstrate how student learning opportunities are stratified within schools. Elementary and more recently middle schools have been the focus of this type of within-classroom research, while the high school has been largely neglected.

Research at the high school level has mainly centered on programmatic and course-sequencing issues (Alexander and Cook 1982; Garet and Delany 1988; Stevenson, Schiller, and Schneider 1994; Lucas 1999) rather than on the types of instructional practices and learning opportunities that are afforded to students within courses. Some newer work has been conducted with a small number of high school programs that are designed to transform classroom practices, but these studies have limited samples and lack control groups. Questions regarding how teachers organize their classes for instruction, the learning opportunities that they provide to their students, and how students respond both cognitively and socially remain a fertile ground for additional theoretical and empirical analyses.

One of the problems with social organizational studies has been that empirical investigations are narrow, restricting their attention to the curriculum—that is, what is taught and how the teacher functions—rather than examining the classroom or the school as social systems. By focusing on what is taught, researchers reinforce the link to education while often ignoring more general sociological issues. A more extensive critique of this point can be found in Bidwell (1973, 1980), which identify several promising areas for sociological studies of classrooms and teachers that continue to be unexplored empirically.

Not all studies of the curriculum are devoid of sociological content. The social class concept is perhaps best understood in the work of Bernstein

(Bernstein 1977; Sadovnik 1991) who has used the nature of the curriculum to explore issues of social class and the dominance of Western culture as it is transmitted through language. Using subject matter as the starting point, Farkas's (1996) studies of reading and Gamoran and his associates' (1995) studies of English combine a sociological organizational and an educational lens to show relationships between fundamental distinctions in learning opportunities, including teacher activities and student socioeconomic backgrounds.

Social and cultural reproduction theorists also argue that the structure and curriculum of schools create an environment of gender bias (Connell 1987). One of the major interests of sociologists of education has been in the access of girls to certain courses and learning opportunities at all levels of the educational system (Hanson, Schaub, and Baker 1996; Muller 1998), differences in achievement between boys and girls (Mickelson 1989), and the cognitive and social advantages of attending a same-sex school (Riordan 1990; Lee, Marks, and Byrd 1994). How elementary and secondary schools and the curriculum are organized to retain and reinforce traditional gender images has received less attention from sociologists of education. Sociologists interested in gender have examined children's play groups at school (Thorne 1993) and women's role in the family and workplace (Hochschild 1989, 1997), but few have focused on the organization of schools and differences in the experiences of girls and boys. Rather, it has primarily been psychologists who have related differences in achievement to the emotional experiences of females and males (Sadker and Sadker 1994). A notable exception is the edited volume by Wrigley (1992).

More organizational conceptual frameworks for studies of the class-room—such as emphasizing the incentive nature of the instruction, the cooperative and competitive characteristics of learning and social activities, the moral order that is reinforced by the teacher, and more general organizational features of how classrooms function—have yet to receive the same attention as the content of the curriculum and stratification of learning activities. This sociological perspective, however, can be found in work by Stevenson (1991) where he shows how deviants can be a collective resource in classrooms. Observing students in several classrooms, he demonstrates how the same number of deviant students are identified and reproached by the teachers in different classrooms regardless of the ability and behavior of the students in each respective class. However, the same students are not necessarily identified as deviant during the school year. Such findings suggest that socialization norms for behavior are directly linked to how classrooms are organized, raising the questions of whether social control needs to be realized rather than abstractly conveyed and, on a more practical level, the question of how deviant students are selected and maintained in classrooms.

EXPANDING THE CONCEPTUAL CORE

While Dreeben's review of the field focused primarily on studies conducted early in the last century, after the 1950s work in sociology of education took on a slightly different cast and three other conceptual strands began to assert a stronger presence in the field: inequality and social justice, globalization and the expansion of schooling, and social networks and their influence on behaviors and social norms. These themes were explored in sociology before the 1950s; however, unlike work related to social mobility, community, and the social organization of schools (where connections to past research are tightly linked), the connections between current work on these ideas and previous studies are weaker and more ambiguous. To a large extent, these themes could be characterized as elaborations and reworkings of the conceptual ideas previously identified by Dreeben. The first two of these themes are directly related to major societal changes resulting from federal actions, including *Brown* v. *Board of Education* (1954) and the subsequent civil rights legislation, the increasing diversification of the American population, and the rapid expansion of the formalized education marketplace. The third arises in part from the sustained interest in the study of mid-level theories that can potentially link microresults to more macrolevel analyses.

In contrast to work conducted in the first half of the last century, investigators sometimes find that the technology available to them is far more sophisticated than their study designs. Researchers can now choose from an arsenal of methods for analyzing data, ranging from event history analysis for longitudinal data to simultaneous equation techniques; statistical programs for analyzing networks of people or clusters of social entities; geographical programs for examining spatial configurations; algorithms for determining global constructs; powerful data-mining techniques for pattern recognition; and qualitative data analysis packages that can sift through reams of interview and observational data in formats that defy conventional patterns, including information obtained through video and audio recordings. Such methodological advances have the potential to apply new statistical power and other forms of compelling evidence to understanding education and constructing social policy.

Inequality and Social Justice

In the 1950s questions regarding social inequality infused the social sciences and sociology in particular as many scholars and policymakers challenged the segregation policies that permeated American society. The Supreme Court's decision in *Brown*, which found that separate schools for white and black children were unconstitutional because separate educational facilities were inherently unequal, established a legal precedent that essentially tied issues of race and schooling to questions of social justice. As Walters (2001) points out, although the *Brown* decision was viewed as a remedy for desegregation, the decision was virtually impossible to enforce. Not until the enactment of the Civil Rights Act of 1964, which prohibited federal funds being funneled to schools that discriminated on the basis of race, did the federal government have a policy tool for challenging racial segregation in public schools. The subsequent passage of the Elementary and Secondary Education Act (ESEA), which provided additional funding for schools with low-income children, produced the monetary incentive that enticed many school systems to change attendance boundaries, thus overriding the inherent racial and ethnic bias found among school staff and parents.

These pieces of legislation demonstrated a historical shift whereby education became publicly identified as a central mechanism for both social mobility and equal access to and participation in society. This shift has resulted in education being more formally recognized as the route into full adult status, and consequently educational quality and attainment have become intertwined with concerns for social justice. The intent of the ESEA legislation was that compensatory education should be provided to children whose economic and social backgrounds prevented them from acquiring the skills that would allow them to compete for jobs against children who had more family and educational resources. How education was being dispersed was in fact inherently unfair, thus making it nearly impossible for those without access to higher quality learning opportunities to subsequently be competitive for jobs. Before students even had the opportunity to enter school, their learning opportunities were compromised. This more instrumental approach to education has led sociologists to focus on determining what the barriers are to educational opportunities and the extent to which such barriers should be removed.

The congressional role in promoting civil rights extended into the scholarly community, and in the early 1960s plans were put in place to conduct a major study to learn about the allocation of resources in schools and their impact on the educational achievement of black students. After some negotiating, Coleman was selected to head the Equality of Educational Opportunity study (Coleman et al. 1966), which produced a set of controversial findings in what later became known as the Coleman Report. At a deeper level, one could argue that this massive study (which surveyed 639,650 students in elementary and high schools and their teachers and administrators) was really an attempt by Congress to use social science to determine the extent to which America's school systems were violating principles of justice and denying specific rights and opportunities to students—in this case, poor blacks.

Coleman's findings indicated that one of the major differences between southern schools and those in the North was the lower quality of their teachers. Although less statistically robust, the findings for desegregation nonetheless showed that black children did better in school when they attended schools with children of other races—a result that was subsequently used in the early 1970s desegregation cases (e.g., Swann v. Charlotte-Mecklenburg Board of Education, 1971). Another finding that also received considerable attention among sociologists of education was that family background characteristics were far more important for a child's academic performance than the teachers or the school. Whereas issues concerning the teachers were relatively straightforward, the regulation of these inequities among families became much more difficult to address. The government could justifiably intervene in schools; this was not the case in families. Despite these rather disappointing school effects results, scholars refused to concede that the educational system was intractable. Coleman's findings merely fueled the desire of researchers to isolate school-related policies that could be changed to level the playing field and channel resources to those who had never even had a chance to enter the game.

Over thirty years ago, Dreeben (1971) made the prediction that we would come to see schooling as an extension of welfare rights. It would appear that this is the case, even though the U.S. Supreme Court has failed to recognize education as a fundamental right as shown in the school finance cases. Despite the actions taken by the Supreme Court, researchers and policymakers have not been swayed from initiating studies and policies that are based on the premise that unequal educational opportunities are a violation of one's rights. Questions in sociology of education now seriously examine whether policies in or out of school are morally and legally just, right, or fair, particularly for racial and ethnic minorities. Much of the work in the field today that relates to desegregation (Wells and Crain 1994; Orfield 2001), busing (Mickelson, Ray, and Smith 1994), immigration (Kao and Tienda 1995; Portes and MacLeod 1996), the adoption of bilingual education (Portes and Schauffler 1996), and analyses of test score differences among diverse populations (Jencks and Phillips 1998) are strongly based on a platform of social justice as a means of social reform. Researchers are interested in the extent to which the denial of opportunity creates situations for individuals and social institutions that are presumed to be ethically and socially unjust.

One could argue that social mobility—the focus of earlier sociologists—had an individualistic emphasis, whereas sociologists interested in social justice are more concerned with collective change. Scholarly work that emanates from a theory of social justice is different in form and content from studies that identify barriers to social mobility for all citizens. In these types of studies, the research has a moral imperative. The intent is to learn which basic liberties—such as freedom of thought and conscience and the rights of individuals, particularly as they relate to child care (Fuller et al. 1996), educational practice (Wells 1997), and occupational opportunities (Wilson 1996)—have been denied and to assure that these liberties are provided to all.

The controversies surrounding studies of school choice have their roots in this theme of social justice (Fuller, Elmore, and Orfield 1996). Two interesting and complementary sociological themes run through the school choice literature. The first is the question of parent choice with respect to education and the socialization of their children and how that may conflict with the interests of the state. This issue is one of parent rights and has its roots in early sociological theory regarding the rights of the individual versus those of the wider community. The second is the denial of choice to those, particularly poor and minority children, who have been denied access to higher quality schools because of the racially segregated attendance boundaries of many public school systems. Sociologists of education have tended to focus on the second theme, examining the constraints of the public system and how students and parents respond to choice options, suggesting that choice in of itself will not achieve a more equitable educational system (Cookson 1994; Lee, Croninger, and Smith 1994; Wells 1996). Another group of investigators, taking a more economic perspective, tends to be more concerned with questions of efficiency. This economic market-based perspective draws investigators to macro-school organizational issues, such as administrative practices, although these studies also relate these practices to student outcomes (Chubb and Moe 1990). As educational reforms continue to target schools as a mechanism for reducing inequalities, investigations of both of these strands are likely to continue.

The causal relationship between choice and achievement seems premature, mainly because of data limitations. We have yet to learn conclusively whether participants in school choice programs achieve greater occupational success in adulthood compared to those who are either denied the opportunity to choose or choose not to take advantage of these programs. Studies of school choice have also not yet overcome the inadequacies we find in studies of the social organization of public schools. One reason may be that the pressure to link school choice with gains in student achievement has placed issues of selection bias and test score differences at the forefront, thus overshadowing serious efforts to examine qualitative differences in the learning opportunities experienced in choice versus other types of school settings.

Theoretically, one of the major constraints facing sociologists of education interested in issues of social justice is the considerable attention paid to the formal structure of institutions and the probable consequences of certain policies as opposed to sources of discrimination, particularly as these relate to racism. Today there tend to be few as bold as Wilson (1996), who demonstrated how discrimination and prejudice play out in the hiring practices of American business with respect to African Americans. Racism and discrimination, particularly within educational research, have often been sanitized by focusing on variations in teacher expectations rather than directly addressing the low level of expectations that teachers typically have for their black students and how they adjust their pedagogy to accommodate their expectations. Increasingly, questions regarding the meaning of race, culture, and socioeconomic class are being pushed to the forefront of the social science agenda. Supported by recent gene research, in 1998 the Executive Board of the American Anthropological Association issued a statement indicating that establishing groups on the basis of physical variations among populations is arbitrary and subjective. Following the AAA, the American Sociological Association has also created a panel to develop a statement on race. Race, it has been argued, does not exist from a scientific and biological point of view, but does exist as a social and political construct (Graves 2001). As more formalized statements are made on the biological and social definitions of race, investigators will be increasingly challenged in their treatment of race as a social construct. How social institutions and the individuals within them cope with this reality will undoubtedly affect our understandings of social justice and the research that is pursued to achieve it.

Studies that have societal reform as their primary aim may not be concerned with whether such reforms benefit all segments of society equally and fairly. As Dreeben pointed out (1994), early sociologists believed that only those few who exhibited unusual talents inconsistent with their social origins should be educated. In contrast, studies of social justice are focused more on fairness for all and attempt to learn which barriers deny individuals or specific groups equal rights or liberties. This emphasis places a considerable burden on analyses that can precisely identify sources of causality. The two major studies by Jencks and his associates (1972, 1979) are perhaps the best examples of this type of work: empirical investigations into the relationships among various kinds of inequality—primarily occupational status and earnings—taking into account family background, ability, and schooling and work experiences. Such studies encourage seeking remedies such as affirmative action policies that obviate existing as well as prior injustices. However, even in the instance of affirmative action, the question of whose rights and liberties are being compromised makes solutions difficult. Studies of social justice, it would seem, require empirical analyses that are longitudinal in nature. This is ironic since it is these types of analyses that are currently becoming unfashionable, just as the need for them seems even more compelling than in the past.

Globalization and the Expansion of Schooling

A second theme that has increasingly become a focus of research in sociology of education is the globalization of education. In its most recent manifestations, this line of study has centered on international comparisons of student achievement that examine schools and schooling outcomes across nation-states. This research is best exemplified by international studies of achievement such as the Third International Mathematics and Science Studies, where U.S. school children have consistently scored lower on tests in science and mathematics than children in other countries (Schmidt, McKnight, and Raizen 1997). The less than sterling performance of U.S. students is attributed to teachers and textbooks that cover too much material and fewer subjects in depth compared to the information provided to students outside the United States. In defense of the teachers and students, some have argued that the size of this difference in U.S. scores is small compared to other countries given the large and diverse client population the U.S. serves. While this may be so, the fact that 32 nation-states can agree on test content across multiple ages, and trust enough in their findings to worry about effect sizes, speaks more to a global curriculum—at least among industrialized and developing countries—than those who believe in local cultural influences might perhaps assume.

Mass schooling has become a standardized activity throughout the world and nearly all nation-states endorse primary education as a fundamental human right (Ramirez and Ventresca 1992). What is perhaps most surprising is that the world's societies are structurally similar in many unexpected dimensions and change in unexpectedly similar ways (Meyer et al. 1997). I would argue that the desire to achieve universal education created a need for a deeper theoretical understanding of the institutionalization of schooling. The work of Meyer is of interest here, for not only did he define schooling and how it operated in the United States, but he also provided the theoretical tools for understanding how these concepts applied to educational systems elsewhere.

Meyer (1977) defined schools and their curricula in institutional terms—that is, as socially constructed objectified symbols that are embedded in organizational structures that are transportable. Despite local cultures, power relationships, and local economic forces, mass schooling assumes a standardized form in various nation-states. What is particularly important about Meyer's concept of the institutionalization of schooling is that it provides us with a frame for comparing particular educational practices among nation-states, such as centralized state control of the curriculum (Stevenson and Baker 1991); "shadow education," the learning resources provided to students by their parents outside of the formalized school environment (Stevenson and Baker 1992; Baker et al. 2001); and female enrollment in higher education (Bradley and Ramierez 1996). Although the institutionalization of models may be similar, they may encounter specific problems in certain locales—for example, providing sophisticated technical university training for nonexistent jobs. The global education marketplace of ideas and practices is as real as any other product market. However, this exchange of practice in many ways merely strengthens the viability and institutionalization of different pedagogies, organizational structures, and assessment practices such as the standards movement and national testing.

Schooling, as we know it, is being dramatically transformed by globalization buttressed by technological support systems. The educational experiences of students, whether in preschool or postsecondary institutions, are being shaped by communication and information technologies. Internet connections bring a global society into American homes with a stark reality that is as compelling as the fantasy world of television and the movies. From learning tools to degrees, the computer opens a window for everyone. This rapid access to worldwide networks of information may more closely align the technical core of instruction to conform with institutionalized notions of schooling.

Meyer's argument about the institutionalization of education is not without critics, and while a standard model of schooling may be found in all parts of the globe, there certainly are instances where the curriculum content seems inappropriate for the population. Some have questioned whether Meyer's conception of schooling allows for a closer analysis of the inner workings of the educational system—that is, how federal, state, and district policies can direct-ly influence schooling outcomes. What seems particularly useful about Meyer's idea is that it is possible to isolate what appears to be universalistic and what appears to be idiosyncratic to individual practice and then to reconcile these differences. The richness of the research lies in identifying which practices are decoupled from the institutionalization of schools and the impact that has, not only on educational outcomes but on the teachers and other education per-sonnel who work within the system. Underscoring this idea, several studies are underway that link administrative acts—that is, standard-based reforms—with teacher practices and student outcomes (Swanson and Stevenson 2002).

In the future researchers will be able to discern if in fact nation-states adopt standard identities and structural forms. More important, it should be possible to learn whether the movement is toward closer alignment with stan-dards or attempts to forge distinctive identities. One of the first changes after the fall of the Taliban government in Afghanistan was the reopening of schools to girls. The admission of girls to educational institutions speaks to the func-tional global view of educating all students. Decoupling concepts facilitates the study of variations in schooling experiences for women and how their educational credentials serve them in the labor market.

Social Networks and Their Influence on Behaviors and Social Norms

Sociology is the study of social systems, and one of the most interesting advances in the field has been in our ability to understand conceptually and empirically how individuals interact with one another and the quality of those relationships. In contrast to the work on status attainment that has been on the individual level, social network studies—particularly those at the level at which observations are made—address both actions and orientations (Coleman 1990). One of the major problems in sociology has been taking these lower level actions and orientations and using them to explain larger system-level problems, the micro to macro problem which is consistent throughout the social sciences. Whereas earlier work in sociology of educa-tion focused on factors that affect achievement—and especially inequality and social justice—by looking at a hierarchy of levels from the student through the class, school, district, and state, social network studies examine these topics through the relationships that link and cut across these different levels of analysis. In several instances researchers have been able to make these link-ages, and in doing so have forged several conceptual advances in descriptions of educational social systems.

In the field of sociology of education, there are at least two distinct types of social network problems. First are those that use formal social network analysis to describe social systems. Examples of this type would be studies of friendships and sexual behaviors among adolescents (Udry and Bearman 1998); studies of relationships among teachers in high schools to understand how information about educational reforms is learned, shared, and adopted (Frank and Fahrbach 1999); consequences of teacher networks on their beliefs and understandings of instructional aims, procedures, and standards (Bidwell and Yasumoto 1999); and student curriculum positions in high schools and their effects on achievement (Friedkin and Thomas 1997). Second are studies that examine the nature of these social networks. These studies do not use formal network methodology, although they are interested in characterizing social relationships to understand more fully the operation of the social system. Examples of this research would be social exchange of student work for teachers' grades (simulated data, Coleman 1990); informational network exchanges among students with limited social resources and their relationship to educational attainment (Stanton-Salazer and Dornbush 1995; Hill 2001); and relational trust among teachers, parents, and administrators (Bryk and Schneider 2002).

One of the key conceptual ideas that form the bases of these studies of social networks is the concept of social capital—that is, a set of relational ties that facilitate action (Coleman 1988). Since the concept of social capital was formally introduced in the late 1980s, the number of published works on this topic has been substantial, although some of the work assumes that social capital is merely the sharing of information. This perspective understates and misinterprets the value of social capital for explaining social behaviors at both a macrolevel and microlevel (see Putnam, Leonardi, and Nanetti 1993; Fukuyama 1995; Putnam 2000). The value of social capital is its ability to provide a mechanism of social control within a social system by creating norms and sanctions that are based on obligations, expectations, and trustworthiness. However, as Furstenberg and Hughes (1995) argue, social capital is not a global concept that ensures a successful and uniform outcome. While promoting certain norms, it may produce negative effects for different aims. For example, strong ties among gang members may encourage deviant behaviors. As a concept social capital has very useful properties for understanding relational ties and outcomes in social systems that comprise our postmodern, technological society. Other forms of capital also have particular importance to sociologists of education. Cultural capital is defined as the resources that are acquired in childhood from one's parents and community that are passed on from one generation to the next. Human capital is defined as the educational resources embodied in an individual as the consequence of additional schooling. Distinctions between human capital, cultural capital, and social capital are discussed by Coleman (1988). Social capital is deliberately highlighted here because it is conceptually germane to relational network studies.

CONCLUSION

From its beginnings as a specialization within the discipline, sociology of education has addressed how education can improve society and by what means. The joining of sociology with education has been problematic primarily because of the low status of education as a field of intellectual inquiry within the social sciences and questions regarding the quality of the teachers and professors who are trained in schools and colleges of education. Despite these questions, sociology of education has been a prolific field, populated with key figures in sociology who have drawn attention to the importance of education for advancing societal reforms, promoting social mobility, stimulating the economy, and rectifying inequities in learning opportunities.

In the early part of the last century, substantive work in the field centered on three topics: status attainment, community studies, and the social organization of schooling (Dreeben 1994). Each of these areas was widely researched, although critics have been quick to suggest that some of this work is flawed because it is not sociological enough in its focus and thus does not sufficiently examine contextual factors, whether in the family, school, or community. Even though there have been methodological advances that allow for exploration of nested contexts that affect individuals, groups, and institutions, some criticisms continue to prevail. One concern has been the limited work on conceptual frameworks for constructing and interpreting the relationships that exist among individuals and their social systems including family, peers, religious groups, and other informal and formal organizations.

One of the few scholars who moved both theoretical and empirical work more deeply into context was Dreeben, whose work focused on the inner workings of schools and classrooms and how organizational differences affected the educational opportunities of the students. Through his work Dreeben provided not only a fuller definition of the field of sociology of education, but also a richer and more comprehensive understanding of how schools work. Dreeben's work and that of his colleague Barr show how the intricate and complex decisions of classroom management and instructional practice profoundly affect the stratification of student learning opportunities within schools and the lasting impact that such practices can have on students' lives in school.

While questions related to status attainment, community, and the social organization of schooling continue to be present in much of today's work in sociology of education, societal changes in the 1960s spurred a renewed interest in social reform that broadened the somewhat narrow focus on social mobility to questions of social justice. Sociologists of education became increasingly interested in education not only because of its long-term consequences for our nation's political strength and economic growth, but also because of more immediate concerns with fairness and social justice as young people experienced it everyday in their schools and communities. These same questions of social justice also transfer to concerns about higher education and affirmative action as it relates to admissions and occupational placements. The broadening of sociology of education also moved outside the United States. As the world shrinks in size from an informational perspective, a pervasive educational model is being replicated throughout the globe, and this may present opportunities and its own set of issues as nation-states accelerate their knowledge production. But as those who work in this area have shown, the hegemonic model of education does not necessarily filter down into local practice and significant discontinuities between goals and actions exist among nation-states. The model of globalization of education continues to develop both theoretically and empirically and can be seen as an expansion of the earlier community studies that were conducted only within the United States. Today our interest is in how local practice, whether it be in the United States or abroad, links to state and national conceptions of education.

Finally, sociology of education shares with the larger discipline a continuing interest in the study of social systems—that is, how individuals interact with one another and the quality of those relationships. Recent work has demonstrated how powerful the quality of relationships can be for stimulating institutional change by linking relationships across various levels, some hierarchical and some horizontal. Social network studies can be especially useful for providing new insights into the operation of social systems by identifying theoretical properties for understanding relational ties and various outcomes—be they school improvement, postsecondary matriculation, or diffusion of instructional practices.

Sociology of education continues to evolve as a subspecialization within sociology. While studies of status attainment previously dominated work in this area, this review shows how sociology of education today includes a wider range of topics, one of the most promising in the area of social networks. Although sociologists of education are unlikely to independently raise the quality of education or ensure that schools provide more equitable services to their clients, they are likely to continue to learn which conditions both within and outside the school are impeding learning and contributing to unequal educational opportunities throughout various levels of the schooling system. That is in large measure because scholars such as Robert Dreeben have continued to encourage us to pay closer attention to microlevel actions and orientations in order to better understand more macrolevel problems.

Acknowledgments

I would like to thank Charles Bidwell, Robert Dreeben, and John Meyer for their helpful comments and suggestions.

REFERENCES

Abbott, Andrew. 1988. *System of Professions: An Essay on the Division of Expert Labor.* Chicago: University of Chicago Press.

Abbott, Andrew. 1999. *Department and Discipline: Chicago Sociology at One Hundred.* Chicago: University of Chicago Press.

Alexander, Karl L. and Martha A. Cook. 1982. "Curricula and Coursework: A Surprise Ending to a Familiar Story." *American Sociological Review* 47:626–40.

Alexander, Karl L. and Edward L. McDill. 1976. "Selection and Allocation within Schools." *American Sociological Review* 41:963–80.

Arum, Richard. 1998. "Invested Dollars or Diverted Dreams: The Effect of Resources on Vocational Students' Educational Outcomes." *Sociology of Education* 71:130–51.

Baker, David P., Motoko Akiba, Gerald K. LeTendre, and Alexander W. Wiseman. 2001. "Worldwide Shadow Education: Outside-School Learning, Institutional Quality of Schooling, and Cross-National Mathematics Achievement." *Educational Evaluation and Policy Analysis* 23:1–17.

Baker, David P. and David L. Stevenson. 1986. "Mothers' Strategies for Children's School Achievement: Managing the Transition to High School." *Sociology of Education* 59:156–66.

Barr, Rebecca and Robert Dreeben. 1983. *How Schools Work*. Chicago: University of Chicago Press.

Becker, Gary S. 1964. *Human Capital: A Theoretical and Empirical Analysis*. New York: National Bureau of Economic Research.

Becker, Howard S. 1952. "The Career of the Chicago Public School Teacher." *American Journal of Sociology* 57:470–77.

Becker, Howard S. 1953. "The Teacher in the Authority System of the Public School." *Journal of Educational Sociology* 27:128–41.

Bernstein, Basil. 1977. *Class, Codes, and Control, Volume 3: Towards a Theory of Educational Transmissions*, rev. ed. London: Routledge & Kegan Paul.

Bidwell, Charles E. 1965."The School as a Formal Organization." Pp. 972–1022 in *Handbook of Organizations*, edited by James G. March. Chicago: Rand McNally.

Bidwell, Charles E. 1973. "The Social Psychology of Teaching." Pp. 413–49 in *Second Handbook of Research on Teaching*, edited by Robert M. W. Travers. Chicago: Rand McNally.

Bidwell, Charles E. 1980. "The Sociology of the School and Classroom." Pp. 99–114 in *Sociological Theory and Research: A Critical Appraisal*, edited by Hubert M. Blalock, Jr. New York: Free Press.

Bidwell, Charles E. 1989. "Willard Waller and the Sociology of Education." Pp. 39–51 in *Willard Waller on Education and Schools: A Critical Appraisal*, edited by Donald. J. Willower and William Lowe Boyd. Berkeley, CA: McCutchan.

Bidwell, Charles E. and Anthony Bryk. 1994. *How Teacher's Work Is Original: The Content and Consequences of the Structure of the High School Workplace*. Unpublished report, National Opinion Research Center and Ogburn-Stouffer Center, University of Chicago.

Bidwell, Charles E., Kenneth A. Frank, and Pamela A. Quiroz. 1997. "Teacher Types, Workplace Controls, and the Organization of Schools." *Sociology of Education* 70:285–307.

Bidwell, Charles E. and Noah E. Friedkin. 1988. "Sociology of Education." Pp. 449–71 in *Handbook of Sociology*, edited by Neil J. Smelser. Newbury Park, CA: Sage.

Bidwell, Charles E. and Jeffrey Y. Yasumoto. 1999. "The Collegial Focus: Teaching Fields, Collegial Relationships, and Instructional Practice in American High Schools." *Sociology of Education* 72:234–56.

Blau, Judith R., Vicki L. Lamb, Elizabeth Stearns, and Lisa A. Pellerin. 2000. "Cosmopolitan Environments and Adolescents' Gains in Social Studies." *Sociology of Education* 74:121–38.

Borman, Kathryn M. 1991. *The First "Real" Job: A Study of Young Workers*. Albany: State University of New York Press.

Bourdieu, Pierre and Jean-Claude Passeron. 1977. *Reproduction in Education, Society and Culture* (Richard Nice, trans.). London: Sage.

Bowles, Samuel and Herbert Gintis. 1976. *Schooling in Capitalist America: Educational Reforms and the Contradictions of Economic Life*. New York: Basic Books.

Bradley, Karen and Francisco O. Ramirez. 1996. "World Polity and Gender Parity: Women's Share of Higher Education, 1965–85." Pp. 63–92 in *Research in Sociology of Education and Socialization*, vol. 11, edited by Aaron M. Pallas. Greenwich, CT: JAI Press.

Brint, Steven and Jerome Karabel. 1989. *The Diverted Dream: Community Colleges and the Promise of Educational Opportunity in America, 1900–1985*. New York: Oxford University Press.

Bryk, Anthony S., Valerie E. Lee, and Peter B. Holland. 1993. *Catholic Schools and the Common Good*. Cambridge, MA: Harvard University Press.

Bryk, Anthony S. and Stephen W. Raudenbush. 1992. *Hierarchical Linear Models: Applications and Data Analysis Methods*. Newbury Park, CA: Sage.

Bryk, Anthony S. and Barbara Schneider. 2002. *Relational Trust: A Core Resource for School Improvement*. New York: Russell Sage Foundation.

Carbonaro, William J. 1998. "A Little Help from My Friend's Parents: Intergenerational Closure and Educational Outcomes." *Sociology of Education* 71:295–313.

220 Barbara Schneider

220 Barbara Schneider

Carbonaro, William J. 1999. "Opening the Debate on Closure and Schooling Outcomes: Comment on Morgan and Sørensen." *American Sociological Review* 64:682–86.

Chubb, John E. and Terry M. Moe. 1990. *Politics, Markets, and America's Schools.* Washington, DC: Brookings Institution Press.

Cohen, Elizabeth G. 1997. "Equity in Heterogeneous Classrooms: A Challenge for Teachers and Sociologists." Pp. 3–14 in *Working for Equity in Heterogeneous Classrooms: Sociological Theory in Practice,* edited by Elizabeth G. Cohen and Rachel A. Lotan. New York: Teachers College Press.

Coleman, James S. 1961. *The Adolescent Society: The Social Life of the Teenager and Its Impact on Education.* New York: Free Press.

Coleman, James S. 1988. "Social Capital in the Creation of Human Capital." *American Journal of Sociology* 94:95–120.

Coleman, James S. 1990. *Foundations of Social Theory.* Cambridge, MA: Belknap Press/Harvard University Press.

Coleman, James S., Ernest Q. Campbell, Carol J. Hobson, James McPartland, Alexander M. Mood, Frederic D. Weinfeld and Robert L. York. 1966. *Equality of Educational Opportunity.* Washington, DC: U.S. Government Printing Office.

Coleman, James S. and Thomas Hoffer. 1987. *Public and Private Schools: The Impact of Communities.* New York: Basic Books.

Connell, Robert W. 1987. *Gender and Power: Society, the Person, and Sexual Politics.* Cambridge, UK: Polity Press.

Cookson, Jr., Peter W. 1994. *School Choice: The Struggle for the Soul of American Education.* New Haven, CT: Yale University Press.

Cookson, Jr., Peter W. and Caroline Hodges Persell. 1985. *Preparing for Power: America's Elite Boarding Schools.* New York: Basic Books.

Counts, George S. 1927. "The Subject Matter of the Curriculum and Sociology." *Journal of Educational Sociology* 1:11–17.

Dance, Lory J. 2000. "'Hard' Like a 'Gangsta': The Impact of Street Culture on Schooling." Unpublished manuscript, Department of Sociology, University of Maryland.

Dewey, John. 1900. *The School and Society,* 3rd ed. Chicago: University of Chicago Press.

DiMaggio, Paul J. 1982. "Cultural Capital and School Success: The Impact of Status Culture Participation on the Grades of U.S. High School Students." *American Sociological Review* 47:189–201.

Dreeben, Robert. [1968] 2002. *On What Is Learned in School.* Clinton Corners, NY: Percheron Press/Eliot Werner Publications.

Dreeben, Robert. 1970. *The Nature of Teaching: Schools and the Work of Teachers.* Glenview, IL: Scott, Foresman.

Dreeben, Robert. 1971. "American Schooling: Patterns and Processes of Stability and Change." Pp. 82–119 in *Stability and Social Change,* edited by Bernard Barber and Alex Inkeles. Boston: Little, Brown.

Dreeben, Robert. 1973. "The School as a Workplace." Pp. 450–73 in *Second Handbook of Research in Teaching,* edited by Robert M. W. Travers. Chicago: Rand McNally.

Dreeben, Robert. 1994. "The Sociology of Education: Its Development in the United States." Pp. 7–52 in *Research in Sociology of Education and Socialization,* vol. 10, edited by Aaron M. Pallas. Greenwich, CT: JAI Press.

Dreeben, Robert and Rebecca Barr. 1987. "An Organizational Analysis of Curriculum and Instruction." Pp. 13–19 in *The Social Organization of Schools: New Conceptualizations of the Learning Process,* edited by Maureen T. Hallinan. New York: Plenum.

Dreeben, Robert and Adam Gamoran. 1986. "Race, Instruction, and Learning." *American Sociological Review* 51:660–69.

Duncan, Otis Dudley and Robert W. Hodge. 1963. "Education and Occupational Mobility: A Regression Analysis." *American Journal of Sociology* 68:629–44.

Durkheim, Emile [1897] 1951. *Suicide: A Study in Sociology* (George Simpson, trans.). New York: Free Press.

Durkheim, Emile. [1912] 1995. *The Elementary Forms of Religious Life* (Karen E. Fields, trans.). New York: Free Press.

Durkheim, Emile. [1922] 1956. *Education and Sociology* (Sherwood D. Fox, trans.). New York: Free Press.

Durkheim, Emile. [1925] 1961. *Moral Education: A Study in the Theory and Application of the Sociology of Education* (Everett K. Wilson and Herman Schurer, trans.). Glencoe, IL: Free Press.

Durkheim, Emile. [1938] 1977. *The Evolution of Educational Thought* (Peter Collins, trans.). London: Routledge & Kegan Paul.

Elder, Jr., Glen H. 1999. *Children of the Great Depression: Social Change in Life Experience.* Boulder, CO: Westview Press.

Elder, Jr., Glen H. and Rand D. Conger. 2000. *Children of the Land: Adversity and Success in Rural America.* Chicago: University of Chicago Press.

Ellwood, Charles A. 1927. "What Is Educational Sociology?" *Journal of Educational Sociology* 1:25–30.

Entwisle, Doris R., Karl L. Alexander, and Linda Steffel Olson. 2000. "Early Work Histories of Urban Youth." *American Sociological Review* 65:279–97.

Epstein, Joyce L. 2001. *School and Family Partnership: Preparing Educators and Improving Schools.* Boulder, CO: Westview Press.

Epstein, Joyce L. and Marvis G. Sanders. 2000. "Connecting Home, School, and Community: New Directions for Social Research." Pp. 285–306 in *Handbook of the Sociology of Education,* edited by Maureen T. Hallinan. New York: Kluwer Academic/Plenum.

Farkas, George. 1996. *Human Capital or Cultural Capital? Ethnicity and Poverty Groups in an Urban School District.* New York: Aldine de Gruyter.

Firestone, William A. 1994. "Redesigning Teacher Salary Systems for Educational Reform." *American Educational Research Journal* 31:549–74.

Frank, Kenneth A. and Kyle Fahrbach. 1999. "Organizational Culture as a Complex System: Balance and Information in Models of Influence and Selection." *Organization Science* 10:253–77.

Friedkin, Noah E. and Scott L. Thomas. 1997. "Social Positions in Schooling." *Sociology of Education* 70:239–55.

Fukuyama, Francis. 1995. *Trust: Social Virtues and the Creation of Prosperity.* New York: Free Press.

Fullan, Michael. 2001. *The New Meaning of Educational Change,* 3rd ed. New York: Teachers College Press.

Fuller, Bruce, Richard F. Elmore, and Gary Orfield, eds. 1996. *Who Chooses? Who Loses? Culture, Institutions, and the Unequal Effects of School Choice.* New York: Teachers College Press.

Fuller, Bruce, Susan D. Holloway, Marylee Rambaud, and Costanza Eggers-Pierola. 1996. "How Do Mothers Choose Child-Care? Alternative Cultural Models in Poor Neighborhoods." *Sociology of Education* 69:83–105.

Furstenberg, Frank and Mary Elizabeth Hughes. 1995. "Social Capital and Successful Development among At-Risk Youth." *Journal of Marriage and the Family* 57:580–92.

Gambetta, Diego. 1987. *Were They Pushed or Did They Jump? Individual Decision Mechanisms in Education.* Cambridge, UK: Cambridge University Press.

Gamoran, Adam. 1987. "The Stratification of High School Learning Opportunities." *Sociology of Education* 60:135–55.

Gamoran, Adam and Robert D. Mare. 1989. "Secondary School Tracking and Educational Inequality: Reinforcement, Compensation, or Neutrality?" *American Journal of Sociology* 94:1146–83.

Gamoran, Adam, Martin Nystrand, Mark Berends, and Paul C. LePore. 1995. "An Organizational Analysis of the Effects of Ability Grouping." *American Educational Research Journal* 32:687–715.

Garet, Michael S. and Brian DeLany. 1988. "Students, Courses, and Stratification." *Sociology of Education* 61:61–77.

Goldstein, Harvey. 1995. *Multilevel Models in Educational and Social Research,* 2nd ed. London: E. Arnold.

Graves, Joseph L. 2001. *The Emperor's New Clothes: Biological Theories of Race at the Millennium.* New Brunswick, NJ: Rutgers University Press.

Grodsky, Eric and Devah Pager. 2001. "The Black-White Wage Gap: Occupational and Individual Sources." *American Sociological Review* 66:542–67.

Groves, Robert, Eleanor Singer, and James M. Lepkowski. 2001. "Survey Methodology." Paper presented at the conference "A Telescope on Society: Survey Research and Social Science at the University of Michigan and Beyond," Ann Arbor, MI.

Hallinan, Maureen T., ed. 2000. *Handbook of the Sociology of Education.* New York: Kluwer Academic/Plenum.

Hallinan, Maureen T. 2001. "Sociological Perspectives on Black-White Inequalities in American Schooling." *Sociology of Education* Extra Issue:50–70.

Hallinan, Maureen T. and Warren Kubitschek. 1999. "Conceptualizing and Measuring School Social Networks: Comment on Morgan and Sørensen." *American Sociological Review* 64:687–93.

Hallinan, Maureen T. and Aage B. Sørensen. 1983. "The Formation and Stability of Instructional Groups." *American Sociological Review* 48:838–51.

Hallinan, Maureen and Richard Williams. 1989. "Interracial Friendship Choices in Secondary Schools." *American Sociological Review* 54:6778.

Hanson, Sandra L., Maryelle Schaub, and David P. Baker. 1996. "Gender Stratification in the Science Pipeline: A Comparative Analyses of Seven Countries." *Gender and Society* 10:271–90.

Hauser, Robert M. and Douglas K. Anderson. 1991. "Post-High School Plans and Aspirations of Black and White High School Seniors, 1976–86." *Sociology of Education* 64:263–77.

Havighurst, Robert J., Paul Hoover Bowman, Gordon P. Liddle, C. V. Matthews, and James V. Pierce. 1962. *Growing Up in River City.* New York: Wiley.

Hedges, Larry V. and Amy Nowell. 1999. "Changes in the Black-White Gap in Achievement Test Scores." *Sociology of Education* 72:111–35.

Hill, Lori Diane. 2001. *Conceptualizing the Attainment Opportunities of Urban Youth: The Effects of Community Context, School Capacity, and Social Capital.* Ph.D. dissertation, Department of Sociology, University of Chicago.

Hochschild, Arlie R. 1989. *The Second Shift: Working Parents and the Revolution at Home.* New York: Viking.

Hochschild, Arlie R. 1997. *The Time Bind: When Work Becomes Home and Home Becomes Work.* New York: Metropolitan Books.

Hollingshead, August B. 1949. *Elmtown's Youth: The Impact of Social Class on Adolescents.* New York: Wiley.

Ingersoll, Richard. 1996. "Teacher's Decision-Making Power and School Conflict." *Sociology of Education* 69:159–76.

Jencks, Christopher, Susan Bartlett, Mary Corcoran, James Crouse, David Eaglesfield, Gregory Jackson, Kent McClelland, Peter Mueser, and Michael Olneck. 1979. *Who Gets Ahead? The Determinants of Economic Success in America.* New York: Basic Books.

Jencks, Christopher and Meredith Phillips, eds. 1998. *The Black-White Test Score Gap.* Washington, DC: Brookings Institution Press.

Jencks, Christopher, Marshall Smith, Henry Acland, Mary Jo Bane, David Cohen, Herbert Gintis, Barbara Heyns, and Stephan Michelson. 1972. *Inequality: A Reassessment of the Effect of Family and Schooling in America.* New York: Basic Books.

Kao, Grace and Marta Tienda. 1995. "Optimism and Achievement: The Educational Performance of Immigrant Youth." *Social Science Quarterly* 76:1–19.

Kerckhoff, Alan C. 1976. "The Status Attainment Process: Stratifications or Allocation?" *Social Forces* 55:368–81.

Kerckhoff, Alan C., ed. 1996. *Generating Social Stratification: Toward a New Research Agenda.* Boulder, CO: Westview Press.

Kerckhoff, Alan C. 2001. "Education and Social Stratification Processes in Comparative Perspective." *Sociology of Education* Extra Issue:3–18.

Lareau, Annette. 2000. *Home Advantage: Social Class and Parental Intervention in Elementary Education,* 2nd ed. Lanham, MD: Rowman & Littlefield.

Lee, Valerie E. and Anthony S. Bryk. 1989. "A Multi-Level Model of the Social Distribution of High School Achievement." *Sociology of Education* 62:172–92.

Lee, Valerie E., Robert G. Croninger, and Julia B. Smith. 1994. "Parental Choice of Schools and Social Stratification in Education: The Paradox of Detroit." *Educational Evaluation and Policy Analysis* 16:434–457.

Lee, Valerie E., Helen M. Marks, and Tina Byrd. 1994. "Sexism in Single-Sex and Coeducational Independent Secondary School Classrooms." *Sociology of Education* 67:92–120.

Lee, Valerie E. and Julia B. Smith. 1995. "Effects of High School Restructuring and Size on Early Gains in Achievement and Engagement." *Sociology of Education* 68:241–70.

Levinson, David, Peter W. Cookson, Jr., and Alan R. Sadovnik, eds. 2001. *Education and Sociology: An Encyclopedia.* New York: Routledge Falmer Press.

Lortie, Dan. C. 1975. *Schoolteacher: A Sociological Study.* Chicago: University of Chicago Press.

Lucas, Samuel R. 1999. *Tracking Inequality: Stratification and Mobility in American High Schools.* New York: Teachers College Press.

Lynd, Robert S. and Helen M. Lynd. 1929. *Middletown: A Study in Contemporary American Culture.* New York: Harcourt, Brace.

MacLeod, Jay. 1987. *Ain't No Making It: Leveled Aspirations in a Low-Income Neighborhood.* Boulder, CO: Westview Press.

Marx, Karl. [1887] 1971. *Capital: A Critique of Political Economy*, 3 vols. (Samuel Moore and Edward B. Aveling, trans.). Moscow: Progress Publishers.

McNeal Jr., Ralph B. 1997. "Are Students Being Pulled Out of High School?: The Effect of Adolescent Employment on Dropping Out." *Sociology of Education* 70:206–20.

Metz, Mary Haywood. 1978. *Classrooms and Corridors: The Crisis of Authority in Desegregated Secondary Schools.* Berkeley: University of California Press.

Meyer, John W. 1977. "The Effect of Education as an Institution." *American Journal of Sociology* 83:55–77.

Meyer, John W., John Boli, George M. Thomas, and Francisco O. Ramirez. 1997. "World Society and the Nation State." *American Journal of Sociology* 103:144–81.

Mickelson, Roslyn Arlin. 1989. "Why Does Jane Read and Write So Well? The Anomaly of Women's Achievement." *Sociology of Education* 62:47–63.

Mickelson, Roslyn Arlin, Carol Ray, and Stephen S. Smith. 1994. "The Growth Machine and Politics of Urban Educational Reform: The Case of Charlotte, North Carolina." Pp. 169–95 in *Education in Urban Areas: Cross-National Dimensions,* edited by Nellie P. Stromquist. Westport, CT: Praeger.

Moore-Johnson, Susan. 1990. *Teachers at Work: Achieving Success in Our Schools.* New York: Basic Books.

Morgan, Stephen L. 1996. "Trends in Black-White Differences in Educational Expectations, 1980–92." *Sociology of Education* 69:308–19.

Morgan, Susan and Aage B. Sørensen. 1999. "A Test of Coleman's Social Capital Explanation of School Effects." *American Sociological Review* 64:661–81.

Mortimer, Jeylan T., Michael Finch, Katherine Dennehy, Chaimun Lee, and Timothy Beebe. 1994. "Work Experiences in Adolescence." *Journal of Vocational Education Research* 19:39–70.

Mortimer, Jeylan T. and Monica Kirkpatrick Johnson. 1998. "New Perspectives on Adolescent Work and the Transition to Adulthood." Pp. 425–96 in *New Perspectives on Adolescent Risk Behavior,* edited by Richard Jessor. New York: Cambridge University Press.

Muller, Chandra. 1998. "Gender Differences in Parental Involvement and Adolescents' Mathematics Achievement." *Sociology of Education* 71:336–56.

National Center for Educational Statistics. 2001. *The Condition of Education 2001.*Washington, DC: U.S. Department of Education.

Natriello, Gary, Aaron M. Pallas, and Karl L. Alexander. 1989."On the Right Track? Curriculum and Academic Achievement." *Sociology of Education* 62:109–18.

Oakes, Jeannie. 1985. *Keeping Track: How Schools Structure Inequality.* New Haven, CT: Yale University Press.

Oakes, Jeannie, Adam Gamoran, and R. N. Page. 1992. "Curriculum Differentiation:

Opportunities, Outcomes, and Meanings." Pp. 570–608 in *Handbook of Research on Curriculum*, edited by Philip W. Jackson. New York: Macmillan.

Orfield, Gary. 2001. *Schools More Separate: Consequences of a Decade of Resegregation*. Unpublished report, Civil Rights Project, Harvard University.

Pallas, Aaron M. 1998. "Scholarly Lives on the Boundary: Markets, Demands, and the Erosion of Identity." Paper presented at the annual meeting of the American Educational Research Association, San Diego, CA.

Parsons, Talcott. 1959. "The School Class as a Social System: Some of Its Functions in American Society." *Harvard Educational Review* 29:297–318.

Payne, E. George. 1927. "Sociological Basis of the Normal School Curriculum." *Journal of Educational Sociology* 1:1–10.

Plank, Stephen. 2000. *Finding One's Place: Teaching Styles and Peer Relations in Diverse Classrooms*. New York: Teachers College Press.

Pong, Suet-Ling. 1998. "The School Compositional Effect of Single Parenthood on 10th Grade Achievement." *Sociology of Education* 71:23–42.

Portes, Alejandro and Dag MacLeod. 1996. "Educational Progress of Children of Immigrants: The Roles of Class, Ethnicity, and School Context." *Sociology of Education* 69:255–75.

Portes, Alejandro and Richard Schauffler. 1996. "Language and the Second Generation: Bilingualism Yesterday and Today." Pp. 8–29 in *The New Second Generation*, edited by Alejandro Portes. New York: Russell Sage Foundation.

Putnam, Robert D. 2000. *Bowling Alone: The Collapse and Revival of American Community*. New York: Simon & Schuster.

Putnam, Robert D., Robert Leonardi, and Raffaella Y. Nanetti. 1993. *Making Democracy Work: Civic Traditions in Modern Italy*. Princeton, NJ: Princeton University Press.

Raftery, Adrian E. 2001. "Statistics in Sociology, 1950–2000: A Selective Review." Pp. 1–45 in *Sociological Methodology*, vol. 31, edited by Ross M. Stolzenberg. Boston: Blackwell.

Ramirez, Francisco O. and Marc Ventresca. 1992. "Building the Institution of Mass Schooling: Isomorphism in the Modern World." Pp. 47–60 in *The Political Construction of Education: The State, School Expansion, and Economic Change*, edited by Bruce Fuller and Richard J. Rubinson. New York: Praeger.

Riordan, Cornelius H. 1990. *Girls and Boys in School: Together or Separate?* New York: Teachers College Press.

Rosenbaum, James E. 1976. *Making Inequality: The Hidden Curriculum of High School Tracking*. New York: Wiley.

Rosenbaum, James E. 2001. *Beyond College for All: Career Paths for the Forgotten Half*. New York: Russell Sage Foundation.

Rosenbaum, James E. and Stephanie A. Jones. 2000. "Interactions between High Schools and Labor Markets." Pp. 411–36 in *Handbook of the Sociology of Education*, edited by Maureen T. Hallinan. New York: Kluwer Academic/Plenum.

Rowan, Brian, Stephen W. Raudenbush, and Yuk Fai Cheong. 1993. "Teaching as a Non-Routine Task: Implications for the Management of Schools." *Educational Administration Quarterly* 29:479–500.

Rumberger, Russell W. and Scott L. Thomas. 2000. "The Distribution of Dropout and Turnover Rates Among Urban and Suburban High Schools." *Sociology of Education* 73:39–67.

Sadker, Myra and David Sadker. 1994. *Failing at Fairness: How Our Schools Cheat Girls*. New York: Simon & Schuster.

Sadovnik, Alan R. 1991. "Basil Bernstein's Theory of Pedagogic Practice: A Structuralist Approach." *Sociology of Education* 64:48–63.

Schmidt, William H., Curtis C. McKnight, and Senta A. Raizen. 1997. *A Splintered Vision: An Investigation of U.S. Science and Mathematics Education*. Dordrecht, The Netherlands: Kluwer Academic.

Schneider, Barbara. 1987. "Tracing the Provenance of Teacher Education." Pp. 211–41 in *Critical Studies in Teacher Education: Its Folklore Theory and Practice*, edited by Thomas S. Popkewitz. London: Falmer Press.

Schneider, Barbara and James S. Coleman, eds. 1993. *Parents, Their Children, and Schools.* Boulder, CO: Westview Press.

Schneider, Barbara and David L. Stevenson. 1999. *The Ambitious Generation: America's Teenagers, Motivated but Directionless.* New Haven, CT: Yale University Press.

Schultz, Theodore W. 1961. "Investment in Human Capital." *American Economic Review* 51:1–17.

Secretary's Commission on Achieving Necessary Skills. 1992. *Learning a Living: A Blueprint for High Performance.* Washington, DC: U.S. Department of Labor.

Sewell, William H., Archibald. O. Haller, and Murray A. Straus. 1957. "Social Status and Educational and Occupational Aspiration." *American Sociological Review* 22:67–73.

Sewell, William H. and Robert M. Hauser. 1980. "The Wisconsin Longitudinal Study of Social and Psychological Factors in Aspirations and Achievements." Pp. 59–99 in *Research in Sociology of Education and Socialization,* vol. 1, edited by Alan C. Kerckhoff. Greenwich, CT: JAI Press.

Shouse, Roger. 1997. "Academic Press, Sense of Community, and Student Achievement." Pp. 60–86 in *Redesigning American Education,* edited by James S. Coleman, Barbara Schneider, Stephen Plank, Kathryn Schiller, Roger Shouse, and Hua-Ying Wang. Boulder, CO: Westview Press.

Shu, Xiaoling and Margaret Mooney Marini. 1998. "Gender-Related Change in Occupational Aspirations." *Sociology of Education* 71:44–68.

Slavin, Robert E. and Nancy A. Madden. 2000. "Roots and Wings: Effects of Whole-School Reform on Student Achievement." *Journal of Education for Students Placed at Risk* 5:109–36.

Small, Albion W. 1897. "Some Demands of Sociology upon Pedagogy." *American Journal of Sociology* 2:839–51.

Sørensen, Aage B. and Maureen T. Hallinan. 1986. "Effects of Ability Grouping on Growth in Academic Achievement." *American Educational Research Journal* 23:519–42.

Sorokin, Pitirim A. [1927] 1963. *Social Mobility* [Reprinted as *Social and Cultural Mobility*]. Glencoe, IL: Free Press.

Stanton-Salazar, Ricardo D. and Stanford M. Dornbush. 1995. "Social Capital and the Reproduction of Inequality: Information Networks among Mexican Origin High School Students." *Sociology of Education* 68:116–35.

Stevenson, David L. 1991. "Deviant Students as a Collective Resource in Classroom Control." *Sociology of Education* 64:127–33.

Stevenson, David L. and David P. Baker. 1991. "State Control of the Curriculum and Classroom Instruction." *Sociology of Education* 64:1–10.

Stevenson, David L. and David P. Baker. 1992. "Shadow Education and Allocation in Formal Schooling: Transition to University in Japan." *American Journal of Sociology* 97:1639–57.

Stevenson, David L., Kathryn Schiller, and Barbara Schneider. 1994. "Sequences of Opportunities for Learning." *Sociology of Education* 67:184–98.

Stinchcombe, Arthur L. 1964. *Rebellion in a High School.* Chicago: Quadrangle.

Stringfield, Sam, Steven M. Ross, and Lana Smith, eds. 1996. *Bold Plans for School Restructuring: The New American Schools Designs.* Mahwah, NJ: Erlbaum.

Swanson, Christopher B. and David L. Stevenson. 2002. "Standards-Based Reform in Practice: Evidence on State Policy and Classroom Instruction from the NAEP State Assessments." *Educational Evaluation and Policy Analysis* 24:1–28.

Swidler, Ann. 1979. *Organization without Authority: Dilemmas of Social Control in Free Schools.* Cambridge, MA: Harvard University Press.

Talbert, Joan E. and Milbrey W. McLaughlin. 1994. "Teacher Professionalism in Local School Contexts." *American Journal of Education* 102:123–53.

Thorne, Barrie. 1993. *Gender Play: Girls and Boys in School.* New Brunswick, NJ: Rutgers University Press.

Trow, Martin A. 1973. *Problems in the Transition from Elite to Mass Education.* Berkeley, CA: Carnegie Commission on Higher Education.

Udry, J. Richard and Peter S. Bearman. 1998. "New Methods for New Research on Adolescent Sexual Behavior." Pp. 241–69 in *New Perspectives on Adolescent Risk Behavior,* edited by Richard Jessor. Cambridge, UK: Cambridge University Press.

Valenzuela, Angela. 1999. *Subtractive Schooling: U.S.-Mexican Youth and the Politics of Caring.* Albany: State University of New York Press.

Waller, Willard. 1932. *The Sociology of Teaching.* New York: Wiley.

Walters, Pamela B. 2001. "Educational Access and the State: Historical Continuities and Discontinuities in Racial Inequality in American Education." *Sociology of Education* Extra Issue:35–49.

Ward, Lester F. [1883] 1968. "Education." In *Dynamic Sociology.* New York: Johnson Reprint.

Weber, Max. [1922] 1947. *The Theory of Social and Economic Organization* (A. M. Henderson and Talcott Parsons, trans.). Glencoe, IL: Free Press.

Wells, Amy S. 1996. "African-American Students' View of School Choices." In *Who Chooses? Who Loses? Culture, Institutions, and the Unequal Effects of School Choice,* edited by Bruce Fuller, Richard F. Elmore, and Gary Orfield. New York: Teachers College Press.

Wells, Amy S. 1997. *Stepping over the Color Line: African American Students in White Suburban Schools.* New Haven, CT: Yale University Press.

Wells, Amy S. and Robert L. Crain. 1994. "Perpetuation Theory and the Long-Term Effects of School Desegregation." *Review of Educational Research* 64:531–55.

Willis, Paul. 1977. *Learning to Labor: How Working Class Kids Get Working Class Jobs.* New York: Columbia University Press.

Wilson, William Julius. 1996. *When Work Disappears: The World of the New Urban Poor.* New York: Knopf.

Wrigley, Julia, ed. 1992. *Educational and Gender Equality.* London: Falmer Press.

VI

Conclusion

12

Classrooms and Politics

Robert Dreeben

From my reading of the chapters in this book, a small number of themes predominate. First is the attention devoted to teaching, which along with curriculum has long been the stepchild of sociology of education. Whether this happened because the nature of the work proved so difficult to formulate, or whether it is the product of neglect, is hard to ascertain. The status attainment view of the landscape, for example, has ignored teaching practices as well as other properties of schools. The view of schools as factorylike bureaucracies tacitly reduced teachers to functionaries bound up in an exercise of class reproduction; the work of teaching accordingly required little or no description on its own terms. However, work on the discourse of teaching did focus on patterns of verbal interaction in classrooms, on teachers as actors, but at the same time paid little attention to the properties and contingencies of classrooms. This volume contains treatments of teaching by considering elements of it that have received minimal attention in the past.

The second is the attention paid to the politics (for want of a better term) of schooling—the problem of school management and change that filters through the hierarchical layers that span the territory between classrooms and agencies of local, state, and federal government and across to private agencies like universities and interest groups. This theme has gained prominence during the past fifteen years or so because the country has been experiencing a frenzy of educational reform—originating in private associations, universities, and government agencies—and sociologists have presented themselves both as analysts of and participants in it. Because the reforms themselves were formulated at all levels of government and educational organization, questions arise about how those levels are connected to each other.

As Barbara Schneider (Chapter 11) documents, substantial headway has been made during the past fifty years in understanding particular aspects of educational organization and its mechanisms based on comparisons of schools,

Robert Dreeben • Department of Education (Emeritus), University of Chicago, Chicago, Illinois 60637.

Stability and Change in American Education: Structure, Process, and Outcomes edited by Maureen T. Hallinan, Adam Gamoran, Warren Kubitschek, and Tom Loveless. Eliot Werner Publications, Clinton Corners, New York, 2003.

classrooms, teaching methods, and curricula. There were also significant advances in demonstrating how schooling is linked to other social institutions—primarily the family and the economy (through employment)—and the social identities of students (especially race, sex, and socioeconomic status). Much less attention, however, has been paid to the connection of education to the polity and to religion. The chapters in this volume make clear that there is a future agenda in exploring relations between the work of schools and the politics of the larger educational domain. At the same time, the past few decades have witnessed an unbalanced preoccupation with school achievement and the future life chances of individuals—a concern that has shaped scholarly investigations as well as reform efforts, particularly those related to standards and testing. This is understandable given the temper of the times, but from the standpoint of understanding the educational enterprise on a broader scale, there is much to be said for enlarging the agenda.

TEACHING AND THE VIABILITY OF CLASSROOMS

While the classroom is where teaching and learning take place, it is also a setting whose viability has proven to be problematic. This is because it is a collective entity with a long life (the duration of an academic year) in which teachers must confront unpredictable contingencies and disruptions associated with maintaining an instructional program and a basic level of social order. The viability of the classroom has implications for learning, but how viability is established and maintained is a problem in its own right.

What does it mean to say that the viability of a classroom is a problem in its own right? First, viability is distinct from whether students learn or achieve academically. A classroom can be a viable setting for instruction even if student learning is minimal, in the same way that a medical treatment can be appropriate even if the patient does not recover or legal counsel can be fully competent even if the client loses. That is to say, more is entailed in producing learning than the efforts of the teacher. Viability represents a condition in which the appropriate activities of a practitioner can proceed according to standards of competent practice, not necessarily that they will succeed. Second, classroom viability has a time dimension. Classroom work occurs on a daily basis during a period of months, with a population that is diverse in its motivations to be present and do the work and in its capacity to do it. Some classroom events are treated as momentary, as expressed in teachers' immediate responses to students—for example, by praise, feedback, rebuke, and the like. Classes have daily life histories that include the alternative ways in which teachers combine sociable and academic activities (McFarland 1999). They also have longer time spans and periodicities related to semesters, academic years, and different portions of the year (like the beginning and the stretch before vacations) during which shifts in classroom organization occur (Smith and Geoffrey 1968; Barr and Dreeben 1983). The combination of long time span and contingency means that actions taken in a moment can ramify in unpredictable ways down the line, sometimes favorably, sometimes disruptively. Third, the viability of a classroom can be influenced by forces that originate outside the school and beyond its control—for example, those located in the family and community that contribute to truancy and long periods of absence and that disrupt both the opportunities for individual students to learn and the instructional and social order of the class.

The viability of a classroom refers to a set of conditions under which an instructional program can be undertaken, a proposition more easily asserted than specified and explained. One such condition, as Philip Jackson (1968) indicated in *Life in Classrooms*, is for teachers to gain and sustain the attention of students. Attention refers at the minimum to students looking alert, a surface indication of what is believed to be active involvement in learning activities. The reasoning goes that students who show interest in their schoolwork and actively do it are more likely to make academic headway than those who lack or feign interest. The empirical work that Jackson cites, completed mostly in the 1920s, has methodological flaws (which he identifies) associated with the difficulty of distinguishing real from dissembled attention and with the fact that most of the classes examined showed extraordinarily high rates (90 percent or more) of students paying attention. What is difficult to sort out in these early studies is whether attention is an individual phenomenon—those who pay attention learn more than those who do not—or a classroom condition whose absence renders it extremely difficult or impossible for a teacher to carry out an instructional program (because students' minds are elsewhere), but whose presence is enabling when favorable conditions obtain. With respect to viability, the matter of attention is inconclusive. Teachers act as if it is important and work hard to gain it. Though the result of its presence may be indeterminate, its absence can be disastrous.

The importance of attention seems almost too obvious to discuss. But lest one arrive too hastily at this conclusion, the question of whether attention per se is a condition of viability or whether it is a by-product of some other condition is an open one. Louis Smith and William Geoffrey (1968), in an ethnography of a junior high school classroom, indicated that the teacher's main task during the first several weeks of the school year is to establish rules of student conduct covering both academic and behavioral matters. This is accomplished, they claimed, by stating expectations clearly, explaining the reasons for them, demonstrating their seriousness, and sanctioning violations. The aim of these actions is to create a consistent set of experiences, including paying attention, which in time students accept as normative premises for their conduct and with which they comply with willingly and routinely (Scott 1995:54–55). Viewed from this perspective, attention is derivative. The logic here is reminiscent of Paul Breer and Edwin Locke's (1965) argument about how task experiences influence beliefs, norms, and values. The teacher establishes routines in the first several weeks of school so that students' participation in them becomes unreflectively normative.

An additional condition for classroom viability is whether students are adequately prepared for the level of curriculum that the teacher presents. An example of this problem appeared in fieldwork that Rebecca Barr and I did in a fourth grade class in the early 1980s. Only two students could read the science textbook that the school had adopted—the only curriculum material available. Instruction during the course of the year consisted of the teacher and the few students who could read reciting the textbook to the rest of the class. (A constructive alternative to that dismal state of affairs could have occurred had the teacher on her own initiative brought in appropriate curriculum materials and employed more imaginative instructional practices. We do not know whether doing so would have exceeded her abilities and level of interest, or run afoul of the district's curriculum guidelines.) Similar problems are currently found in the Chicago public schools when students two or more years behind in reading and math begin high school. (This is one of the problems that prompted the Chicago school reform efforts that Kenneth Wong discusses in this volume and to which I will turn later.)

Adam Gamoran and Sean Kelly (Chapter 7) focus on the viability of a class as an instructional setting. Their approach to instruction entails a characterization of classroom activity based on the extent to which teachers rely on "dialogic" instruction consisting of authentic questions, student-initiated questions, and teachers taking students seriously by following up on what a student says. The method of analysis abstracts from the ebb and flow of classroom activities to identify a measure of instruction by averaging across four observations over the year. In effect, a single dimension of instruction is taken to endure for the year even though its frequency in the same class might vary day to day and week to week. One might infer from this that the teacher is primarily (perhaps solely) concerned with the academic component of instruction and classroom life, and that variation in reliance on techniques of instruction (like the dialogic method) are the central components of teaching practice contributing to classroom viability.

This may be a powerful theory, because if verified it suggests that sustained effort devoted to a particular method brings good results without effort wasted on subordinate considerations. Instructional method is what speaks to viability: if the method succeeds in motivating engagement, then the class is viable to the extent that students participate actively in mastering the curriculum. Of course both engagement and lecture and recitation methods may be passive. And while these latter forms of instruction are conventionally in bad odor, has anyone shown that classes employing them are not viable or that students do not learn from them? It has long been a source of dismay among educators that evidence has consistently confirmed how infrequently teachers employ discussion methods in general, let alone the sophisticated ones entailed in dialogic instruction. No doubt viable classrooms can be run on a dialogic basis, but perhaps primarily by teachers sufficiently talented to employ the curriculum imaginatively as well as to manage the social relations of the classroom. Classrooms run more routinely by lecture and recitation can also be viable (though not necessarily exciting). If this were not so, perhaps the higher education system would then collapse. Viability in routinely run classrooms is maintained by keeping social order, while the conveyance of academic content comes as much through students studying textbooks, writing reports, and studying for exams as by the wonderful orchestrations of their teachers.

Charles Bidwell (Chapter 3) addresses classroom viability in another way. His focus is not foremost on academic instruction but on conditions that enable instruction to proceed. Goodwill from his point of view is not only a condition supporting instructional activity, but also a social condition that underlies the legitimacy of the classroom enterprise itself, including the teacher's position of authority. In the primary grades, the teacher's initial task is to establish authority, both for himself or herself but also with a longer time span that covers the authority of teachers generally. More likely than not, the teacher can count on help from parents who might be pleased to have their five or six year old out of the house and in someone else's care. Smart parents who undoubtedly do not want to be called by the school will sing the teacher's praises and tell their child to be good. But once (and if) a teacher has gained a stable position of authority, it is his or hers to lose—something easily done in a classroom.

Bidwell reminds us that goodwill has academic implications as "a condition of effective instruction" as well as social implications in promoting both academic and social engagement in the classroom. At stake is the stability of the teacher's authority. Part of the teacher's difficulty is that there is no reliable recipe—or perhaps too many recipes of dubious reliability—for creating goodwill, and innovative techniques like charismatic teaching or exciting new curricula become shopworn and lose their shine. What exacerbates the goodwill problem are the prolonged stretches of time through which students and teachers face each other in the course of activities that do not differ much from one week or month to the next. Given current knowledge the time dimensions of goodwill are difficult to identify, particularly those pertaining to goodwill over the long haul.

Goodwill is not the whole story. Alongside it runs a regime of "exchanges of sanctions for performance or conduct." Nor should goodwill be considered only a product of the school. As Bidwell's comparison of an academically selective and a working-class high school indicates, some students carry their goodwill with them. These examples bring together different components of the school's problem of gaining the willing participation of students in the academic enterprise. How is goodwill established, maintained, and replenished? How is a linkage established between the regimes of goodwill and exchange? How does this linkage form at different levels of schooling (elementary, middle, and high) in schools whose student bodies vary in social composition, as well as during different phases of the school year? At present we lack answers.

These ideas refer in different ways to classroom authority in which teachers maintain a sufficiently peaceful social order and create the conditions that permit an instructional regime to go forward. They are about classroom viability. Student compliance—made salient by the fact that school attendance is not voluntary—is the key issue, and spending days on end doing academic work without much variety is not necessarily what young people would choose if given a choice. When teachers succeed in involving students actively in classroom activities, as illustrated in the Gamoran and Kelly chapter, one can assume that the authority problem has been largely solved.

An authority perspective, implicit in the studies just discussed, represents a Weberian take on the case of school organization. Daniel McFarland (Chapter 8) brings a different line of reasoning to the viability question that does not draw its inspiration primarily from Weber. While high school classrooms are clearly hierarchical settings, McFarland's reasoning suggests that they yield more readily to an analysis based on flows of activity—those of academics and sociability—than one based on authority and compliance. He shows that the default position between these flows favors the students and their penchant for sociable activities. This means that while teachers occupy the formally superordinate position, students to a significant degree hold one of dominance. Teachers in each meeting of a class must accordingly draw students out of their sociable state in order to get on with academic instruction. This is not a Weberian scenario of bureaucratic administration based on voluntary compliance (either by teachers or students) to rules and directives, legitimized according to rational-legal principles. The teachers' authority position *in the school system*, of course, is legitimized in bureaucratic terms based on credentials and indications of competence at the time of hiring. It provides teachers with the right to assign schoolwork, grade papers, mete out sanctions, call in parents, and the like. Weber's principle of bureaucratic administration applied to a school system subordinates teachers—not students—to the bottom of its *academic* hierarchy. But teachers' nonbureaucratic, superordinate position in the classroom, the one entailed in instruction and keeping order, is vulnerable. They must work to establish and reestablish it on a continuing basis precisely because the sociability agenda of students takes primacy in reality (except in the limited case of classes whose students possess academic motivations of a high order).

The teacher's job, according to McFarland, consists of using different kinds of speech, task structures, and activities, and of forming alliances with various segments of a class in order to bring the academic agenda to the forefront and keep it there so that the agenda of student sociability does not monopolize class time. From this perspective gaining the attention of students appears to be an indicator of the ascendancy of academics. The question of goodwill, however, is more complex than that of attention, if only because it is hard to put one's finger on it or identify exactly where it resides. In Bidwell's usage, at a minimum one knows it by its results. In juxtaposing goodwill and "social capital," Bidwell implies the relational character of goodwill. But more than that, goodwill has collective properties: "common enterprise," "collective engagement," "common observance of norms," reminiscent of Durkheim's noncontractual elements of contract in that they are collective and not subject to negotiation, action by action.

McFarland notes teachers' use of alternative means to classroom viability (i.e., gaining the ascendancy of the academic program over the sociable for most of the time). One is to acknowledge the presence and appropriateness of the students' sociability agenda and to participate in it to a limited extent. This is to concede the legitimacy of student society. The uncertainty in doing this is whether the students will grant the legitimacy of the teacher's role as advocate and agent for the academic agenda. A second is to get absorbed by student society, to be a good guy—essentially sue for peace and sacrifice the instructional program. A third alternative is to give no quarter to student sociability, a strategy that consists of all academics all the time or all discipline all the time. Dialogic instruction, for example, may be feasible under the first alternative, but only if students consider class discussion to be a sufficiently satisfying form of sociability; it is probably impossible to carry out under alternatives two and three. The second alternative appears in Ann Swidler's (1979) description of Group High School, which was dedicated to erasing hierarchical distinctions between teacher and students but ended up putting a teacher under relentless pressure to be interesting, entertaining, and charismatic in the eyes of students. The third alternative can be found in many Chicago schools under the mandate for scripted teaching and test preparation as accountability measures under the reform regime.

Lest one believe that the viability of class instruction rests solely in the hands of a teacher, caution is in order. Prevailing social conditions, outside the control of teachers, impinge on their work in the form of opportunities and constraints. Among the significant conditions is the social composition of students in a class, the product of neighborhood and catchment area characteristics, and school administrators' decisions about student and teacher class assignments. (I recall a conversation with a principal who had to decide which grades to assign her most and least competent teachers. The most competent she assigned to first and eighth, the least to fourth and fifth.) Classes composed of students with strong academic records, motivations, and plans pose different instructional issues from those composed of students without such interests or who enter unprepared, uninterested, or disruptive. Other conditions are the scope, range, and difficulty of the school's curriculum. The viability question revolves around which combinations of these conditions beyond the teachers control represent "hard" classes (e.g., those with weak teachers assigned to academically inclined students; any teachers assigned to classes whose students cannot abide the regime of schooling or who, for whatever reason, cannot do the level of work required).

While the works just described consider the class as a collective entity organized to carry out a program of instruction, classes are composed of individuals whose characteristics matter for both immediate and long-term outcomes. The status attainment tradition, which emphasizes short- and long-run achievements, fastens on those individual characteristics that have the most common-sense bearing on school achievement: social status, race/ethnicity, sex, ability, past achievement—essentially elements of human and cultural capital. This bundle of characteristics has become conventional, most of it representing indexes of social stratification, an outgrowth of the preoccupation of sociologists with education in the context of mobility. While there is no reason to gainsay the importance of this tradition of work, there is also no reason to be bound by it. Inkeles and Leiderman (Chapter 4), for example, argue for the inclusion of what they call "psychosocial maturity," net of social status, among boys and girls separately to explain variation in grades and college-going expectations. They show an association between maturity and the outcomes, but given their design they cannot tell whether maturity is a capacity that adolescents bring to school, a product of their experience in school, or both. If we think about Inkeles and Leiderman in the light of Gamoran and Kelly, dialogic teaching may presuppose a threshold level of maturity; or perhaps dialogic teachers aim to encourage the development of maturity as a condition supporting their pedagogy. One can also speculate about whether maturity is germane to classroom life because of its relevance to academics, to patterns of sociability that support the academic agenda, or to some other considerations.

Pallas, Boulay, and Karp (Chapter 2) also argue to extend the range of individual characteristics worthy of consideration beyond the standard variety expressed in status attainment models. But unlike Inkeles and Leiderman, their interest is in distant outcomes: the contribution of schooling to the life course experiences of adults, at least as they remember schooling. Pallas and his colleagues focused on their respondents' reports about what they learned from school subject matter and whether it became relevant later in life; the subjects also discussed the school's disciplinary regime, what school taught them about themselves as well as people who differ from them, and the like. Their perspective is not one readily translated into a quantitative design intended to isolate school experiences and relate them to specific views held later in life, but rather one in which school experience is already absorbed into an adult point of view and is part of a cognitive framework for thinking about the past.

THE POLITICS OF SCHOOLING

Part of the agenda of *How Schools Work* (Barr and Dreeben 1983) was to explore how the organizational levels—from district administration to individual student—are connected to each other. The approach left untouched the forces operating on local school systems that originate outside district boundaries, from higher levels of government and laterally placed private and voluntary associations. Although these forces were always in place, it has taken the recent preoccupation with reform to stimulate analytical attention to them. This was a mixed blessing, because while the research on educational reform brought political considerations beyond the level of school districts to the fore, much of it also consisted of thinly disguised advocacy. The field of education, moreover, lacked an overall mapping of its major institutional and organizational components similar to what can be found, say, in Laumann and Knoke's (1987) book *The*

Organization State that treats the policy domains of energy and health in terms of their major corporate actors and the relations among them, though without emphasis on how policies are effected through practices occurring within the organizations located in each domain. (See Caves [2000] for a different take on similar issues based on contractual relations among, for example, consumers, producers, performers, marketers, audiences, and patrons in the arts industries.) The present volume contains three efforts that deal analytically with the external environments of school districts from a vertical organizational perspective that educational reform makes available.

At irregular intervals since the end of World War II, criticism has arisen that the public (not the private) schools were doing an inadequate job: that students were not learning enough, not learning the right things, or both. The criticisms have been accompanied by policies intended to improve the curriculum, teachers, and school management, and the policies have usually specified remedies: government action at different levels, various kinds of curriculum schemes, university-generated reform schemes and changes in the preparation of teachers, actions by interest groups and voluntary associations, and the like. There seems to be a stockpile of these remedies that reappear from time to time, albeit under different names. Not too long a memory is necessary, for example, to see the parallels between the attempts to upgrade the mathematics, science, and social studies curricula in the 1950s and 1960s and the current standards reforms. The same is true with performance contracting of yesteryear and accountability reforms of today.

Chapters in this volume by William Firestone, Kenneth Wong, and Tom Loveless all analyze a recent reform syndrome commonly known as the standards movement, treating it in different but overlapping ways. The opening shot in this movement was *A Nation at Risk*, the 1983 report of the U.S. National Commission on Excellence in Education, which listed national educational goals set out in standardslike language. The document was neither a piece of legislation (or even a congressional resolution) nor an executive order: it was an exhortation. Although the federal government can pass laws that influence the conduct of the educational system—the National Defense Education Act and the Elementary and Secondary Education Act being cases in point—the Constitution makes no provision for the government to legislate the means and ends of schooling, tasks that under the Tenth Amendment are reserved for the states. The standards movement is national in scope because interest groups, professional associations, and private foundations with national constituencies took up the cudgels for it. *A Nation at Risk* provided ideological impetus, not legal sanction.

Although the federal government can try to enforce educational legislation by withholding funds (as in cases of racial discrimination), it takes a back seat in the design and enforcement of educational policies—mainly curriculum and instruction—that involve practice, leaving those matters to the states, localities, and schools themselves (Meyer 1983a:235–37). In this context Firestone writes about the translation of national into state standards aimed to change how teaching is done in local schools; Wong focuses on the movement toward mayoral control of urban education, in accordance with state standards, intended to raise student performance in schools; and Loveless deals with alternative models of standard setting promulgated by different professional and voluntary associations designed to alter the conduct of teachers through regulation. What stands out in all of these accounts is the degree of indeterminacy in the translation of policy principles into policies and then into practice.

Firestone (Chapter 9) describes the sloppy connections between what states prescribe in putting accountability schemes in place and how school districts respond to them. He draws a distinction between machinery designed to enforce accountability for meeting standards generally, such as rewards and punishments for schools (e.g., raising criteria for high school graduation, merit pay schemes, state takeovers of schools, and the like), and accountability for meeting curriculum content standards. "The accountability stream is strong," he maintains, "on ensuring responsiveness to state standards but does little to clarify the content of standards." This suggests that while states possess the machinery to enforce standards, and presumably thereby achieve accountability, they have difficulty defining the content of those standards. States can specify which courses and levels are required for high school graduation, but they cannot readily define the particulars or the pedagogy entailed. Substantively, then, what is enforced? To answer this question, states and districts turn to national curriculum associations in mathematics, English, science, and social studies that define content standards in the abstract but do not address the related instructional practices necessary to produce the results expressed in the standards. The California experience with whole-language reading instruction is a case in point. An ideological movement in the reading community inspired whole-language instruction, which until its collapse won out as a state mandate in California. Although some of the practices that it includes represent sound principles in the abstract, carrying it out instructionally places heavy demands on teachers' knowledge (e.g., of children's literature) and skills of instruction and classroom management—demands that many teachers, especially the inexperienced, lack the capacity to meet.

The part of accountability that bears on the enforcement of standards winds up in the laps of school district administrators and teachers. States and districts, with the resources of enforcement at their disposal, have little to enforce because there is no reason to believe that changing graduation and promotion requirements, stopping funding, closing schools, firing teachers and administrators, introducing testing, and so forth have anything to do with classroom teaching and changes designed to make it more effective. In effect, the policy apparatus does not reach the points of educational practice in classrooms where improvements in learning are supposed to occur. This is not to say that it is impossible for the policy apparatus to work; rather, making it do so requires a sequence of linkages and mechanisms, which for the most part were beset with gaps in the connections. Most conspicuous among these is the inability of the federal government to press the states to act as the former may direct, of the states to do likewise with the diversity of local school districts, and the extreme difficulty of inducing local administrators and teachers to act in ways that differ from what their training and experience (or the inadequacy of it) has prepared them to do.

Wong's discussion of mayoral control over the Chicago school system (Chapter 5) traces the policy process from the mayor's office to the classroom; it has two main components. The first deals with the incorporation of the public schools into the governmental machinery to provide city services. (Heretofore the schools had a quasi-independent budgetary and bureaucratic existence apart from, say, parks, sewers, transportation, street repair, and other municipal services.) This move, approved by the state legislature, was designed to address a host of problems that plagued the system in the past, among them the failure to put the schools on a sound financial footing; the vulnerability of the system to pressures exerted by political constituencies whose influence was guaranteed by their inclusion in the appointment machinery; waste and mismanagement; yearly financial crises previously "solved" by jury-rigged, last-minute political settlements between the mayor and governor; and so on. The mayor created a businesslike structure to run the school system, took control of the appointment process, and brought in top executives with budgetary skills and experience from noneducational sectors of city government. In these efforts, as Wong reports, the mayor succeeded in bringing a substantial degree of stability to governing the system; in addition, he worked out a longer term and more pacific contract with the Chicago Teachers Union than had been negotiated in the past.

The second deals with attempts by the school system to increase the level of academic performance of the schools themselves. The remedies proposed for doing this were again drawn from the world of business. Chicago's chronic problems of governance (noted previously) did yield to businesslike approaches, most probably because they pertained to the economic aspects of running the system—especially to budgets and labor negotiations—for which there were precedents in other branches of city government. The academic reform of the schools, however, was another story. The new executive officer of the Chicago public schools introduced a set of changes, guided by the principle of "accountability," in order to raise the academic performance levels of schools as indicated by scores on basic skills and achievement tests for elementary and secondary schools, respectively. Wong describes these remedies as the "remediation" and "reconstitution" of schools; they included the introduction of a summer school "bridge" program to eliminate the practice of "social promotion" of third, sixth, and eighth graders who failed to score high enough on year-end tests.

Introducing a businesslike organizational structure under the mayor's direction successfully addressed the economic problems of the school system; it also served to reduce the vulnerability of the public schools to the veto politics of interest groups that were encouraged by the previous flawed procedures for nomination and appointment to school system offices. These reforms entailed changes in governance; whether business-oriented governance reforms would also address and solve problems of academic performance, "the regulation of teaching"—as Loveless (Chapter 10) calls it—was another matter. The Chicago reforms are clearly premised on the regulation of learning outcomes, but in order to regulate outcomes, instruction itself has to be regulated. And while there are some well-understood principles—given the political will—for rationalizing the economics of public school governance, there are no comparable principles or procedures for regulating the instructional and curriculum components in order to increase learning outcomes. In that situation the rhetoric of accountability became the guiding principle. What conduct it actually guides becomes the core issue.

The Chicago case, even with its own peculiarities, should be seen as part of a larger national movement of reform, which in turn finds expression in a variety of state ventures—Illinois's among them. Loveless explains the principles of the regulation of learning outcomes.

> Responding to the public clamor for greater accountability and increased student learning, a state legislature, state board of education, or local school board defines a set of desired outcomes, devises a testing system for measuring student achievement, and offers incentives [or punishments, as with Chicago's remediation and reconstitution] to schools for achieving goals.

This describes the Chicago case. The logic is transparent: define goals, provide incentives, measure whether the goals were achieved, fix the cases that remain broken. The assumptions in this scenario are that teachers and administrators will respond appropriately once they know the level of the school's performance (based on test scores) motivated by avoiding penalties and seeking rewards, and that the incentives per se will provide *substantive* guidance for practice intended to remedy the shortfall.

These assumptions, however, are highly suspect, especially in schools where much of the school population enters unprepared or has other characteristics that make carrying out an instructional program difficult. The fact that there are two ideologically inspired and competing positions on regulation—instruction and results based, according to Loveless's argument—is part of the problem. In reality, if not in ideology, the two entail each other. In order to increase the learning outcomes, the means for doing so must be explicitly addressed. If not done explicitly (not to mention viably), then one sees the kind of situation found in Chicago where the district thrashes about looking for remedies in school organization and instruction that have no necessary connection to the test outcome-oriented regime that it has put in place. What drives the Chicago reforms is the mayor's dependence on the state legislature for funding; it was the legislature, after all, that enabled a system of mayoral control to exist in the first place. With satisfaction the legislature has witnessed the rationalizing of the business component of the system's reform. It remains waiting for significant academic improvement, and the mayor and his school executives have yet to deliver on that front. The pressure generated by that situation galvanizes the school system in search of academic remedies. It must bring together the means and ends, both for academic and political reasons.

But bringing the means and ends together is itself problematic given the unsettled state of teaching practice as applied to difficult classrooms (Dreeben and Barr 1988; Dreeben 2001). In the Chicago case—the same is true wherever there is a strong commitment to testing—there is a search for solutions that show achievement gains even in the absence of sure-fire methods to produce them. Chicago has accordingly adopted the following approaches: employ instructional methods that prepare directly for taking tests, both in terms of content and test-taking skills; bring into individual schools what are called "external partners" who are purveyors and advocates of various approaches to school reorganization and instruction; and establish a demotion policy to preclude social promotion for students who do not pass the tests (Anagnostopoulos 2000).

At least in Chicago, the policies of the school system executive—under mayoral control—has generated a set of practices that reach into classrooms. The emphasis on accountability has led to the joining of scripted teaching and test preparation and test taking, reducing them to virtually the same activity in the expectation that test scores will be raised sufficiently to convince the public and the legislature that progress is being made. The "no social promotion" policy, which requires demoting students who do not test well enough, has the unannounced effects of either creating student superannuation, a gradual way to increase the likelihood that students drop out (and accordingly reduce the proportion of low-achieving students with whom the schools must cope), or of undermining itself through noncompliance. The external partner procedures introduce elements of random search into the system on the chance that some workable solutions will emerge. Whether the remediation or reconstitution of schools turn out to be effective policies remains to be seen. These moves trade on the cultural resonance of an ideology of accountability that places responsibility for failure on teachers and students and on the idea of "social promotion," which taps into the principle that individuals are not entitled to anything they do not earn even if demotion has little or nothing to recommend it as an effective educational practice (Anagnostopoulos 2000).

Consistency with an ideology is what gives these practices syndromelike coherence. But nothing in this sequence of elements in the reform is determinative. Mayoral control does not automatically lead to scripted instruction nor does it necessarily entail a "no social promotion" policy; recent newspaper accounts already indicate the policy being abandoned on a large scale (*Chicago Tribune*, June 2, 2002). These are choices, and there are alternatives. Moreover, the practices employed in schools under mayoral control intended to improve academic outcomes have no inherent connection to the economic reforms save for the fact that any financial savings under the latter can support activities entailed in the former. That is to say, governance based on mayoral control can countenance a variety of approaches to raising academic performance. For example, the initial Chicago reforms of 1988 introduced a scheme of governance that placed unprecedented control in the hands of elected local school councils. By 1995 this arrangement was almost completely scrapped, having accomplished little or nothing. In the fourteen years since the beginning of the reforms, well-designed programs to address problems in reading and math instruction in the elementary schools might have reduced the proportion of students more than one year below grade level entering high school, moreso perhaps than attempts to remediate the learning shortfall once students entered high school. In sum, changes in governance—even those that proved effective in stabilizing the economic circumstances of a school system—leave most options open as far as the academic instructional agenda is concerned. This must be addressed in its own terms, and experience has shown that it is a difficult matter to confront.

COUPLING: LOOSE AND TIGHT

The chapters in this volume, taken collectively, raise the issue of how the parts of an educational system are connected. The literature already contains one answer, expressed in Karl Weick's (1976) article "Educational Organizations as Loosely Coupled Systems." But is it the right answer? Can we characterize educational organizations globally as loosely or tightly coupled systems? And is that the right question? I would argue "no" in each case. Maureen Hallinan's discussion (Chapter 6) about a breakdown in scheduling opens up the problem of what is coupled to what in the organization of schools. Although schools differ from "high-risk technological systems" characterized by "complex interactivity and tight coupling" as well as by susceptibility to human error, they are still vulnerable to human error—as Hallinan's study shows— and still have tight connections among some of their parts. A school's time schedule is a document that ties together the plan for assigning students and teachers to classrooms according to the subject matter curriculum and the scheme for tracking. In the case she describes, for example, a feedback loop— student schedules that revealed class and time conflicts—was not only in place, it was the conduit through which the counselor's error brought the system to its knees as students showed up at the wrong classes. The case also shows which parts of the school's organization and operation were tightly linked to the schedule and which were not.

The crisis was set off because of a counselor's error and because that error occurred in one of the tightly coupled areas of school practice: between the schedule as a document and the actual class assignments of students and teachers. The mess *was* that students went to the wrong classes, study halls, or no classes; it was exacerbated and extended in time because the guidance system was inadequately staffed to cope with the emergency. By contrast, the impact on learning as assessed by grades—Hallinan notes that this was not the best possible measure—was minimal. Had the crisis lasted until or beyond Christmas, the damage to learning might have been greater. Why was the damage to learning not so great? Plausible conjecture suggests that perhaps students who went to study hall rather than class actually read their textbooks and studied. What they missed was the classroom instruction component of their schooling, while retaining other parts of it. Perhaps the results would have been worse had the students been out of school entirely. In any case one can argue that there is a weak relation between the time schedule and individual learning, at least for the duration of the breakdown, and a strong one between the schedule and actual class attendance. Class attendance is a key element in a school's operation; it assures students' *direct exposure* to the curriculum (even though exposure does not guarantee learning). Hence if the schedule is in disarray, students miss class; but they may learn in spite of that. The difference in coupling depends, then, on which elements of school organization and practice are under consideration. Coupling means little more than whether relations between two or more components of an organization are weak or strong (in the statistical sense). What matters more is whether, as in the case just described, the schedule leads to curriculum exposure—it was severely attenuated during the crisis—and what conditions are in place (as Gamoran and Kelly, Bidwell, and McFarland show) that bear on the linkage between exposure and learning.

Coupling problems also exist across as well as within levels of the educational enterprise. A case in point is the reform strategies employed in Chicago high schools intended to increase student achievement by following the principle of accountability promulgated by the mayor's office and implemented by the chief executive officer through the administrative apparatus. As I argued earlier, the use of scripted instruction and test preparation was an attempt by the administration to constrain the conduct of teachers with respect both to curriculum and instructional method, to tighten the linkage between administrative policy pronouncements and teaching practice. Attempts to change teaching practices that follow directives from the central offices of school districts tend to have mixed consequences, as shown by the following examples from (unpublished) fieldwork done by Barr and me. In one school system, the superintendent—in order to improve reading achievement—hired a reading consultant who revamped the existing program in all elementary schools by adopting a good eclectic basal reading series, providing guidance on how to use it and lengthening the time devoted to reading. Despite the consultant's somewhat officious manner, which caused initial resistance, the new scheme caught on and teachers realized improvement in both instruction and learning. This looks like a case of tight coupling, but labeling it as such does not explain its success. Even though imposed from the center, the new reading program was sound in its conception: it included a wide range of reading skills, required sufficient time for the teaching and mastery of concepts, and was put in the hands of a capable staff of teachers. In a contrasting case, a superintendent—having heard about popular ideas at the time that touted increasing curriculum coverage—announced that prevailing rates of coverage were too low and ordered the rates increased across the board, but made no provision for increasing instructional time. The result was to proceed too rapidly for students who were already having difficulty. This too was an example of tightly regulating instruction by administrative directive, but with negative results. In both cases, however, the results become comprehensible by examining the mechanisms (the actual classroom procedures and their consequences) rather than the tightness or looseness of coupling.

The recent Chicago reform experience also provides telling examples of why the global characterizations of tight and loose coupling have little analytical bite. The idea of accountability that justified the use of scripted instruction in the late 1990s was also used to justify the 1988 reform; the latter mandated an extreme form of decentralization in which local school councils and their agents (the principals) were responsible for accountability in order to raise the level of student performance. This move severely attenuated the connection between the central administration and the schools; it aimed at accountability by limiting central controls, while counting on those exercised by community-based amateurs elected to local school councils. And with the 1995 reforms, the attempt in troubled schools to script instruction was accompanied by the invited participation of "external partners" who tried to implement their own disparate remedies—a decoupling of reform efforts from the central administration at the same time that the administration was recentralizing after the sorry performance of the local school councils. Similar patterns can be found in events initiated from beyond the school level of the educational system by federal and state governments, foundations, and subject matter-based curriculum organizations—the latter two lacking governmental provenance but with national reach nevertheless. Firestone shows how state efforts at accountability by implementing standards have little impact on teaching practice. Loveless makes a similar case, paying particular attention to the weak technological condition of teaching to explain why reforms that rely on changes in teaching founder.

The concept of mechanism might be more useful than that of coupling insofar as the former refers to *how* the parts are related, including how they influence one another. To illustrate this consider an example drawn from the early twentieth century history of the Du Pont Company, described in Alfred Chandler's (1962) book *Strategy and Structure*, to explore how parts of an organization are connected to each other and how they change when alterations in the organization's practices are introduced. Du Pont in the 1910s was a centralized company that manufactured black powder, high explosives, and smokeless powder. It sold to large buyers like the government, railroads, contractors, and mining firms, not to consumers through retail outlets. It hired its own technically informed salespeople rather than relying on jobbers to handle marketing. Manufacturing, engineering, and purchasing were located at the same level in the hierarchy under the jurisdiction of a general manager who—along with managers for development, legal matters, and sales—was subordinate to the corporation's president (Chandler 1962:62). At the conclusion of World War I, the demand for smokeless powder—a propellant for artillery shells—declined leaving an excess of plant capacity. Du Pont had previously experimented with product diversification using pyroxylin, the base for artificial silk and oilcloth, whose manufacture employed the same nitrocellulose technology used for explosives. In the postwar period, using the same technology, it diversified into the production of varnishes and paints for retail sale. The result was that adopting these new product lines, despite the similarity of production technology, caused unexpected administrative problems for the centralized structure. It also led to financial losses that were ultimately traced to inadequacies in the procedures for marketing the new retail products—this in a company whose strength was based on marketing to large industrial producers, not to hardware stores.

Du Pont was governed by an Executive Committee with a keen interest in organizational structure and operation as well as skill in gathering and using information diagnostically about the corporation's workings (Chandler 1962:94, Stinchcombe 1990). One of its self-discoveries was that marketing procedures suitable for the explosives business were inappropriate for the distribution and sale of consumer items like paint and varnish. The difficulties experienced led to a redesign of the corporation's structure more in keeping with the diversified nature of its production. The solution was to decentralize the single structure into product divisions, and to centralize each division so that its separate lines of production and their respective requirements for marketing were joined under the same unit of management. In effect, the prior system—integrated around a single manufacturing technology applicable to a variety of products—gave way to an organizational arrangement that linked production to the marketing of each product. Key to this reorganization was the fact that marketing practices applicable to diversified products were a known "technology" in manufacturing firms, even though Du Pont had no previous need to employ them.

School systems are not manufacturing firms, but this excursion into the business world still has implications for how to think about school system organization. It is not illuminating to describe the structures and practices of the Du Pont Corporation as tightly or loosely coupled. The case shows that Du Pont underwent a fundamental change in its structure, from a monocratic hierarchy to a division-based one, as a result of introducing a new product line. Du Pont's problem was resolved by linking related activities previously not seen to be related, and by discarding the assumption that the corporation's actions could be governed by a single manufacturing technology underlying all production. Chandler (1962) reports this understanding as follows.

> The basic "principle" was rather "that it is related effort [manufacturing and marketing] which should be coordinated and not 'like things' [items manufactured by the same technology]. In fact it is often more necessary to combine related efforts which are unlike." (p. 70)

Particularly interesting in the Du Pont case, especially seen in contrast to efforts to change educational organizations, was the reliance on analysis. As Stinchcombe (1990) observes:

> The standard [organizational] theory at the time of the innovations at Du Pont was one that ordinarily gave centralization and specialization as its answer. . . . But at least the theory's concrete manifestation at Du Pont was one that *could* diagnose a pattern in the data (e.g., the fact that other companies were making money in lines where Du Pont was losing money . . .) as requiring an organizational solution. (p. 111)

In other words, centralization and specialization were the ideological corporate watchwords at the time; in today's educational lingo, for example, they would correspond to "decentralization," "accountability," "standards," and the like—remedies that do not necessarily have much connection to the problems of schooling. The story in principle was similar to the case of the scheduling crisis described by Hallinan. At issue was the mechanism connecting production to marketing. In the school case, no change in organizational structure occurred with the end of the crisis, while in the Du Pont case, establishing a workable mechanism "required" a redesigned structure.

What bearing does the Du Pont experience have on the analysis of classrooms and the linkages across levels of educational organization? There is a long, fragmented line in the policy sequence from the federal government to the classroom. Government-originated programs can traverse that line, or at least parts of it, in different ways. One example is through legislation aimed first at the states but intended to reach the classroom, such as the Reading First initiative of the current Bush administration designed to raise levels of literacy in the primary grades. It works by soliciting programmatic grant proposals from the states that, if accepted, in turn solicit applications from local school districts that must conform to the provisions to which the state has already agreed. (Other models of federal policy implementation can be found, for example, in the GI Bill, National Defense Education Act, and Elementary and Secondary Education Act [ESEA]—all of which began with legislation— and in court action such as desegregation cases. Some were aimed at individuals, others at schools and school districts.) The first test of the initiative is at the state level; success in implementation is indicated by U.S. Department of Education approval of a grant application. The second test is state approval of local district applications through a replicated process within states. The main analytical point about these procedures is that the sequential application process across federal, state, and local levels *defines* the political linkage; the substance is defined in principle by what is in the application and in actuality by the specific changes (if any) that occur in the schools. A variant procedure can be found in the Bush administration's testing program. The administration is making receipt of ESEA funds contingent on states adopting the testing program, but there is resistance in some states (e.g., Vermont) now debating whether to forego ESEA funds as the price of opposition. In such cases the political linkage breaks down, and the government's policy does not get implemented (although some other one does).

These remarks refer to linkage or coupling in a process of political transmission across levels of the educational system. Also at issue is the substantive nature of what is proposed at the national level: whether the reforms of Reading First, for example, even if transmitted and implemented, will make the difference in primary level literacy that they are intended to make. For in the classroom the content of the federal proposal meets the vicissitudes of classroom life that Bidwell, Gamoran and Kelly, and McFarland identified. At issue here is whether the Reading First proposal contains an adequate diagnosis of what is depressing the acquisition of literacy among young children and whether it has formulated a workable remedy. The latter concern is not one of coupling but of developing viable practices. Du Pont made a good diagnosis and solved its problem by changing the linkages among parts of the corporation. Meyer (1983b) has argued that the policy transmission belt in nations with education ministries operates differently from that in the United States. A ministerial system reduces the indeterminacies across levels of the system through bureaucratic controls exercised down the line by civil servants. At the level of schools and classrooms, contingencies arise much like those in the American system, but ideas about standard practice and acceptable remedies for problems are far more limited; the vetoes of ministerial officials and their local agents limit changes that they consider to be out of bounds according to practicality, efficacy, politics, or tradition.

What made the reorganization of Du Pont a successful venture was its possession of three key capacities: a production technology for manufacture, a management cadre with analytical talents, and the availability of effective marketing procedures for markets in which it did not previously participate. These considerations were key to the implementation of new practices and they do not easily fit into a coupling framework. In the educational realm, the key technological issues center around classroom instruction, the counterpart to manufacture. Particularly important in this regard is teaching student populations whose members have difficulty dealing with the academic regime—the hard cases. For example, whether the dialogic methods described by Gamoran and Kelley will succeed with populations lacking academic interests and insufficiently prepared for their grade level is an open question—as are the procedures capable of solving problems of goodwill and sociability that Bidwell and McFarland described. Surely there are practices for dealing with such problems, but not standard ones representing a basic technology of occupationwide scope. With such uncertainties at the level of classroom practice, questions must be raised about how seriously we should take the political process of transmitting educational policies from higher levels of the educational system to the activities of teachers. Anyone entering the explosives business would employ a manufacturing technology similar to Du Pont's (or a better one). Anyone entering the teaching business with an interest in increasing literacy among primary grade children, especially those experiencing difficulty, would select from among a wide array of practices—none with a consistent track record of effectiveness, most with a record of effectiveness somewhere but under unknown conditions.

One of the key differences between industrial firms and school districts (the educational analog of manufacturing firms) is the extent to which they generate and control the flow of ideas that shape their own operation and changes in it. Du Pont is a good example of a company possessing such a capacity as well as an ability to analyze itself. (This is not to suggest that all industrial firms have good ideas.) In contrast, school districts have not been known for any comparable capacity. This is partly because of the unsettled state of educational technology, but also because of the untrammeled flow of educational ideas from multiple sources that are publicized as remedies, but usually without a carefully formulated diagnosis of the educational problems that they are supposed to fix. One might think that universities would be a productive source of influences on educational practice, but since their contact with teachers-to-be is brief and the practices of teaching are so poorly understood, universities have little influence over the shaping of teaching activities—unlike the case of medical, law, and engineering schools. Moreover, university-based research has had minimal relevance to teaching practice and teachers tend to be highly skeptical of its value. For reasons little understood, district school systems themselves were involved only minimally in the analysis of educational work in schools, the codification of teaching practices, and the conditions that call for variations in them. In the case of Du Pont, Stinchcombe (1990) remarks that the analysis carried out by the Executive Committee cut through the prevailing business rhetoric of the time. In the case of school organization, the rhetoric reigns.

Each chapter in this volume addresses a portion of the question of how the parts of educational systems are linked together, with primary emphasis on the vertical elements of the political process and the activities entailed in classroom practice. The two are entailed in each other, but how remains an open question.

REFERENCES

Anagnostopoulos, Dorothea M. 2000. *Setting Standards, Failing Students: A Case Study of Merit Promotion in Two Chicago High Schools.* Ph.D. dissertation, Department of Education, University of Chicago.

Barr, Rebecca and Robert Dreeben. 1983. *How Schools Work.* Chicago: University of Chicago Press.

Breer, Paul E. and Edwin C. Locke. 1965. *Task Experience as a Source of Attitudes.* Homewood, IL: Dorsey Press.

Caves, Richard E. 2000. *Creative Industries: Contracts between Art and Commerce.* Cambridge, MA: Harvard University Press.

Chandler, Alfred D. 1962. *Strategy and Structure: Chapters in the History of the American Industrial Enterprise.* Cambridge, MA: MIT Press.

Dreeben, Robert. 2001. "Teaching and the Competence of Occupations." Paper presented at a conference "The Social Organization of Schooling," Chicago, IL.

Dreeben, Robert and Rebecca Barr. 1988. "Classroom Composition and the Design of Instruction." *Sociology of Education* 61:129–42.

Jackson, Philip W. 1968. *Life in Classrooms*. New York: Holt, Rinehart and Winston.

Laumann, Edward O. and David Knoke. 1987. *The Organization State: Social Choices in National Policy Domains*. Madison: University of Wisconsin Press.

McFarland, Daniel A. 1999. *Organized Behavior in Social Systems: A Study of Student Engagement and Resistance in High Schools*. Ph.D. dissertation, Department of Sociology, University of Chicago.

Meyer, John W. 1983a. "Innovation and Knowledge Use in American Public Education." Pp. 233–60 in *Organizational Environments: Ritual and Rationality*, edited by John W. Meyer and W. Richard Scott. Beverly Hills, CA: Sage.

Meyer, John W. 1983b. "Organizational Factors Affecting Legalization in Education." Pp. 217–32 in *Organizational Environments: Ritual and Rationality*, edited by John W. Meyer and W. Richard Scott. Beverly Hills, CA: Sage.

Scott, W. Richard. 1995. *Institutions and Organizations*. Thousand Oaks, CA: Sage.

Smith, Louis M. and William Geoffrey. 1968. *The Complexities of an Urban Classroom: An Analysis toward a General Theory of Teaching*. New York: Holt, Rinehart and Winston.

Stinchcombe, Arthur L. 1990. *Information and Organizations*. Berkeley: University of California Press.

Swidler, Ann 1979. *Organization without Authority: Dilemmas of Social Control in Free Schools*. Cambridge, MA: Harvard University Press.

U.S. National Commission on Excellence in Education. 1983. *A Nation at Risk: The Imperative for Educational Reform*. Washington, DC: U.S. Department of Education.

Weick, Karl E. 1976. "Educational Organizations as Loosely Coupled Systems." *Administrative Science Quarterly* 21:1–19.

Author Index

Subject Index